Environmental Protection and Coastal Zone Management in Asia and the Pacific

Environmental Protection and Coastal Zone Management in Asia and the Pacific

Edited by Ichirō Katō, Nobuo Kumamoto,
William H. Matthews, and Ariffin Suhaimi

UNIVERSITY OF TOKYO PRESS

Publication assisted by a grant from The Toyota Foundation.

Contents

The Marine Environment and the Coastal Zone

Human Activities and the Coastal Zone

Preface

Coastal zone management has been considered an environmental problem in Asia and the Pacific because its various aspects affect the environment. It covers marine pollution, wetland protection, coral reef ecosystem and mangrove protection, aquatic resources exploitation, beach mining, offshore oil exploration, fisheries, protection of natural scenery and land-use plans for recreational facilities, housing and industrial activities on the sea coast. This means that effective countermeasures toward coastal zone management should be wider and deeper than any single environmental problem such as air or water pollution. This also means that interdisciplinary studies and cooperation among concerned countries is strongly required for promoting environmental protection along sea coasts.

From this point of view, coastal zone management needs not only basic studies on each subject but interdisciplinary cooperation at both domestic and international levels. This brought our attention and interest to the idea of organizing a conference to promote these types of studies at domestic and international levels in the Asian region.

Considering this problem, participants at the second Asian-American Conference of Environmental Protection recommended "Environmental Management of the Coastal Zone" as the theme for the third conference in Malaysia. Members of the conference agreed unanimously on the theme after discussing its meaning. Common recognition by the participants who approved the idea stems from the fact that environmental problems of our coastal waters had received much attention due to the increasing stress upon such environments from the rapid rate of land-based developments, population pressures on coastal settlements and the tendency to overexploit marine resources.

They also recognized that stress on the marine environment had been further aggravated by the use of the seabed for mineral extraction, offshore drilling for oil and gas and the release of noxious and hazardous materials from ships and cargo boats. Readers of this book may also agree with the fact that the Straits of Malacca, by virtue of being one of the busiest sea lanes in the world, is most vulnerable to oil pollution risks in the light of the high density of tanker traffic passing through it.

Travelers to Thailand easily see that the depletion of the marine resources in the Gulf of Thailand serves as a constant reminder of the need for control and regulation of the human activities to which the coastal waters are vulnerable. These environmental stresses—besides endangering the marine flora and fauna—also tend to affect the livelihoods of thousands of people who depend on the rich resources of coastal waters. Thus, awareness of the dangers of environmental degradation of the marine environment has resulted in increased studies on the management of coastal waters and activities to promote protection and conservation of marine resources.

For the past seven years, we have organized Asian-American Conferences on Environmental Protection in Sapporo, Japan (1978); Jakarta, Indonesia (1980); Kuala Lumpur, Malaysia (1982); and Bangkok, Thailand (1984). Results of the first and second conferences have been published by the University of Tokyo Press as *Environmental Law and Policy in the Pacific Basin Area* (for Sapporo) and *Water Management and Environmental Protection in Asia and the Pacific* (for Jakarta). This book is the third publication from the conferences, and it concentrates on coastal zone problems. The previous two publications were mainly devoted to general law and policy on environment and problems arising from water management.

No one can deny that international cooperation is the most fundamental activity of people who are concerned about protecting our environments. The phrase "international cooperation" generally calls our attention to that of Europe because of its long history and various experiences. International cooperation in Asia and the Pacific area, however, is considerably different from that of Europe.

We may call it Asian diversity, which relates to geography (island or continental countries), population (size or density), political systems (relation of central and local governments, independence of these governments), presidential or parliamentary systems, separation of powers (especially independence of the judicial branch), legal systems (dual or unit judicial system), the role of laws (private vs. public law), the citizens' ability to bring suits to court and the presence or absence of environmental laws and institutions.

The diversity also covers education (i.e., its system, standard, the social role of higher education, budget allocation for education) and industry and economy (kinds of industry such as agriculture, fishery, timber, mineral or coal, light or heavy industry, skills of workers or quality of products). A study of international cooperation in these areas therefore needs to consider these elements in order to find basic common aspects of cooperation for environmental protection.

The North-South dilemma in economics can be cited as an example of the gap between developed and developing countries. The difference in the quality of workers in advanced and developing countries draws attention toward a possible exchange program for promoting environmental protection. International cooperation in this area must include the particular forms and styles of the countries involved. Bilateral or multilateral programs for environmental protection need to be reconsidered to satisfy the problems raised here.

Recent international cooperation has been promoted by various international organizations, government-supported institutions, or nongovernment organizations. Roles and aims of these groups can be seen in activities such as the ones supported by USAID (the U.S. Agency for International Development), ODA (Overseas Development Administration) in the United Kingdom, CIDA (Canada International Development Agency) or JICA (Japan International Cooperation Agency), or worldwide cooperative programs such as the ones supported by the World Bank, the Asian Development Bank or IDA (International Development Association).

Coastal zone management is an area in which such activities have been most effective. Recipient and donor countries have both shared and played their own roles in achieving common goals. The aim of this book is to discuss such international cooperation among social and natural scientists in Asia and the Pacific. This book consists of four parts: environment and water, coastal zone management and law, marine environment and coastal zones and human activities and coastal zones.

The first part, environment and water, indicates the general relation between environment and water in several parts of Asia. Water is one of the most important elements of our environment. Coastal zone management cannot be discussed without a general consideration of water and environment. From this point, recommendations on the national water resources code will give us an integrated concept for effective production and preservation of water resources.

The second part, coastal zone management and law, deals with the legal process toward coastal zone management which generally needs integrated coastal zone development strategies. Human efforts are another key element for integrated coastal zone management. Research and training are the most well-known examples of international co-operation for fostering human efforts.

The third part, marine environment and coastal zones, discusses the broad area of coastal zone management programs where marine resources including fauna, flora and minerals are the objects of study and protection.

The final part, human activities and coastal zones, covers recent tendencies of human activities moving increasingly into coastal zones. These activities include offshore oil exploration and production, industrial activities and human settlement, including construction of recreational facilities.

Thus, coastal zone management includes various problems that require basic study and research and need appropriate approaches toward better environmental protection. This book gives a general view of the problems and discusses possibilities for improvement in the future.

In addition to the chapters, we have adopted excerpts of important statutes in this book as appendices. The Environmental Quality Act of Malaysia is an example that provides coastal zone management in a general statute as one of the key elements among environmental problems. A Law Concerning Special Measures for Conservation of the Environment of the Seto Inland Sea (Japan) is an example of integrated measures that can be adopted in a regional or limited area. The Coastal Zone Management Act (U.S.A.) is an example that provides a broad and systematic statute for protecting coastal zones. These statutory provisions also may be of value as we consider basic ideas, concepts, and legal measures to be followed for coastal zone management programs.

We wish to put on the record our sincere appreciation to the Toyota Foundation; ESSO Production (M) Inc.; the East-West Environment and Policy Institute, Honolulu, Hawaii; the Japan Center for Human Environmental Problems, Tokyo; and Hokkaigakuen University, Sapporo, Japan, which supported the conference.

We also acknowledge the help of Universiti Pertanian Malaysia, the Ministry of Science, Technology, and Environment (Malaysia), the World Health Organization Regional Centre for the Promotion of Environmental Planning and Applied Studies and the Institute Technology MARA for providing facilities and for the cooperation that made the conference possible.

We are grateful to the organizing committee of the Third Asian-American Conference on Environmental Protection promoted by Dr. Ariffin Suhaimi and members of the committee including Dr. Mohd. Ismail Yaziz, Dr. M. Nakamura, Mr. A. Maheswaran, Ms. Hasmah Harun, Ms. Amimah Abas, Dr. M.W.R.N. De Silva and Mr. Alexander Ritchie.

We wish especially to acknowledge the invaluable assistance of Mrs. Jane Crane of Honolulu in preparing this book, as well as the first and second books in this series, for publication.

This publication was greatly assisted by the Toyota Foundation, Universiti Pertanian Malaysia, the East-West Environment and Policy Institute, the Japan Center for Human Environmental Problems, Hokkaigakuen University, Professor Masao Morimoto of the University and Mr. Kazuhiko Kurata of the University of Tokyo Press. Mrs. Lyn Moy of Honolulu and Ms. Mikiko Hirosawa of Sapporo did most of the typing of the papers.

Environment and Water

Environmental Protection Efforts in Malaysia

Stephen Yong Kuet Tze

I. The Threat to the Marine Environment

The advances in science and technology have no doubt raised our standard of living, made our life easier and possibly increased our lifespan, but in their wake we see harmful side effects caused by interference with the ecosystems, particularly where unplanned and indiscriminate developments take place. In the light of rising aspirations of the people for an improved standard of living, accelerated development continues as a global phenomenon of our times. The hopes for the future of the 57 percent of the world's population who live in the Third World are increasingly pinned on accelerated national development. It is important, therefore, to ensure that with proper concern for the environment, development will result in a significant increase in the flow of benefits with minimal damage and disruption to the ecosystems.

With intensified population pressures, fast growing urban centers, rapid industrialization and the increasing tempo of economic activities on a world-wide basis, and particularly in this region of ours, it can be reasonably expected that the damage to and disruption of the human environment will gain in significance from year to year. We need to take remedial action to check and reverse this trend. The seas and oceans have been treated as one huge garbage dump. It is a myth to think that the vast oceans have an infinite capacity to dilute all manner of man's wastes indefinitely.

The threat to the marine environment comes from abroad and from within. Tankers, cargo ships, wind, current and drift bring in external pollutants. Developmental activities within a country or a group of countries spew forth internal pollutants. With the growing use of sea lanes for commerce, the ever-increasing size and variety of cargo vessels and tankers such as the very large crude carriers (VLCCs), the ex-

3

ploitation of the seabed for minerals, oil and gas, and the release of noxious and hazardous materials from ships and cargo boats, whether deliberate or accidental, are threatening the marine environment every day.

A number of dramatic events in recent years has brought home the real menace that pollution poses to the marine environment. Various tanker disasters and oil spillages in oceans, causing extensive pollution of coastal waters and tar residues on beaches, the detection of pesticides in the marine environment and marine organisms have demonstrated the devastation and havoc that can result from pollution.

It is, therefore, clear that the protection of the environment from pollution is urgent and vital. Most countries in the Asian region have indeed shown sensitivity to the environment and are taking measures to restore, protect and preserve the environment. They are at the same time making the most effective use of the natural resources with the objective of providing a better life for ourselves and for our children. In this respect, the emphasis of this conference, that is, "Environmental Management of Coastal Zones," is most apt and timely.

II. Development Planning and Environmental Policy

For centuries mankind has lived seemingly confident of the permanence and nurturing capacity of nature. This tendency has equated development with the more narrowly conceived objective of economic growth as measured by increases in gross national product from year to year. In essence, development and growth were measured by physical indicators only. Since the epochal Stockholm Conference on Human Environment in 1972, it has become increasingly recognized that nature is by no means an infinite asset to be exploited at will, but rather a fragile and finite resource in need of comprehensive protection and environmentally sound management. Though the major environmental problems in developing countries stemmed predominantly from relative lack of development and inadequate infrastructure, it was increasingly recognized that the high rates of economic growth did not in themselves guarantee the easing of urgent social and human problems. The environment must be considered as an integral part of development. This has served to provide new dimensions to the development concept itself, and in the light of the many advances in science and technology, developing countries can today be said to have better access to the means and "know-how" of effectively dealing with environmental issues before they assume crisis proportions.

It was once generally considered that environmental protection was the pastime of some woolly-minded idealists who set their minds against progress, and that taking environmental factors into account in making decisions in production and consumption served only to add to the costs of development. Thus concern for environmental factors did not feature as an integral element of development, let alone be given prominence.

The environmental policies of developing countries must necessarily cope with the twin problems of overcoming the lack of development and of avoiding disruption and degradation of the environment resulting from the development process being carried out in haphazard fashion. There is, therefore, a need for harmony between economic goals and policies and those of environmental protection and improvement. Developing countries today have the opportunity—and in some cases the resources, even allowing for the current economic recession—for better allocation of their environmental resources. Environmental protection can help developing countries optimize social benefits for present and future generations by sound planning and policy formulation.

This has, in recent years, led to some serious rethinking among developed and developing countries alike on the directions and thrust of economic and social development programs. While antipollution measures and conservation do feature in environmental management, its major concern should be with optimal resource use, maintenance and enhancement. In point of fact, efficient environmental management can generate the resources to help defray the costs of development.

It is important that environmental policy should aim at sound management of both renewable and nonrenewable resources so that exploitation of these resources does not place in jeopardy or impoverish the environment. The capacity of the environment to produce essential renewable resources must be carefully husbanded, restored and improved, as otherwise counter-productive side effects on the environment could reduce the expected benefits from development. This is something we can ill afford, particularly at a time of general economic slowdown. It is imperative that environmental policies be integrated into development planning and regarded as part and parcel of the overall framework of economic and social planning.

III. Environmental Management in Malaysia

In Malaysia, the objectives of environmental management have to be pursued within the context of generating economic growth and employment opportunities and a fairer distribution of income to all within the framework of improving the quality of life. The major objective of most projects has been economic and social improvement, and assessments of their desirability have centered mainly on comparisons of the economic costs and measurable benefits expected from them.

There has been a rapid evolution of methods to evaluate these costs and benefits, and choices have no doubt improved as a result. With greater experience, more thorough investigations of past projects and increased understanding of natural systems, it is now apparent that many development projects can and do have significant, and often unanticipated, effects on the natural environment and the use made of it. These effects can add to the real costs or real benefits of the undertaking.

It is now recognized that if the direct and measurable economic costs and benefits of projects remain of prime importance, the effects on the natural environment which are not included in the economic sums cannot be ignored. It is crucial for developing countries to protect the source of their wealth, both current and future, so that renewable resources can best be extracted from a healthy environment. In addition, these countries must be constantly aware that, because of their limited size, their most basic resources are finite and thus farsighted husbandry is of paramount importance. It is also important for developing countries to pay particular attention to social costs of development.

If this concept of environment and development is to become the starting point of planning policy, two broad conclusions emerge: one is that development projects should assess the environmental implications fully and provide for the required ameliorative or reinforcing actions; the other is that any properly planned strategy for overcoming environmental problems can accelerate development and optimize benefits.

The analysis of the relationship between environment and development is embodied in the environmental assessment of development projects. Quite often this analysis tends to be carried out within the framework of traditional cost-benefit calculations. We need to transcend the limits imposed by the traditional framework and strike out towards new paths which bring out the interrelationships between environment, development, resources and population.

IV. Environmental Impact Assessment

From this point of view, the environmental impact assessment (EIA) has been the most noteworthy response as environmental values are taken into account and weighed together with other more easily measured impacts. At the same time, alternative options can be generated for consideration. It is, therefore, no surprise that the environmental impact assessment has become part and parcel of the decision-making process and forms an important environmental management tool.

However, developing countries in doing so must continue to look for ways and means of assuring that:

(1) it will contribute to improving project evaluation, taking into account environmental effects;

(2) it will lead to a clean evaluation of the project;

(3) it will not add to the project evaluation work load unnecessarily;

(4) it will not be cumbersome and time-consuming;

(5) it will not lead to undue restriction on development.

We have already developed an environmental impact assessment procedure appropriate to Malaysia as an aid to the environmental planning of new development projects or to the expansion of existing projects. In this regard, it can be said to have taken care of the above issues through a procedure providing for:

(1) integrated project planning in which economic, technical and environmental factors are considered together;

(2) a two-step procedure, involving a preliminary screening and if necessary, followed by a detailed assessment. The preliminary screening will help identify projects that do not have inherent and significant adverse environmental impacts so that these need not be subjected to detailed assessment. These will in turn lead to only a few projects subject to full EIA procedure;

(3) proper timing of environmental impact assessment, preliminary screening being carried out at the prefeasibility study stage and the detailed assessment at the feasibility study stage; and

(4) appropriate terms of reference, such as keeping the duration and cost of environmental impact studies to levels which are reasonable in relation to the type and scale of the project.

Specialists in specific fields will assess environmental effects and provide the necessary information on the likely environmental effects for informed decision making. As the machinery and commitment to planning already exist, there will be no change to the existing institutional arrangements for project submission, evaluation and approval process. What is needed is only an enlarged planning methodology for the environmental dimension to be integrated into development planning right from the early stages of planning.

V. Implementation of Environmental Protection

The procedure is being implemented gradually—partially in the Fourth Malaysia Plan and fully in the Fifth Malaysia Plan—once more trained manpower and more experience in environmental impact assessment is available. The procedure will be administered by an independent review panel assisted by the Environment Division of the Ministry of Science, Technology and Environment.

It is encouraging to note that our planners, decision makers and project implementors are beginning to be environmentally conscious. Basically, the most effective method of controlling environmental problems lies in the advance planning in environmentally related activities in terms of the long-term conservation of environmental assets. To this end, this Ministry will continue to strive to ensure that environmental protection is integrated into development projects to avoid environmental degradation and costly and time-consuming remedial measures. Testimony to this Ministry's firm resolve to deal appropriately with the polluters of the Malaysian environment, including our marine environment, is the successful prosecution in Malacca, on 15 April 1982, of the M.V. *Dragon King* for the deliberate discharge of oil into Malaysian waters when a fine of 5,000 ringgit was imposed by the court.

However, the successful implementation of this strategy calls for nothing less than a basic reform in the way our society looks at problems and makes decisions. We need new knowledge, new perceptions, new attitudes—and these must extend to all levels of government and throughout the private sector as well; to industry; to the professions; to each individual citizen in his job and in his home.

Our educational system has a key role to play in bringing about this reform. We must train professional environmental managers to deal with pollution, land planning, and all other technical requirements of a high quality environment. It is also vital that our entire society develops a new understanding and awareness of man functioning in harmony with the environment.

Southeast Asian Waters
Present Status and Future Scenarios

Mark J. Valencia

I. Background

More than a quarter of humanity resides in the political entities bordering the South China Sea, and 75 percent of Southeast Asia's population lives on islands. Due to infertile or rugged forested hinterland, much of the population is crowded into river valleys and available coastal plains. The average national rate of population increase of 2.7 percent per year greatly diminishes per capita benefits derived from annual percentage increases in gross national product, creating a growing gap between expectations and results of "development."

World and future views of many policymakers in the region have long been bound by "landmindedness." However, within the last decade there has been a marked enhancement of "marine awareness" on the part of many, due principally to expectations of the potential of ocean resources in aiding "development." This increased marine awareness has resulted in the unilateral extension of jurisdiction over resources and certain activities up to 200 nautical miles (nm) or more from shore by almost all coastal nations of the South China Sea, leaving almost no marine area left unclaimed, and many areas where claims overlap.

Kampuchea (Cambodia), Burma and Vietnam have claimed the entire suite of maritime zones consisting of a 12-nm territorial sea, a 12-nm contiguous zone, a 200-nm exclusive economic zone (EEZ) and a continental shelf, in January 1977, April 1977 and May 1977, respectively. The Philippines, Taiwan, Indonesia, Malaysia and Thailand have each claimed all these zones except a contiguous zone. The claims were made by the Philippines in June 1978, by Taiwan in September 1979, by Indonesia in March 1980, by Malaysia in April 1980 and by Thailand in May 1980. The Philippines defines its territorial waters as

9

those lying between the archipelagic baselines and the limits set in treaties between the United States and Spain in 1898 and 1900 and between the United States and Britain in 1930. This means that the territorial waters of the Philippines have a maximum width of 284 nm and a minimum width of 0.5 nm. China also claims these three maritime zones proclaimed by the above five countries, although a Chinese fishing zone 12 nm wide coincides with its territorial waters. Brunei at present claims only territorial waters 3 nm wide.

Most of the coastal nations in Southeast Asia are now actively engaged in efforts to identify and to pursue their national interests in the ocean arena. For these developing nations, the new resources, activities and associated management rights and responsibilities in the zones of extended jurisdiction create new challenges and opportunities for national development. The historic Third United Nations Conference on the Law of the Sea, which took place from 1973 to 1982, and its Convention on the Law of the Sea (CLS), is expected to serve as a framework within which nations will carry out their ocean management rights and responsibilities. Clearly the "coastal zones" can now be considered as extending seaward to the limits of national jurisdiction.

The South China Sea has been used by man for eons for war, for trade and for its natural resources, particularly protein. However, recent rapid acceleration of marine transport and nonrenewable resource extraction activities, together with increasing agricultural, industrial and human waste disposal, is producing increasing conflict with the traditional harvesting of marine protein, human health and coastal recreation. With extension of jurisdiction the conflicts are intranational and international in scope, and within and between use sectors.

II. Status of Primary Uses

1. Coastal Ecosystems

With the spread and increased pace of coastal and marine development has come an increasing recognition of the value and vulnerability of particular marine organisms and ecosystems. The prime coastal ecosystems of present concern are estuaries, mangroves and coral reefs. Species associated with these ecosystems and already officially listed as endangered and vulnerable to pollution include: (1) sea turtles, dependent on inshore seagrass and reefs for feeding and undisturbed sandy beaches for nesting; (2) crocodiles, which frequent estuarine swampy areas near large river mouths; (3) dugongs, dependent on seagrass fields for feeding; (4) certain seabirds, dependent on small undisturbed islands for breeding and inshore reefs and offshore waters for feeding; and (5) whales and dolphins, which inhabit deep water and migrate in and out of the region. Numerous nonendangered but vulnerable marine plants, invertebrates and vertebrates comprise inshore reef communities typical of most coastal areas in the region.

Another factor is the growth of the indigenous middle class, together with government and private tourism campaigns and investment. Some tourist sites are closely linked to coastal population centers and certain attractive coastal features. As a response to these trends and as evidence of a growing recognition of the value and vulnerability of these resources, marine and coastal parks and reserves have been declared in a number of countries in the region. Selection and implementation of reserves in the region have been based on tourist destinations, accessibility or political or local community interest. There is little organization of their distribution from a geographic, environmental, national or regional perspective. The sites with existing management are very few, with no single country having more than thirteen. The legislated areas without management are much more numerous, with Indonesia and the Philippines having the most. Proposed sites, although not clearly defined, are also numerous.

2. Marine Fishery Resources

The Southeast Asian seas support some of the world's most productive marine fisheries. Total annual marine catch from the region in recent years has been approximately 7 million metric tons or roughly 11 percent of the world's total marine catch. Total landings in 1978 were about 8 million tons—3.4 million tons demersal, 2.6 million tons coastal pelagic and 1.57 million tons oceanic. Since 1979, Thailand, Indonesia and the Philippines have had the highest total marine landings. Historically, these abundant fishery resources have been harvested in inshore and coastal waters with a variety of traditional fishing gears and have been an important source of food, animal protein and employment for many of the region's coastal peoples. Whole market and barter systems with networks extending to the interior are based on these fisheries.

Increasing local and international demand for the region's marine fishery resources will likely encourage even greater production in the future. However, while certain fisheries are capable of providing still greater yields, many other fisheries now appear to be fished near or at their maximum, or are overfished. In 1979, demersal landings decreased 7 percent and crustacean and coastal pelagic landings each decreased 5 percent, due mainly to decreases in Thai and Chinese landings. Increased fishing effort or pollution stress on any of the already heavily exploited stocks may well result in long-term damage to the given stock and a net decrease in the local and regional catch. Already, increased fishing pressures on such stocks have resulted in local and international conflict over these resources, total bans on particular species for large areas, and consequent scarcity and high prices. Another consequence has been a shift by national fisheries agencies to emphasis on deeper waters and on aquaculture. Suitable sites for major aquaculture enterprises are not plentiful and the pressure for this use of precious coastal areas will increase, including the clearing of mangroves. Mariculture may remain a long-range dream, if suitable marine areas are allocated to other uncomplementary uses such as waste disposal.

With extension of jurisdiction, responsibility for management of the region's marine fishery resources now rests fully with the governments of the region. The future of the region's marine fisheries may therefore be determined to a large extent by the decisions of the region's policymakers on fishery resource ownership allocation and management, and ultimately on the quality and quantity of information available to the region's policymakers as they formulate national and international policies.

A significant portion of the catch in the region in the past has been taken by distant-water fishing fleets, both from within the region—Thailand, Macao, Hong Kong and Singapore—and from outside—Japan, Korea, Taiwan and others. In many assessment areas, total catch could be decreased by reducing or eliminating distant-water catch, thereby reducing fishing intensity, or, alternatively, distant-water catch could be replaced by local catch, thus increasing local catch without increasing fishing intensity. As a result of extended maritime jurisdiction and increased fuel costs, distant-water fishing is being replaced by joint-venture arrangements with a majority of local equity and participation.

Migratory and shared stocks are of increasing importance to fishery managers and policymakers of the region. The most highly migratory fish appear to be the valuable oceanic species, particularly the yellowfin and skipjack tuna marketing at about U.S. $1500/ton, which are capable of migrations of several thousand miles. But migrations are also made by coastal pelagic fishes such as mackerels and sardines.

The movements and distributions of fish stocks in and around the Southeast Asian seas are not well known. Overfishing or desecration of nursery grounds in one country may adversely affect the fishery of another country if based on the same stock. Also, several nations may be unknowingly developing deep-water fleets to fish the same resource. Similar problems may occur with nonmigratory stocks which are shared by virtue of having their areas of distribution divided by new national jurisdictional boundaries.

3. Pollution of Coastal Waters

a. Land-based Sources

Pollution of coastal waters from land-based sources is substantial. Unlike developed areas, the biochemical oxygen demand from domestic pollutants is much greater than that from industrial sources. Major coastal cities in the region lack sewage systems and the wastes from their very large populations enter Southeast Asian waters either directly or via rivers; sewage is also derived from nonpoint sources; pesticides, fertilizers and sediment from the extensive rural and agricultural areas are also important pollutants. However, the effects of industrial pollution are becoming more direct and visible. Although the major industrial pollution sources are food and beverage manufacturing and textile and paper mills, heavy metal and oil pollution are also becoming quite significant. Deliberate waste disposal, particularly of hazardous wastes, is a problem of the near future.

b. Oil Pollution

Oil pollution from drilling accidents and tankers is becoming recognized as a serious problem in the region. Daily production in 1980 for the region was about 1.2 million barrels of oil and 515 million cubic feet of gas; about 30 percent of the crude oil production was from offshore. The predominant offshore discoveries and production to date are from basins on the central and southern Sunda Shelf, and in the Northwest Palawan and North Sumatra Basins.

For the Sunda Shelf alone total reserves, excluding Indonesia, are 3.8 to 5.3 billion barrels of oil and 56 to 67 trillion cubic feet of gas; if the gas is converted to oil-equivalent units, total hydrocarbon reserves are of the order of 13.5 to 17 billion barrels of oil equivalent. Offshore Indonesia adds some 57 billion barrels of oil equivalent to the total, although more than half is in water deeper than 200 m; the Mainland Shelf of southern China adds perhaps 10 billion barrels of estimated ultimately recoverable oil reserves to the total. High potential for oil is indicated for the Brunei-Sabah, Kutei and Makassar Basins and a small area between the Central and South Sumatra Basins. High gas potential is indicated for the Central Luconia Platform and the Baram Delta, and the Malay Basin. With extended jurisdiction some petroliferous basins are now shared or disputed by two or more nations.

High pressure gas pockets are common in the region and blowouts have occurred with increasing frequency in recent years. As wildcat drilling moves into deeper and less well known environs, the possibility of an accident and a consequential oil spill increases. With extended jurisdiction it is likely that a major spill would cross national boundaries. Many of the areas under petroleum rights are understandably situated on and around areas of known deposits like the Gulf of Thailand, the southwestern and southeastern Sunda Shelf and the North Sumatra and the Kutei Basins; others are situated in unproved areas such as the central Philippines, the Mainland Shelf, the Gulf of Martaban, Central Sumatra, the eastern Java Sea and the Vogelkop. Areas under waters deeper than 200 m with petroleum rights include more than half of those on the outer Mainland Shelf and part of the Northwest and Southwest Palawan, Reed Bank, Kutei and Madura Basins.

The major transportation route for oil imported into the region is from the Middle East and Africa through the Strait of Malacca to Japan with offshoots to Thailand, Taiwan and the Philippines. The 920–km long, 15– to 232–km wide Strait of Malacca is the world's second busiest seaway; over 100 vessels transit the Strait every day, including ten very large crude oil carriers (VLCCs). Significant oil shipment occurs within the archipelagic nations and between countries in the region, including transshipment in Singapore; export from Indonesia, Malaysia and Brunei to Japan and to the United States is also important. Operational discharge from tank cleaning is routine and numerous accidental spills have occurred. Petroleum discharge during tank cleaning and from transfer operations at wells, terminals, storage tanks and refineries also contributes significant petroleum to the region's marine environment.

Eighty to ninety percent of ship-generated marine pollution incidents are due to human error. The world of shipping is expected to experience significant technological changes in the 1980s and thus to become more complex. Mariners will have to rely more heavily on instrumentation and be more highly trained. Some new equipment may prove to be dangerous, if it is not properly used. With the encouragement of The United Nations Conference on Trade and Development (UNCTAD), a number of developing states will begin to build their own merchant fleets, and thus a greater number of states will become involved in shipping. Consequently, it will become more difficult to attain and maintain uniformly high standards for the training of seamen. Further, the shift to indigenous refining by OPEC nations may mean more and smaller tankers carrying more environmentally dangerous refined products.

4. Law of the Sea and Marine Pollution

A major impact of the new Law of the Sea on marine pollution may be manifested through the new powers given to coastal states to set standards for ship-generated marine pollution. The designation of sealanes, traffic separation schemes, vessel traffic management systems and areas of special environmental significance by coastal states will require cooperation with international organizations like the Inter-governmental Maritime Consultative Organization, neighboring coastal states and user states, as well as a new awareness on the part of mariners. Promulgation of environmental or other regulations in claimed areas with respect to oil tankers, may, as in the case of the Strait of Malacca, result in a shift of transportation routes for certain vessels.

So far, the coastal states of the South China Sea have emphasized a strengthening of their national legislation instead of seeking regional solutions to reduce ship-generated marine pollution. Thus an initial patchwork of environmental policy initiatives seems likely, possibly leading to double standards for indigenous versus through carriers, variation in navigational aids, contingency plans for disaster situations and disparities in environmental management experience.

III. Conflicts

1. Efficent Utilization of Resources

The myriad increasing activities and usage of the coastal and marine environment in the region is producing conflicts within one use, such as fishing, and between uses such as fishing and waste disposal. When, in addition, extended jurisdictional claims are superimposed on this mosaic of resources, uses and conflicts, some conflicts have become international. There are basically four categories of coastal and marine resource use conflicts: competition for space itself, synchronic competing uses of the same resource, present dedicated use *versus* future use of the same resource and uses at some distance away affected by uses that modify the coastal environment. Some priority areas of concern may be delineated as urgently requiring coastal area planning for the most efficient utilization of the available resources.

Certainly, the coastal areas enveloping the region's major cities are of concern due to the concentration of many resource uses in a small area: dense human habitation, commerce and industry, highways, airports, ports, land reclamation, unrestricted domestic and industrial waste disposal, power facilities, disease control and logging, terrestrial mining and agriculture in the hinterland. Priority urban areas would include Manila, Jakarta and all of north Java and Bangkok. Although controls on existing coastal resource uses may be difficult to implement due mainly to nontechnical reasons, new or additional uses might be regulated or at least planned for, especially in new "development" areas. The upper Gulf of Thailand, particularly the Bight of Bangkok, is a case in point. Circulation is extremely weak, and a new deep-water port is planned with attendant domestic and industrial/commercial activity, adding further stress to the coastal resources in this area. Areas of potential conflict in coastal resource use also include the greater Gulf of Thailand and northwest Palawan, where aquaculture, petroleum exploitation and offshore fisheries may coincide.

2. Development of Sea and Coastal Utilization

The constricted, shallow Malacca Strait is a priority area for a coordinated international approach by the four bordering nations—Thailand, Malaysia, Indonesia and Singapore. This area is a microcosm of the coastal activities and conflicts of the region. The Strait is a major transport route for petroleum tankers. Coastal petroleum exploitation is ongoing in north Sumatra, with exploration off southwest Thailand; and coastal depots and refineries are situated in Dumai, Port Dickson and Singapore. Bottom mining is ongoing from Phuket northwards and exploration is underway off Malacca and Penang. Terrestrial tin mining is scattered throughout the Thai isthmus and the Malay Peninsula. Logging activity is significant on Sumatra, generating much sediment and contributing to coastal accretion. In addition to Singapore, the west coast of the Malay Peninsula is rapidly becoming urbanized, and much of Malaysia's population and industrial agricultural processing activity is concentrated there, discharging wastes into the Strait, including those from disease control. The ports of Penang, Port Swettenham, Port Dickson and Singapore are situated on the Strait.

Aquaculture is being expanded in north Sumatra and may be expanded in suitable locations along Malaysia's west coast, and mangrove harvesting is locally significant throughout the coastal area of the Strait. Much of the West Malaysian coastal plain above the high-tide mark is under cultivation, and an agricultural scheme utilizing reclaimed land is planned for southeast Sumatra. Artisanal fishing including shellfish harvesting is widespread in the nearshore areas, and significant offshore fishing is conducted in the northern Strait. Tourism/recreation centers bordering the Strait include Phuket, Penang and Pangkor; marine research stations are located at Phuket, Penang and Singapore.

IV. Opportunities, Challenges and Responses

1. Coastal Zone Management and Multiple Resource Uses

From a realistic politicoeconomic perspective, it is clear that certain activities in the region will have priority, such as extraction of hydrocarbons and minerals. However, such activities could be planned so as to minimize adverse impacts on other coastal resources and uses; also other uses, such as tourism/recreation, might be geographically situated in areas less likely to be exploited for other purposes. However, it remains to be seen whether and when governmental philosophies, so geared to growth development on the Western model, will also incorporate the concept of planned growth and optimum allocation of coastal resources, so recently and painfully adopted by the West.

Southeast Asia has witnessed in recent years a significant growth of national agencies and legislation pertaining to environmental protection. However, existing coastal zone management planning is based on interagency links rather than on any comprehensive overview of pollution and multiple resource uses, and as a result management is fragmentary both at the national and at the regional level. There is also a debilitating gap between national legislation and implementation.

Environmental baseline studies are necessary for monitoring of ecosystem deterioration and for compensation to states for pollution. Without such benchmarks it is difficult later to determine and to prove the extent and cause of any damage. Long-term ecosystem effects remain particularly difficult to quantify in economic terms. Already the possibility of establishing pristine environmental baselines in some areas is greatly diminished or precluded because hydrocarbon exploration and development and other exploitive uses of the coastal zone have been underway for years.

Anticipated economic benefits may be a prime motivation for jurisdictional extension, but such extension will produce unanticipated economic and political side effects. First, the zones of extended jurisdictions will bring more area and more types of activity under the control of coastal states, which will have to develop policies and efficient management designs for the environment, resources and the increasing varieties of activity within these zones.

For example, the protection of the environment of the entire South China Sea is now the responsibility of the coastal states. In particular, these states are required to take all necessary measures consistent with the Convention to prevent, reduce and control pollution of the marine environment from any source, using for this purpose the best practicable means at their disposal and in accordance with their capabilities, individually or jointly as appropriate, and they shall endeavor to harmonize their policies in this connection. This responsibility includes land-based, atmospheric and offshore sources.

Second, the need is also apparent for increased bilateral and multilateral consultations, as well as a new degree of coordination to meet the challenge of these impending changes in marine use patterns and concepts. Many marine resources are transnational in distribution; the ocean, a continuous fluid system, transmits environmental pollutants; and maritime activities often transcend the new national marine jurisdictional boundaries. Management policies for these national zones of extended jurisdiction may be developed and implemented with insufficient scientific and technical understanding of the transnational character of the ocean environment and the resources and activities it harbors and supports. Diversity of management regimes for transnational resources or activities can lead to intra- and inter-regional compromise, or to conflict. The superimposition of a mosaic of national jurisdictional claims and regulations on transnational resources and activities thus creates possibilities for transnational conflict, as well as opportunities for cooperation.

2. National Interest and the Law of the Sea

The Convention on the Law of the Sea, in Article 123, provides that states bordering enclosed or semienclosed seas should cooperate with each other in the exercise of their rights and duties under the Convention. Specifically they "shall endeavour directly or through an appropriate regional organization:

(a) to co-ordinate the management, conservation, exploration and exploitation of the living resources of the sea;

(b) to co-ordinate the implementation of their rights and duties with respect to the protection and preservation of the environment;

(c) to co-ordinate their scientific research policies and undertake where appropriate joint programmes of scientific research in the area;

(d) to invite, as appropriate, other interested states or international organizations to co-operate with them in furtherance of the provisions of this article."

Indeed, it is becoming evident that appraisals of most changes in the ocean environment are most meaningful on a regional basis, where the intertwining of biological, physical and social factors can be fully appreciated.

But which specific issues and which aspects of marine policy can really be more effectively addressed by a regional approach, and at what level and degree of formality? Should regional approaches be pursued for, say, dispute settlement, management of migratory fish, surveillance and/or enforcement regarding fisheries or environmental regulations, access for fishing or marine scientific research, environmental regulations for transiting vessels, response to transnational oil spills, hazardous waste disposal or regional preserves? What is the appropriate "region" for each of the opportunities for cooperation? What are the various national interests in regard to these opportunities, and what are the likely advantages, disadvantages and trade-offs for each nation and party involved in, or affected by, regional approaches to particular marine policies? Which recurring issues might benefit from a regional institutional arrangement? What might be expected of such institutions and what would be their likely structure and function? How much would they cost and who should, could or would pay? What are the possible roles of the existing international organizations? What relevant lessons have been learned elsewhere, and what aspects should and could be adapted to the region?

3. Regional Efforts

There have been some regional efforts regarding marine matters by the Association of Southeast Asian Nations (ASEAN). Permanent ASEAN committees of marine importance include Fisheries (as a part of food production and supply), Meteorology (as part of air traffic service), Science and Technology and Shipping. The Federation of ASEAN Shippers' Council sponsored the formation of a Federation of ASEAN Shipowners' Association, presumably to present a united bargaining position *vis-à-vis* the European-dominated Far Eastern Freight Conference, which controls trade and sets rates for transport of goods between Europe and Asia.

The ASEAN Committee on Science and Technology (COST) has a Subcommittee on Marine Sciences which has discussed the possibility of a cooperative approach to extraregional access for marine scientific research and has approached Canada, Japan and the United States regarding priority assistance for funding of cooperative marine scientific research. COST has also spawned an informal committee on pollution and a proposal for an ASEAN Subregional Environment Programme. As part of this program, the member nations have discussed a coordinated approach to marine environmental protection with the Regional Seas Programme of the United Nations Environment Programme (UNEP). The Regional Seas Programme has the goal of producing for the "East Asian Seas" a Mediterranean-type protocol and to upgrade awareness and capabilities for its implementation. But the program has encountered difficulties due to conflicting offshore claims and nonparticipation of some main claimants; its budget is also very small and the proposed projects are really more national than international in character. The ASEAN Council on Petroleum (ASCOPE) also has within its terms of reference the development of subregional contingency plans for oil spills and the implications of a transnational spill, and has been discussing standardization of environmental and safety regulations concerning offshore oil exploration. The Malacca Straits Safe Navigation Scheme between Malaysia, Singapore and Indonesia, and the concomitant U.S. $1.3 million revolving fund established by Japanese shipping interests and these nations to cover the cost of cleaning up and preventing oil spills from tankers, are the most concrete indigenous examples of marine regionalization to date.

There are also several marine-relevant international organizations operating in the region. These organizations are not indigenously derived or majority-funded, and included among their membership are both extra-ASEAN and South China Sea states. Nevertheless, these organizations may serve as models, platforms or stimuli for indigenously initiated, intergovernmentally functioning marine regional arrangements. For example, a new body sponsored by the Intergovernmental Oceanographic Commission (IOC), the Working Group for the Western Pacific (WESTPAC), includes the South China Sea within its geographic terms of reference for coordination of marine scientific research by participating countries.

However, in general, the Southeast Asian states are only now beginning to perceive clearly their own national marine interests and how these differ from those of neighboring states or major maritime powers. At this juncture, commonalities are neglected and differences emphasized, particularly regarding the place of environmental protection in national priorities. Functional marine regionalism or subregionalism is incipient at best and perhaps a hopelessly idealistic goal at worst. When it comes to protection of the marine environment, necessity may be the mother of cooperation.

V. Future Scenarios

Indeed, extremely optimistic and extremely pessimistic scenarios for the next twenty years can be projected from the present status of Asian waters.

1. Optimistic Prospects

In an extremely optimistic scenario, the region's people can be quite satisfied with their accomplishments. The marine environment is being managed as a sustainable use system. National political purpose and the will to achieve a sustained environment have triumphed over conflict and confusion. A Regional Ocean Management Authority (ROMA) with credibility and enforcement powers provides an umbrella for the resolution of all international ocean management disputes. All major ocean boundary disputes have been resolved without lingering bitterness. Multiple use conflicts are prevented or quickly resolved. Responsibilities and benefits of transnational resource and environmental management have been allocated and agreed upon. Regulations and standards have been harmonized. The politically powerful ROMA negotiates with extraregional maritime users on behalf of the region's states regarding shipping, fisheries and environment issues.

In particular, environmental regulations and enforcement for land-based, atmospheric and offshore pollution sources have been standardized by the Environment Arm of ROMA (EAROMA) on a sliding scale related to stage of development. Discharge of substances dangerous to human health and the environment, e.g., metals, synthetic chemicals and sewage has been controlled, and pollution incidents are infrequent, short-lived and promptly remedied. Pollution control has become largely a system of prevention rather than response. Extensive monitoring systems ensure the health of coastal dwellers and the environment. Regional contingency systems for combatting spilled oil are well organized and coordinated, and work well in the few instances required. Regional systems for disposal of hazardous waste and toxic chemicals have been established. All nuclear materials have been banned from the region. Extensive national marine and coastal park systems have been established for the enjoyment of recreationers and tourists. Extensive tracts of pristine, valuable and vulnerable ecosystem have been set aside as preserves as part of a regional system based on genetic variety and endangered and threatened species. In the offshore area these preserves are known as "special areas" and are accorded special status under the Caracas Convention on the Law of the Sea which has been signed by all countries. As a result of these efforts, all species endangered back in the early 1980s have been saved and no new species have been added to the list.

Many of these accomplishments have been made possible by enhanced knowledge of marine ecosystems and their interactions with pollutants, particularly long-term, sub-lethal effects. Baseline knowledge of pristine environments is well-established as comparative points for the monitoring system. In a series of global precedents, courts deliberating on international oil spill cases now accept claims to long-term ecosystem damage. Using such precedents, the ROMA persuaded the oil and shipping industry to establish a billion-dollar-per-incident, no-fault compensation fund to compensate for such damage.

In fisheries, all species stressed in the early 1980s are now being managed at optimum sustainable yield. Aquaculture continues to fill the gap between supply and demand for fish protein and provides a community-based industry for rural areas as well as an outlet for surplus fisheries labor. The techniques used are a blend of traditional and Western technology. Some offshore areas which were cleaned of pollution are now being used for ocean ranching of grouper, tuna, mackerel and the like; expansion further offshore is envisioned, possibly linked to the many Ocean Thermal Energy Conversion (OTEC) plants planned throughout the archipelagic countries.

New species like the midwater shrimp are harvested and so-called trash fish are used for fish paste. Access to a regional network of freezing, landing and marketing facilities prevents spoilage; standardized prices and hydrofoil transportation of catch prevents geographic misallocation of landings. A regional fishing license for EEZs obviates the questions of transnational access and surplus, and prevents conflicts. Good fishing practice and fisheries management are ensured by standardized or regional agreed regulations on gear, mesh-size, seasons and quotas, established and enforced by the Fisheries Arm of ROMA (FAROMA).

Again, this revolution in international cooperation was made possible by excellent knowledge of the biology of migratory and shared species, their distinctive stocks, their migration routes or distribution patterns and the relationships between breeding areas and adults. With this knowledge and the incentive, indeed the necessity, for better fisheries management that followed, the numerous offshore/inshore conflicts of the '80s were resolved by limited entry and the subsidization of retraining and geographic movement of surplus fisheries labor to other pursuits. Instrumental in this transformation was the definition and articulation of clear, nonconflicting national fisheries goals and policies designed to maintain the resources and enhance the quality, not the quantity, of the industry.

In shipping, major changes have occurred as well. Indigenous cargoes are now carried by indigenously owned ships in the 40:40:20 ratio suggested by UNCTAD in the '80s; and the Shipping Arm of ROMA (SAROMA) is lobbying for a 50:50 split. SAROMA has established regional regulations for tankers for safety, manning and discharge, and a combined satellite, air and sea surveillance and enforcement system. SAROMA requires that all mariners serving on tankers be certified by SAROMA's Mariner Training Center and that all tankers use Load on Top II (LOT II) systems. Regional waste oil receiving stations have been established at strategic points throughout the region as well as have safe harbors and routes for crippled tankers (tanker hospitals). Safe navigation schemes exist for all major straits, and navigation devices and guides are modern and well maintained.

Scientific research has been the underpinning of many of these remarkable advances. National capabilities have been greatly enhanced and supported by the Research Arm of ROMA (RAROMA), which maintains two regional training and research centers, for marine science and affairs, to strengthen national capabilities through research focused on truly regional systems, e.g., currents, typhoon generation, ecosystem pollution effects, regional genetic resources and regional disposal of hazardous waste. Developed countries participate in and support these scientific endeavors on invitation for specific purposes under specific conditions set by RAROMA.

Finally, multiple use and its many problems are nightmares of the past. MUAROMA, the Multiple Use Arm of ROMA, as a separate arm of ROMA with overriding authority, represents each of the Primary Arms of ROMA. MUAROMA plans multiple use and prevents and resolves multiple use conflicts in close consultation with the nations and parties concerned.

In the area of hydrocarbons, all disputed areas with hydrocarbon potential have been equitably divided or jointly developed. Hydrocarbons have been discovered and developed throughout the "Dangerous Ground," the Mainland Shelf including the Paracels and Macclesfield Bank area, the Vietnamese Shelf and the eastern Gulf of Thailand, and from some parts of the continental slope, increasing the offshore contribution to the region's production and reserves to about 50 percent. The region is the world's leading exporter of LNG with ten LNG plants in operation. A plethora of seafloor production systems and floating LNG plants, refineries and storage systems further add an offshore flavor to Asia's hydrocarbon industry. The Hydrocarbon Arm of ROMA (HAROMA) sets prices and arranges markets for HAROMA crude and LNG, and allocates subsidized supplies on a regular and emergency basis among its members, including nonproducing countries. However, the industry is almost entirely export-oriented as ROMA's members have made the transition to alternative energy systems. Drilling procedures are standardized, strictly regulated and enforced by HAROMA for safety and environmental protection. Systematic environmental impact analysis must be developed and approved before major field development is undertaken. Accidents as well as unexpected impacts are rare and their effects investigated and promptly mitigated.

2. Pessimistic Prospects

The extremely pessimistic scenario is rather unattractive. States treat their extended jurisdictional zones like territorial seas, which are jealously protected. A mosaic of widely differing regulations, enforcement procedures and capabilities presents a crazy-quilt obstacle to management of transnational resources and activities. Each new international ocean management issue creates a political trauma for the countries involved, particularly for political adversaries in this deeply divided region. There are no common policies vis-à-vis external users and thus certain external powers are able to achieve their aims through divide-and-control strategies.

As for environmental management, the initiatives of the '70s and '80s have been abandoned. In short, quick economic growth took precedence over a sustained environment. Regulations vary widely within and between countries; moreover, enforcement is weak and variable.

The coastal strip of the South China Sea is packed with people and raw material processing and manufacturing industries which use the seas as a "free" waste disposal area. No extensive tracts of mangrove or coral reef are left around the South China Sea, and most estuaries are heavily polluted. All species listed as endangered in the early '80s have been eliminated from the region and twice as many species have taken their place on the list. The turtles have stopped returning in large numbers to Trengganu, and the crocodile and dugong are only legends, as none have been seen for many years.

Pollution of coastal seas is thought to be heavy, and apparent environmental effects of heavy metals, synthetic chemicals and oil pollution are common. The Operation Mussel Watch back in the '80s had sounded the alarm but to no avail. Although initially there were some warnings by environmental groups and others, government suppression of these outcries as antidevelopment and therefore antipatriotic soon curtailed these movements. Government environmental agencies either remained powerless or were abolished. As a result, no new systematic information on the state of marine pollution has been available for a decade and now no pristine areas exist to provide comparative baseline information for analysis and decision making.

There have been several Minamata-like outbreaks but the specific cause has not been identified. There is even some evidence of pollution-related genetic defects among peoples living in close proximity to particular industries. Fish kills due to unknown causes are common. Red tides are now frequent and persistent—too much so to be of purely natural origins; shellfish throughout the region are eaten only by the foolhardy or the unaware.

Large areas have been declared biological deserts, like New York Harbor: e.g., offshore major cities, Bight of Bangkok, Manila Bay, Malacca Strait. Needless to say, marine tourism never really got started and many former coastal tourist destinations have been abandoned, e.g., Penang, Phuket, Pattaya, Batangas, Pulau Seribu. The national marine park systems initiated in the 1980s have deteriorated through misuse and neglect.

The picture in fishing is, if anything, worse. Most stocks have been overfished and stressed by pollution to the point where they have been replaced by undesirable species. Towards the end of this tragedy of the commons, mesh sizes became smaller and smaller and blast fishing predominated, with only the high-priced species being kept. As fish grew scarce, conflicts between inshore and offshore fishermen grew increasingly violent, requiring bans on fishing and military intervention to quell the civil strife. After years of jailing one another's fishermen, impounding or driving away each other's fishing vessels and accusing each other of various deliberate sins and general bad faith, a plethora of fisheries wars—the tuna war, the mackerel war and others—erupted between once-friendly neighbors.

Whole industries based on these stocks collapsed—fishing, preservation, processing, marketing—and some fifty million people and their dependents in the region were deprived of income, doubling unemployment and urban migration rates. Cultural traditions based on fisheries were also largely lost and fisheries artifacts became valuable, fetching high prices among expatriate tourists in various Thieves' Markets. *Ikan bilis* and *belachan* became high-priced entrees at fancy restaurants.

The worst effect of the failures was, of course, protein malnutrition. Protein deficiencies among the rural poor greatly increased as they had no other source of income to purchase replacement for their traditional fish. As the shortages became frequent and prices increased several hundred percent, citizen demonstrations forced costly government subsidies of fish imports, largely "cheap" fish, e.g., milkfish, tilapia and catfish, cultivated in the West under a massive and lucrative campaign to provide "medium-priced fish" for the "developing" world.

As impending disaster became apparent, governments had desperately shifted their emphasis to aquaculture, but much of the rare suitable land was already committed to industrialization. Although programs were pushed ahead, aquaculture ponds and products became heavily polluted; milkfish fry and gravid female prawns became extremely scarce. Productivity decreased and foreign market resistance to the polluted products set in. A few sites dedicated to production of luxury species for export, like shrimp, were protected from pollution by the machinations of foreign investors and their local business partners. The governments' attempts at transfer of labor from capture fisheries to aquaculture thus became a cruel joke, and the region's demand soon exceeded supply. For a while, distant-water fishing nations from outside the region used the confusion and disunity to fish migratory and shared stocks intensively; however, they soon overfished the stocks and moved their facilities elsewhere, leaving their hosts holding the unreturned investment on unemployable boats and people.

As for shipping, foreign lines continue to dominate the region's trade and to dictate freight rates. Through tanker traffic cleans tanks and ballast with impunity in the region. Equipment, safety, manning and discharge standards have been lowered to save money. The coastal trade is dominated by indigenous fleets which are poorly manned, equipped and maintained. Both through trade and intraregional oil trade is now dominated by smaller ships carrying refined products which are environmentally more hazardous. Port areas continue to be congested, inefficient and hazardous. Navigation aids and traffic safety schemes are outdated and poorly maintained; "rogue" ships operating outside safe channels are common.

The results have been spectacular accidents and accompanying oil and product spills—three major events in the region in 1972 alone. These incidents were typical of the last decade. Each spill moved across international boundaries and there were confusion and mutual accusations, but no clean-up or protection until the oil had already come ashore. Indeed, one of the incidents again underscored the need for cooperation. A supertanker, damaged in a collision in the Malacca Strait, limped from port to port along the Strait but none would accept her. In desperation her captain headed for the open sea but she sank just east of Singapore, spilling her 200,000 tons of oil into the waters of three countries.

The region boasts two notorious firsts—a serious accident involving a vessel carrying nuclear spent fuel and the first serious LNG spill. In the first instance, a British government vessel carrying Japanese nuclear spent fuel for reprocessing in Europe burned and sank after colliding with an oil tanker at night in the Strait of Malacca. The U.S. military immediately and unilaterally blocked off the Strait and recovered most of the nuclear cargo, although some was lost and presumably has entered the ecosystem. In the LNG incident, a specially built carrier was taking on LNG at the floating Natuna plant when one of the lines ruptured, spilling the fluid onto the dock area. Apparently the gas vaporized and an open fire set off a series of tremendous explosions and fires; there were no survivors.

The region continues to have one of the world's highest undiscovered oil potentials because nations cannot agree on splitting or sharing of disputed areas. Further, a spill similar to the IXTOC-1 incident (where 140 million gallons of oil escaped from an offshore oil rig in the Gulf of Mexico) occurred on the Macclesfield Bank area off China where a well blew out of control for three months, creating an oil slick which eventually reached Malaysia. Such blowouts on a smaller scale have become frequent as companies cut their safety margins to obtain as much oil as quickly as they can before the region's instability again devolves into open conflict. There are no uniform safety standards and enforcement is weak and variable. "Best company practice" has become a public joke.

As one might imagine, multiple use conflicts have become a nightmarish maze resembling an '80s space-invaders video game, although the kills are real and the effects long-lasting. Frankly, national and international ocean management is in chaos.

Neither scenario is likely to be entirely accurate; the reality will be somewhere in between. The relative emphasis of optimistic and pessimistic elements in this future reality is in the hands of present policymakers and their political will.

Note

This paper is based in part on the accumulated work of the Program on Marine Environment and Extended Maritime Jurisdictions: Transnational Environment and Resource Management in Southeast Asian Seas, a project of the Environment and Policy Institute, East-West Center, Honolulu, Hawaii, U.S.A.

Water Management in the Malaysian Coastal Zone and Its Socioeconomic Implications

Cheong Chup Lim and Sieh Kok Chi

Coastal zones, including deltaic and estuarine areas, possess a number of natural advantages for socioeconomic development which are not found or do not occur to the same extent in the hinterland. The nearby seas and rivers are natural sources of fish and other foods and the rivers provide fresh water for domestic usage as well as for irrigation. Lands in the coastal zones are usually fertile and flat, and are suitable for the cultivation of rice—the staple in the tropics. A further advantage is the availability of water transport which facilitates communication, not only locally but also with the outside world. Thus in the past coastal zones have provided opportunities for the establishment of human settlements and the development of population centers.

In spite of these advantages coastal zones are not without inherent drawbacks, such as being exposed to flooding by rivers and the sea, drought which occurs from time to time, river pollution due to development and activities in the hinterland and other water problems. As population expands and as the demand of human society for water increases and becomes more complex, relevant water problems come into sharper focus, and the need for water management in these areas arises.

Water management is concerned primarily with the efficient use and control of water resources for beneficial purposes such as flood protection, drainage, water supply for agricultural, municipal and industrial uses, water quality control, navigation, hydropower generation, fish and wildlife conservation and recreation. Since water flows from upstream to downstream, there exists an intimate relationship between the interests of the coastal zone and those of the hinterland. As such, water management in the coastal zones should be an integral part of the overall river basin or regional water management program.

I. Background

Malaysia comprises Peninsular Malaysia and the States of Sabah and Sarawak on Borneo Island, with a total land area of about 336,000 square km. The two regions are separated by some 640 km of the South China Sea. It has a long coastline, and about half of the total land area of Malaysia consists of coastal and river plains. In Peninsular Malaysia, the coastal plains average about 30 km in width along the west coast, but are narrower along the east coast. In Sabah and Sarawak, the coastal plains are broader, averaging 50 km in width.

Settlement in Malaysia first began in the coastal zone in and around deltaic and estuarine areas. With the availability of abundant natural resources in the area, both the settlements and agricultural activities flourished rapidly. Today, areas of high population densities are found along the whole of the west coast and in the estuarine areas of Kelantan and Trengganu on the east coast of Peninsular Malaysia, as well as in the coastal zones of Sabah and Sarawak. Most of the major towns and state capitals are located in the coastal zone. About 70 percent of the total population of 13.5 million and major agricultural areas are found in this zone. In 1980 the gross domestic product (GDP) of Malaysia was M$25,376 million. The manufacturing sector contributed 21.2 percent to this and 22 percent in export earnings, while the agricultural sector's contributions for these were 22.9 percent and 40 percent, respectively. The labor force in Malaysia in 1980 was 5.4 million, with an unemployment rate of 5.3 percent. Total employed labor was estimated at 5.1 million with the agriculture, forestry and fishing sectors engaging 41 percent of the labor force.

The agricultural sector therefore plays an important role in the economy of Malaysia, although its relative importance is declining as the country proceeds toward industrialization. The agricultural population includes some of the most economically and socially depressed sectors of the Malaysian community. In 1978, it was estimated that 36 percent of the population in Malaysia had incomes below the official absolute poverty line, and of those, two-thirds were in agricultural households where the incidence of poverty was about 55 percent. Among *padi* (rice) farmers, it was estimated that 74 percent have family incomes below the absolute poverty line.

II. Water Resources Management

The control and use of water resources are essential to the undertaking of agricultural and industrial activities, and the management of these resources is therefore important in order to sustain economic growth and to raise the living standard of the people.

The main activities of water resources management in the Malaysian coastal zone are in the fields of irrigation and agricultural drainage, domestic and industrial water supplies, flood mitigation, water quality control and hydropower development.

1. Drainage and Irrigation

Irrigation and agricultural drainage works in Malaysia constitute a basic infrastructure on which the settlement, continued habitation and prosperity of large tracts of land in the coastal areas depend. The most productive *padi* as well as large tree-crop areas were developed from coastal swamp jungles and tidal lands. Drainage works give protection from sea and river floods and prevent tidal intrusion into settlements and agricultural lands. Irrigation works provide water to meet crop requirements. In general, irrigation and drainage create the physical conditions conducive to crop growth.

There is a total of about 530,000 ha of wet *padi* lands in Malaysia, out of which about 330,000 ha have been provided with irrigation facilities. The major irrigation schemes include Muda (95,860 ha), Krian (23,490 ha), Sg. Manik (6,000 ha), Tanjong Karang (19,260 ha), Besut (5,060 ha), Kemubu (17,990 ha) and North Kelantan (11,640 ha) which are by far the more productive. All are located in the coastal areas.

Irrigation in Malaysia has undergone several stages of development. Early irrigation works provided for simple water control and management systems whereby water from direct rainfall and nearby streams and rivers is conserved and used for the growing of *padi*. In some schemes, where a source of irrigation water was readily available, supplemental irrigation was provided.

With the advent of double cropping, the main effort was devoted to the development of an adequate water supply for the second crop (the dry-season crop). To bring about double cropping in existing major *padi* areas, the construction of storage reservoirs and large irrigation pumping stations involving major engineering works was undertaken. Canal and drainage systems were constructed to handle the full irrigation supply from the controlled source. This stage of development resulted in the rapid increase in rice production.

To exploit the full potential in crop yield in these areas, the development of tertiary irrigation and drainage facilities is being undertaken to permit proper water management at the farm level, i.e., to enable effective water distribution and control in the field—a condition necessary for the introduction of advanced cultivating practices and high yields.

Besides the main irrigation projects, major drainage projects for agricultural development have also been carried out. The main objectives of these projects are to improve agricultural productivity and to raise the farmers' income through improvement of drainage and flood control facilities. The major agricultural drainage projects are West Johore, 133,600 ha; Northwest Selangor, 77,000 ha; Bruas, 8,770 ha; Bagan Datoh, 24,220 ha; Kelang, 17,028 ha; Kuala Langat/Sepang, 31,469 ha; and Nonok, 15,663 ha. Except for the Nonok project, which is along the Sarawak coast, the rest of the projects are located on the west coast of Peninsular Malaysia.

2. Domestic and Industrial Water Supply

The provision of domestic and industrial water supply is to meet the basic human needs to enhance the quality of life, and to facilitate industrial and manufacturing processes. The annual growth in demand for water, both for domestic and industrial use, has been increasing rapidly over the past few years and its rate is now more than 11 percent per annum. Between 1959 and 1980, due to rapid development, increase in per capita consumption, increase in urban and rural coverage and industrial expansion, water demand has increased several fold. In 1980, 64 percent of the population was provided with public water supply, with the service factor for urban areas being around 90 percent and that for rural areas being about 40 percent. With further increase in population and the growth in GDP in the future, the demand for water will be even heavier, especially for industrial water.

The provision of a water supply is achieved either through the rather simple system of abstracting water from upstream portions of rivers that are free from saline intrusion, or through the construction of storage dams in upper catchments. Development first began with the readily available water sources near population and town centers, and as these are progressively committed to use, water has to be brought from further afield and the system becomes more complex and costly.

There are certain rural settlements which are rather small and scattered in the coastal areas and at the same time are situated far away from a source of fresh water. This situation has presented a special problem in water supply. Piped water supply is not readily available and is rather costly to provide. The problem is most acute in some coastal areas in Sarawak where more than 100,000 people periodically face the difficulty of water shortage. Suitable measures remain to be found to resolve this problem.

3. Flood Mitigation

Flooding is one of the negative aspects of water resources, and from past records the total flooded area in Malaysia amounts to about 29,300 sq. km, or some 9 percent of the total land area of Malaysia, affecting 2.8 million people. Of significance is the fact that the flooded areas are mostly located in the coastal zone and inland valleys where traditionally population centers and settlements are situated. As a result, flood damage and loss is significant, and the total annual average flood damage has been estimated to be about M$110 million. In order to reduce flood damage and hardship to the affected people, flood mitigation projects have been planned and implemented for the coastal zone. The bunding (diking) of river banks and sea coast, ring bunds, river channel improvements, bypass floodways and the construction of upstream flood control dams are the usual structural measures. Nonstructural measures include change in land use and land use control, and the setting up of flood forecasting and warning systems.

4. Water Pollution Abatement

The other negative aspect of water resources is pollution. Population and industrial growth has increased and will continue to increase the pollution load in rivers. The main sources of pollution are in the form of domestic and industrial sewage and effluents from oil palm mills and rubber factories. In the absence of control, many rivers in the west coast of Peninsular Malaysia will be heavily polluted in the future. In order to combat this the need to construct sewerage systems in towns and population centers is urgent. In addition, stringent measures should be taken to control effluent discharge from oil palm and rubber factories. It is only through these measures that the pollution of water resources and the coastal areas can be reduced to a manageable level.

5. Hydropower Development

Demand for power has been rapidly increasing over the past years, with an annual growth rate of between 10 percent to 12 percent. The major demand centers are the urban and industrial areas located in the coastal zone. In recent years, the rural electrification program has been intensified with the implementation of mini-hydro projects. In 1980, the share of hydropower was about 29 percent, with a total installed capacity of 614 mw. Another 750 mw of hydropower is being developed and will be completed by 1985.

Water management with regard to hydropower generation is relatively simple as it is a nonconsumptive user of water. However, since hydropower dams could also be integrated with other users, it is important that during the planning stage close coordination with other potential water users is carried out, so that multi-purpose storage projects would be developed for optimum usage of available resources and for maximizing economic efficiency.

III. Socioeconomic Implications

Water resources development activities are undertaken in support of the development of several major socioeconomic sectors. Irrigation development is linked to the production of food and the raising of farmers' incomes. The development of a public water supply contributes to industrial development and public health as well as rural development objectives. Pollution control ensures the preservation of river water in quantity and quality for various uses and the preservation of environmental quality. Flood mitigation contributes towards the social well-being of the people in the flood-prone areas and provides a better physical environment to permit socioeconomic activities to continue to take place. Hydropower development contributes towards the production of energy for the country essential for industrial, urban and rural development.

The management of water resources therefore has far-reaching socioeconomic implications and its direct impacts include the improvement of both urban and rural environment, the increase in employment opportunities and the increase in income levels of the people. By far, the above impacts are greater on the rural community who benefit directly from the agricultural development projects, the provision of rural water supply and rural electrification.

1. Improvement of Urban and Rural Environment

Water resources management will improve the overall environment through better drainage facilities, flood control measures, prevention of tidal intrusion and water pollution abatement measures. The drainage of swamp and low-lying areas has generally improved the health environment of the areas and this is borne out by the fact that diseases such as elephantiasis and malaria, which were very common in tidal areas in the past, have now been greatly reduced if not eradicated, while the provision of public water supply has greatly reduced the incidence of cholera outbreaks. The provision of electricity, flood control and water pollution abatement measures have enhanced the quality of life and social well-being of the people.

2. Increase in Employment Opportunities

Water resources development projects will not only create employment opportunities during the construction period of the projects, but will also generate employment opportunities for the population through increased land use and farming activities. They permit expansion of the manufacturing and industrial sectors, leading to increased employment. Increased agricultural production will increase the general wealth of the people and will have a catalytic effect on the generation of further employment opportunities. As an example, the Western Johore Agricultural Development Project provides, among other things, flood mitigation and improved drainage to 133,600 ha of existing and potential agricultural lands and it is projected that as a result some 24,000 full-time jobs would be created by the year 2000.

3. Increase in Income Levels

With the implementation of the various water resources projects, the income of the population will be substantially increased. Agricultural development projects have the most direct impact on the raising of the income of farmers. For the West Johore Agricultural Project, the farmer's income has been projected to increase from the present level of about M$2,100.00 from a 2.0-ha area of oil palm and rubber to about M$4,800.00 on completion of the project, while for the *padi* scheme in Muda, the farmer's income will increase from the present level of about M$3,000.00 for a 1.4-ha area to about M$5,200.00 on completion of the Muda II project.

IV. Future Trends in Water Resources Management: Conclusions

Given the objectives and targets set for continued socioeconomic development in Malaysia, the scale of water resources development and management must necessarily increase in the next two decades. Thus, water demand for domestic and industrial uses has been projected to increase by 3.5 times between now and the year 2000, while irrigation water demand will almost be doubled. The increased use of water will result in a corresponding increase in the volume of sewage and waste water. This, together with increased effluent from oil palm mills and rubber factories, will impose very heavy pollution loads on rivers and waterways, which need to be controlled.

At present, the readily available portion of water resources has already been committed for use and the development of additional sources will be more costly in the future. Unless water resources development is planned and undertaken to meet domestic, industrial, agricultural and other uses, competition among the various water use sectors will arise.

In order that water will not be a constraint to socioeconomic development, the planning of water resources development projects should be based on a long-term perspective of problems and needs as well as available resources. To avoid conflict among water use sectors, the planning should coordinate and integrate the requirements of various water use sectors to achieve optimum use of available resources in a river basin, in a state or in a region covering several states. There is therefore a need for the preparation of a water resources master plan at national and regional levels. At the national level, the planning should be guided by the targets for the development of various water use sectors in consonance with social development goals, taking into account available resources. At the regional level, the planning should be based on the national water resources master plan and should formulate specific water resources development programs, identify projects, carry out feasibility studies and determine the priority ranking of projects for implementation.

The above underlines the need for an integrated approach to the management of all water resources activities. Accordingly, a framework needs to be established for the orderly planning and implementation of water resources programs and projects and for rational water resources management. Such a framework not only provides for the necessary institutions and procedures for the planning, execution and management of water resources projects, but also includes the water administration systems and legal provisions to facilitate implementation and management of water resources programs and projects in an orderly and efficient manner.

Water Quality in the Coastal Area
The Jakarta Bay Experience

R. T. M. Sutamihardja

The role of the sea in the history of mankind has been proved. It is very important in supporting and meeting essential human needs, as can be seen in various activities like fisheries, marine transportation, dredging, offshore drilling, tourism and education. There is apparently a trend in Indonesia, during its economic development, to generate various economic activities near the shoreline such as tidal rice field farming and electric power generation. Consequently, its population and industrial activities are shifting to the coastal regions.

The increased utilization of marine resources is a remarkable phenomenon of technological progress and of human dependence on it. This two-fold or manifold use of marine resources, however, can result in serious consequences from the possible resulting conflict of interests, which could happen in extensively used marine waters like estuaries, bays, straits and inner or closed sea waters. With increased economic development to meet the demands of social welfare, harmful side effects will also tend to increase, resulting in environmental degradation and pollution, especially of the marine biota.

To protect and to save the marine biota, total and integrated preventive measures are required to give benefits to each sector of economic activity without harmful effects to any. However difficult this may be in practice, these measures must gradually be applied if conservation of marine resources for continuous and optimal utilization is our ultimate goal. The most difficult problem we have to face, however, is the problem of how to control marine pollution.

The problem of marine pollution as a whole, however, cannot be approached from one aspect only. It is clear that during the history of mankind the sea has been considered as a "waste basket" (*keranjang sampah*). Until now the view has existed that the sea is a convenient and economical place for depositing waste materials. However great and dynamic the potentialities of the seas are in dissolving, decomposing and diffusing waste materials and recycling their reproduced nutrients to the ecosystem, there will be a time when these potentialities reach their limits, and at that stage the seas will become incapable of performing their recycling function properly. This is especially true for narrow marine waters not directly connected with oceans or open seas. When this happens, foreign matter, especially that which is insoluble, will accumulate and will change the marine habitat, which in turn will cause serious injuries to the biota. The insoluble matter must therefore be subjected to special cautionary measures to avoid harmful effects on other economic and social aspects like fisheries, public health and tourism.

The Jakarta Bay region as a whole cannot be considered separately from other surrounding regions, particularly from the city of Jakarta, with its watershed and rivers running into Jakarta Bay and adjacent marine waters. The human factor in this case constitutes the most active component of the system. Discussions on the water quality of Jakarta Bay, therefore, must be related to human activities directly or indirectly affecting its aquatic environment.

In this report information obtained from studies conducted on the water quality of Jakarta Bay and other related subjects has been put together to give a clear illustration of the status of the aforementioned aquatic environment resulting from various interactions. This information was derived from secondary data without critical evaluation. The conclusions, therefore, should not be used as guidelines for entirely solving and tackling the water quality problem of Jakarta Bay.

I. General Features of the Area

Parjaman (1977) and Nontji and Supangat (1977) have stated that Jakarta Bay is a shallow water system, with a water depth near the shoreline of less than 10 m, and further from it, i.e., outside Jakarta Bay, about 10–30 m. The sea bottom slopes gently towards the Java Sea. The increase in depth from the shoreline to the Java Sea is gradual and regular. The more or less flat topography of the sea bottom of Jakarta Bay, 200–600 m from the shoreline, is covered with muddy sand, and further towards the Java Sea by sandy mud. In the center and western parts of Jakarta Bay, some coral islands are located. The isobaths are 5, 10 and 20 m, and are more or less parallel to the shoreline. The opening of Teluk Jakarta (Jakarta Bay) is about 22 miles wide. The deepest inlet, measured from the imaginary line connecting the extremes of the opening, i.e., from Tanjung Karawang (Cape of Karawang) at the east to Tanjung Pasir (Cape of Pasir) at the west, is about 10 miles.

The coastal area is generally covered by mud, sand, muddy sand and sandy mud. There are many great and small rivers flowing into this bay, such as the Citarum, Kali Bekasi, Kali Sunter, Kali Asin, Ciliwung and Cisadane. At the river mouths (estuaries) of the great rivers, there are sandbanks. The coast gently sloping into the sea is generally covered with mangroves, coastal shrubs and swamps.

Like the Java Sea, Jakarta Bay waters are heavily affected by the monsoons. The east monsoon, occurring in June, July and August, is generally dry and drives the sea westward. The west monsoon, on the other hand, occurring in December, January and February, is wet and drives the sea eastward. In between is the first transitory season, occurring in March, April and May, and the second transitory season, occurring in September, October and November, with winds of irregular direction and generally of low intensity.

The average yearly rainfall for the Jakarta region and its hinterland, up to Tangkuban Perahu and the Salak Mountains, ranges from 1,500 mm to 6,000 mm. This rainfall level greatly affects the water volume of Citarum, Ciliwung and Cisadane rivers, all of which flow into Jakarta Bay.

The highs and lows of the sea level in Jakarta Bay have been studied since the Dutch administration, and it was concluded that there are only the daily ebbs and tides. The lowest sea level ever recorded in the study (for more than twenty years) was not more than 0.6 m below the central point of position.

The stream characteristics in Jakarta Bay during the west monsoon (October–April) affects the shoreline facing westward in terms of erosion and translocation of the land surface, resulting in sedimentation and formation of sandbanks and movement of depth lines.

II. Causes of Marine Pollution

1. Jakarta Bay as a Terminal of River Water

In Indonesia and in other maritime countries, the occurrence of marine pollution may result from terrestrial activities like manufacture, urban life and watershed destruction, and from marine activities like offshore drilling, dredging, sea mining and marine transportation. The type and level of pollution are determined by various factors like the kind, amount, and extent of the activities and the location and interaction of various systems.

Jakarta Bay, which functions as a region for transport activities (local, national and international), fisheries and tourism, as well as a place for terminal accumulation of river waters with all the transported materials and thermal wastes, clearly has a heavy duty. Various activity sectors contribute to the pollution of Jakarta Bay, such as industry, urban dwellings or agriculture.

To determine the quality of a water system (aquatic environment), some parameters have to be measured. The water quality parameters can be classified into the chemical, physical and biological (including microbiological). The chemical parameters include the data on organic materials (carbon compounds), inorganic materials (mineral compounds) and toxic substances. Data for the physical parameters are on turbidity, suspended material, temperature, salinity, conductivity, color, foam, water flow, stream velocity, pH and substrates. Finally, the biological parameters give us the data on bacteria, viruses, animals, plants, soluble foodstuffs, competition and diversity among various biota, or predatory cycles, interdependency in the food chain, smell and taste.

The normally accepted parameters in various criteria for water quality are: temperature, total suspended solids (TSS), total dissolved solids (TDS), electric conductivity, dissolved oxygen (DO), pH, biological oxygen demand (BOD), chemical oxygen demand (COD), alkalinity, hardness, color, phosphate, nitrate and ammonia concentrations, coliform count, clarity/turbidity, free carbon dioxide, hydrocarbons, benthos, planktons and heavy metals. The parameters to be determined depend on the use of the aquatic environment.

Based on results from various studies, the Cisadane, Ciliwung and Citarum effluents, aside from the other small rivers running into Jakarta Bay, have contributed greatly to the degradation of water quality. Various activities like clear cutting in the upper regions, and sand and gravel mining in rivers, have caused a great deal of mud (*lumpur*) and other small particles to be transported (or suspended) by the river streams, resulting in shallowing of rivers and irrigation canals, and obscuring river waters, which in turn will affect their biota. The most seriously affected regions are those waters near estuaries where heavy sedimentation occurs.

2. Clarity and Turbidity in the Bay

To determine the clarity/turbidity, color and salinity of water, the seston level may be used. Waters with a seston level of more than 0.5 mg/1 and with salinity of less than 32 percent have low levels of clarity. Based on studies conducted in 1975–1976, the Jakarta Bay waters, particularly near the river mouths up to 250 m from the shoreline, have a very low degree of clarity (Sinegar and Hadiwisastra 1976). The turbidity is not due only to the suspended solids like clay and mud, but also due to organic matters like planktons and microorganisms which prevent the penetration of solar radiation and thus inhibit photosynthetic processes. If this suspended matter precipitates at the bottom or decomposes, the utility value of waters will decrease, and the aquatic environment for spawning ground of fishes and benthic organisms will undergo degradation. Aside from this, the suspended solids will also inhibit the process of respiration of aquatic biota.

3. Agriculture as a Cause of Pollution

Agriculture is another factor in determining the quality of the aquatic environment. The amount of pesticide residues and fertilizer resulting from efforts to increase agricultural production is proportional to the extent of rice fields, cropping frequency and amount of agrochemicals used. Utilization of short-life pesticides with higher toxicity like phorate, malathion, dimethion and parathion has been increased. Goldsmith (1979) has shown that utilization of pesticides has grown due to the increasing need for their continuous application. Predatory species unfortunately develop immunity to pesticides so that more and newer varieties must be used. Of all pesticides, DDT has been the most used, and this chemical now occurs in almost all lipid substrates (*serat lemak*) of animals in the world. All water is now a terminal for accumulating all DDT compounds and their residues, and about 25 percent of all DDT compounds produced has now been dissolved into the seas.

Some short-life pesticides with high toxicity can survive for only one or two months, but in the short run these chemicals will kill all creatures without exception. Most herbicides can survive also for a relatively short period, from two to twelve months. Other pesticides possibly do not have high primary toxic capacities, but have the ability to survive during a long period and, therefore, create cumulative effects. It is hard to imagine the impact of the delayed cumulative harmful effects on the environment. This is the problem, however, with chlorinated hydrocarbons (mostly DDT, dieldrin and endrin), accumulating along the food chain with increasing concentration. Due to the need to increase agricultural production, it would be a problem to forbid the use of long-life pesticides of all kinds.

Pesticides and fertilizers applied to increase food crop production in Bogor Regency consist of diazinon and zinc phosphate (ZP), whereas in the Tengerang area, trisodium phosphate, diazinon, endrin and ZP are used. Residues of these pesticides and fertilizers, from both regions, will accumulate in Jakarta Bay waters. The types of fertilizers applied contain nitrogen (N) and phosphorus (P) which could result in fertilization of the aquatic environment, and which will induce the excessive development of algae and seaweeds, due especially to a P content higher than that normally needed by aquatic plants. According to Perkins (1974), the dissolved P content in natural waters is not higher than 0.1 mg/1, except in water systems receiving waste effluents from certain households or industrial areas, and from agricultural areas with fertilizer application.

4. Criteria for Biological Oxygen Demand

One of the criteria for determining water quality is the BOD. According to the Japanese standard for fisheries, agricultural water and environment conservation, the permissible BOD level is 5 ppm. Studies have shown, however, that offshore areas of Jakarta Bay tend to have a heavier pollution burden than those at the river mouths. This means that pollution in these areas has not yet reached the defined pollution level resulting from domestic waste, as can also be seen by the DO level (4.9 ppm), which is still good enough. The BOD at the Cakung River mouth was 6.4 ppm; the BOD in its offshore areas, however, was quite higher, i.e., 15.8 ppm. The possible reason, aside from the higher pollution burden of the latter, was that gravel mining activities near the river mouth resulted in shaking of the settled organic matter at river bottom, causing upward movement.

The dissolved oxygen level at the river mouth and offshore was 4.9–6.1 ppm. The DO level at the Sunter River mouth, however was only 1.5 ppm, and this was possibly due to heavy domestic waste pollution. The Federal Water Pollution Control Administration has set the standard DO level for water systems with living organisms at 5 ppm. Based on the fact that the DO level at offshore areas of Jakarta Bay was 4.9–6.1 ppm, whereas the DO level of the sea was normally 6–7 ppm, the water quality of this area could be categorized as degraded.

Because most of the fecal waste discharged through septic tank effluents has reached the open waters, the potential for symptoms of infectious disease is obvious. Areas near the river mouths and near the coasts of some islands have shown coliform levels higher than those found in other areas. The MPN (most probable number) coli level ranged from $3-110 \times 10^{14}$, meaning that these areas were already polluted because of a level higher than that defined by the World Health Organization in 1967, which was not more than 24×10^2. Microorganisms having disease potential have also been found contaminating the sea products, mud and water.

To prevent water quality degradation caused by sewage and waste materials, measures for sewage treatment and a system for wasting/ destroying through sanitary landfill and composting have to be found, since organic waste material from households is still the dominant waste component. The negative mental attitude that considered water bodies as "waste baskets" must be eradicated through various means, including legislative measures with clear sanction.

5. Oil Pollution

The level of hydrocarbons can also be used as a criterion for water quality. The tolerance limit defined by Pescod (1973) for living organisms in fresh water, for tropical regions, is oil content of less than 0.4 ppm. In Jakarta Bay, the source of hydrocarbons could be from marine transportation activities, urban waste, effluents from rivers, dry docking and ships (bilge and bunkering).

The study group on pollutants of the Indonesia Oil and Gas Institute (LEMIGAS) and the Smithsonian Institute (1973) has found that the high hydrocarbon levels were due to oil pollution. Tanjung Priok and Pasar Ikan harbors were already polluted by oil, especially due to transportation activities. The high hydrocarbon level was also due to effluents in the form of tar residue and diesel oil from industries and households in Jakarta.

The highest hydrocarbon concentration was found in the water of Tanjung Priok (100 ppm), whereas the lowest (less than 20 ppm) was found in the area of Nirwana, Ayer Besar, Sakit and Kelor islands. Tar balls, characterized by black layers found on sandy grounds at the coast, were also found on coral pieces around the islands of Jakarta Bay. In 1972 the hydrocarbon level in the area of Tanjung Priok harbor was 3–25 ppm and in areas outside of it the level was 6–100 ppm (Wisaksono and Bilal 1976). However, Santosa et al. (1977) found that the hydrocarbon level in areas at the river mouth was 0–1.23 ppm, and offshore 0–1.76 ppm. Studies made by Bilal et al. (1979), however, found that the oil level in river waters was 10–18 ppm and in the offshore areas 0.39 ppm. In the offshore areas, the oil content level tends to be higher at eastward and westward directions from the harbor. Parallel to the coastline, the average figure was 1.1 ppm. From this information it appears that the contribution of river mouths to marine pollution is not very clear, since hydrocarbon levels offshore were higher than those at the river mouths. This might be due to the activity of the sea, or from run-off accumulation in other areas outside Jakarta Bay.

6. Water Temperature

Water temperature is an important factor in determining the existence and behavior of the organisms. For poikilothermal animals like fishes and seaweeds, water temperature is a determining factor in regulating their metabolic rate. Within the tolerance limits of temperature, the metabolic rate of poikilothermal animals will be increased twofold if water temperature is increased by 10°C. The operation of PLTU Tanjung Priok (Tanjung Priok Center for Electric Power Generation by Steam), therefore, with its continuous wasting of heat effluent into Jakarta Bay, has increased the water temperature at the wasting area, and even at areas far from it. The temperature increase of cooling water resulting from heat exchange in the condensors reaches about 9.8° C; the effluent flow is 17,600 m³/hour, and this has already resulted in thermal pollution of waters around this area. The temperature rise of 9.8° C is able to increase the metabolic rate of aquatic animals twofold if they congregate near or in the area of thermal pollution. Otherwise they will fail to survive or escape from this area. The ecosystem in this area, therefore, has undergone serious changes which could be seen by the decrease of species and number of fishes in the thermally polluted areas, as compared with the fishes living in areas with lower temperatures and which are sheltered by coral reefs.

7. Pollution by Heavy Metals

The content of heavy metals, especially mercury (Hg), lead (Pb), cadmium (Cd), copper (Cu), and zinc (Zn), at the surface of Jakarta Bay waters generally reveals that this aquatic environment is polluted by these metals (with reference to water quality standard defined by the U.S. Environmental Protection Agency (EPA) for marine waters and its biota). This was especially true for Pb and Cd, although Hg, Cu and Zn are reaching or surpassing the defined permissible limits for these metals, i.e., 0.1, 0.05 and 0.1 ppm, respectively (U.S. EPA 1973).

The levels of heavy metals appear to fluctuate greatly during the year, possibly due to transportation of heavy metals by streams, absorption of heavy metals by sediments or aquatic organisms through the food chain or degradation of heavy metals, physically and chemically as well as biologically.

III. Conclusion

The waters of Jakarta Bay, functioning as a main gate for marine transportation from other parts of Indonesia and from the world to the capital of Indonesia, and as a natural resource for fisheries, as well as a receiving place for waste materials, have already undergone changes in quality. This was due to the ever increasing level of population density of Jakarta and its surroundings, the continuous growth of the industrial sector and of the land use pattern and the increase of marine transportation in this region. All of these factors contribute to the increasing burden upon the aquatic system. Also, Jakarta Bay waters are a part of the Java Sea, and changes undergone by the Java Sea, therefore, will affect the aquatic system of the bay.

Based on recorded data, we strongly suggest that the water quality of rivers flowing into Jakarta Bay has already undergone degradation. However, we also suggest that these river systems still have the potentialities to counterbalance the pollution. The water quality around Tanjung Priok and Pasar Ikan harbors has also undergone degradation, but this was due particularly to high hydrocarbon levels.

Studies in the western part of Jakarta Bay have revealed that the degradation of water quality in that area was due to household wastes (the population factor), whereas the studies in the eastern part have revealed that water pollution was caused by hydrocarbons and heavy metals (the industrial factor).

Levels of Hg, Pb, Cd, Cu and Zn content in Jakarta Bay waters have fluctuated greatly from year to year. This phenomenon was highly related to the physicochemical characteristics of the aquatic system, aside from absorption of those metals by sediments and aquatic organisms of the system. The highest level of pollution was due to Pb and Cd, both of which showed levels far higher than those defined by the U.S. Environmental Protection Agency. The other heavy metals, like Hg, Cu and Zn, have also reached or surpassed the permissible limits defined for standard water quality. The determination of heavy metal levels was generally restricted to the measurement of heavy metal content in water only; there were very few studies or observation of heavy metal contents in aquatic organisms until recently.

Despite the prohibition on coral exploitation, such activities and others like uncontrolled sand or gravel mining still exist, which can cause serious deterioration of the environmental system. To recover the water quality of Jakarta Bay, integrated management of both terrestrial and marine activities should be taken to counteract the possible sources of aquatic pollution.

References

Bianpoen. 1977. Masalah lingkungan Jakarta, kondisi slum satusatunya alternatif? [The environmental problem of Jakarta: Is slum improvement the only alternative?]. *Wydiapura* 1 (5–6):3–14.
Bilal, J. et al. 1975. Inventarisasi kualitas air permukaan berbagai perairan daerah Teluk Jakarta [Inventory of surface water quality of various waters of Jakarta Bay region]. Jakarta: Indonesia Oil and Gas Institute.
Bilal, J. et al. 1979. *Report on environmental quality*. Jakarta: State Ministry of Development Supervision and Environment.
Burhanuddin and Birowo. 1979. Pengaruh air panas PLTU Tanjung Priok terhadap komposisi menis ikan di pelimbahannya [Effect of thermal waste effluent from the Central Electric Power Steam Generator in Tanjung Priok on fish composition in the thermal polluted water]. Seminar Biologi V, Bandung.
Cautrier, P. L. 1976. Pencemaran laut [Marine pollution]. *Proceedings of a Seminar on Marine Pollution, Jakarta, July 1976*, 2:174–183.
Coyne et Bellier and Sogieah Consulting Engineering. 1978. Cisadane Jakarta-Cibeet water resource development study. Draft final report. Annex C: Environment of the Republic of Indonesia. Jakarta: Ministry of Public Works, Directorate General of Water Resource Management.
Directorate General of Irrigation. 1974. Pre-survey polusi air di Pulau Jawa: Pengawasan polusi air dari managemen kualitas air [Pre-survey on water pollution in Java: Water pollution control in water quality management]. Second Report of the Directorate for studies on water problems, Department of Public Works and Electric Power, H. K. 4, 3. Bandung.
Goldsmith, E. 1979. Menuju kelestarian lingkungan hidup [Towards environmental conservation]. In M. T. Zein, *Menuju Kelestarian Lingkungam*, 103–165. Jakarta: Gramedia.
Mahbub, B. 1979. Kriteria mutu lingkingan hidup air [Criteria for the quality of aquatic environment]. Paper presented at the National Technical Meeting on Living Environment, Jakarta, June 1979.
Menasveta, P. 1975. Aquatic environmental mercury contamination. *Journal of the Science Society of Thailand* 1:167–177.
Nontji, A. and I. Soepangat. 1977. Seston di Teluk Jakarta [Seston in Jakarta Bay]. In *Teluk Jakarta*, 219–232. Jakarta: Lembaga Oseanologi Nasional.
Paramajan, Dj. 1977. Akresi dan abrasi Teluk Jakarta disebabkan kondisi fisik dan sosial [Accretion and aberration of Jakarta Bay due to physical and sociological conditions]. In *Teluk Jakarta*. Jakarta: Lembaga Oseanologi Nasional–Lembaga Ilmu Pengetahuan Indonesia (LON–LIPI).

Perkins, E. J. 1974. *The Biology of Estuaries and Coastal Waters.* London: Academic Press.

Pescod, M. D. 1973. Investigation of rational effluent and standards for tropical countries. Bangkok: Asian Institute of Technology, Interior Research Report.

Santosa, W. et al. 1978. Inventarisasi kualitas air permukaan daerah Teluk Jakarta Timur [Inventory of water quality of Jakarta Bay waters]. In *Teluk Jakarta,* 179–218. Jakarta: LON–LIPI.

Siregar, M. S. and S. Hadiwisastra. 1976. Penyelidikan sedimen di Teluk Jakarta [Sediment research in Jakarta Bay]. In *Teluk Jakarta,* 107–137. Jakarta: LON–LIPI.

Smithsonian Institute International and Environmental Programs. 1974. *Coastal Zone Pollution in Indonesia: A Reconnaissance Survey.* Washington, D.C.

Soegiarto, A. 1976. Aspek penelitian dalam pencegahan dan penanggulangan pencemaran laut [Research aspects in preventing and overcoming marine pollution]. *Proceedings of a Seminar on Marine Pollution, Jakarta, July 1976.*

Thayib, S. S. and J. T. D. Listiawati. 1976. Perarian Teluk Jakarta dan mikroorganismenya yang berpotensi menyakit [Jakarta Bay waters and its pathogenic microbiological organisms (or microorganisms)]. In *Teluk Jakarta* 233–244. Jakarta: LON-LIPI.

Thayib, S. S. and F. Suhadi. 1974. Suau usaha isolasi *Vibrio parahaemolyticus* dari rumpur dan beberapa macam hasil laut yang berasal dari perarian Teluk Jakarta [Isolation of *Vibrio parahaemolyticus* from mud and from various samples of fishery products of Jakarta Bay]. *Oseanologi di Indonesia* 2:41–55.

Thayib, S. S. and F. Suhadi. 1976. Preliminary study on the distribution of heterotropic bacteria and the microbiological indicators in Jakarta Bay. Paper presented for the International Symposuim on the Biology and Management of some Tropical Communities, Shallow Water, Coral Reefs, Tidal Forest and Estuaries, Jakarta, 28 June–3 July.

Thayib, S. S., W. Martoyudo and F. Suhadi. 1977. Beberapa bakteri penyebab penyakit perut manusia pada kerang *Anadara* dan *Crossotrea* [Some gastropathogenic bacteria in *Anadara* and *Crossotrea* shellfishes]. *Oseanologi di Indonesia* 7:49–55.

Tjia, H. D. et al. 1968. Coastal accretion in western Indonesia. *Bulletin of the National Institute of Geology and Mineralogy* 1(1):15–45.

United States Environmental Protection Agency. 1973. *Water Quality Criteria: A Report of the Committee on Water Quality Criteria.* Washington, D.C.

Widya Pertiwi Engineering. 1975. Studi dasar pengembangan das Ciliwung–Cisadane (JABOTABEK) [Basic study for the development of Ciliwung–Cisadane watershed (JABOTABEK)] Vols. 1 and 2. Jakarta: Proyek Pengelolaan Sumber-sumber Alam dan Lingkungan Hidup.

Wisaksono, W. and J. Bilal. 1976. Masalah pencemaran minyak bumi ditinjau dari aspek pengelolaan, penlitian dan pendidikan [The problem of earth oil pollution, viewed from environmental management, research and educational aspects]. *Proceedings of a Seminar on Marine Pollution, July 1976*, 2:163–170.

Wood, J. M. 1975. Metabolic cycles for toxic elements in the environment: A study of kinetics and mechanism. In *Heavy Metals in the Aquatic Environment, Proceedings of the International Conference, Nashville, Tennessee, 1975*, 105–117. Oxford: Pergamon Press.

Recommendations on the National Water Resources Code for Malaysia

Akira Kimizuka

Malaysia is equipped with dozens of laws and regulations, both federal and state, for water resources development and management. Several decades have already passed since the enactment of these laws. They have prevailed over the whole country and the lives of the people, not only in domestic and industrial water supplies, irrigation, drainage and hydroelectric power, but also in flood mitigation, water pollution control, watershed management and so on. For water resources development and management, considerable efforts are being made by various kinds of water-related agencies at federal, state and local levels. Several statutory bodies were also set up, and plans and projects are sometimes coordinated through the committee system. Thus, water resources development and management is a federal/state/local matter, not only within the present constitutional framework but also in the sense of administrative practice. Hence, these various water-related laws and institutions come to form an intricate complex in which they are fulfilling their own functions while having close relations with each other.

The Five-Year Plan includes not only socioeconomic but also various kinds of sectoral development programs. This results in the scattering of components relating to water resources development and management into various sectors, where they are only briefly described. It is, therefore, difficult to confirm the detailed programs of each water resources development project, not only at the federal level but also at the state level. On the other hand, there seems to be no specific planning system and procedure in which water supplies, irrigation and drainage, flood mitigation and so on are categorized in a comprehensive and detailed form.

These sectoral plans are, as will be explained hereinafter, expected to be integrated from the viewpoint of the comprehensive water resources development plan at the federal level as well as at the state level. The background and circumstances which increase the necessity for a national approach, i.e., a comprehensive integrated approach from a national viewpoint or for national interests, are as follows:

(1) new tendencies in water resources development such as a number of large-scale water resources developments in a definite period, water resources development and use in larger regions, multi-purpose-oriented or jointly planned water resources development;

(2) integral part of national development policy and national development planning, such as national standards for projection of water demands for domestic and industrial uses, a national approach for drainage and irrigation projects and hydroelectric power development;

(3) conservation of the environment and the nation's land, such as supporting the national environmental policy through water pollution abatement, and conservation of the national land conditions through flood mitigation measures.

In order to ensure the integrated approach for water resources development and management, it is worthwhile to consider, in the near future, the comprehensive legal/institutional system, temporarily called a national water resources code, while, alternatively, revising the existing respective laws concerned as the needs become pressing, for the following reasons:

(1) Water resources development and management is a federal/state/local joint matter in the aspects of not only its jurisdiction within the present constitutional framework and existing legislation but also institutional and financial arrangements; and these factors should be integrated as much as possible.

(2) The law on water resources development and management could be seen as an indispensable instrument for the implementation of water resources policies and plans, spelling out the basic principles, establishing the fundamental rules and providing the constitution and functions of institutions.

(3) It is necessary to maintain and promote uniformity among the water-related laws enacted by the states, by amending them in accordance with the needs arising from the changes and progress of the country.

(4) There will appear some deficiencies in such existing laws as the Waters Enactment, as well as the necessity for an integrated approach to water resources development and management.

I. National and Interstate Policies

1. National Water Policy Guideline Plan

With reference to the long-term plan at the federal/national level, all water resources developments are finally planned and authorized in the Five-Year Plan. In this plan, the sectoral programs such as drainage and irrigation, energy, water supply and sewerage follow the outline perspective plan which comprises mainly project demand and needs within a macroeconomical framework. With regard to the planning process, the drafts for water resources development projects are prepared by each respective agency and submitted to the Economic Planning Unit. At the state level, plans are integrated by the State Planning Unit and submitted to the Federal Unit. This Unit is engaged in preparing a five-year plan and an annual development budget for approval by the National Development Planning Council and finally of the Cabinet. The Unit plays the role of adjusting sectoral plans from the viewpoint of overall national policy and budget allocation. In order to prepare the optimum water resources development plan, it will be necessary to take an approach for reviewing, adjusting and making the plan not only from the long-term viewpoint but also in an integrated manner on every mutually related water resources development.

For these purposes, the following recommendations should be considered.

It is necessary:

(1) to establish a national water policy where all those concerned, not only federal, state, local and the public, rely on, refer to and endeavor to attain the targets and objectives;

(2) to prepare the guideline plan which consists of, on the one hand, a national water resources development plan for the identification of present and future needs, problems and available sources and, on the other hand, of a regional/basin water resources development plan for clarification and identification of details of water resources development in some specific area;

(3) to strengthen the role of the existing agencies concerned with the formulation of the national water policy and the preparation of the long-term/integrated guideline plan.

2. Interstate Water Resources Development and River Management

There are seventeen interstate river basins (including one international river basin), at least from the geographical viewpoint. Some of the river utilization ratios in these river basins will rapidly increase up to the year 2000. In addition, several interstate diversion and dam construction programs are included in the recommended plan. It is anticipated that it will take a considerably long time for the preparation of the interstate water resources development plan and implementation after consultation of the states concerned with each other. In this respect, the federal government is expected to play a positive role in coordinating the states concerned as well as promoting interstate water resources development from the national viewpoint.

For the purpose of providing legal and/or institutional arrangements, the following are recommended:

The state governments shall initially draft a plan for interstate diversion and/or the agreement of interstate river management and consult with each other. The federal government may, at the request of a state government concerned, coordinate, arbitrate and/or make plans or agreements after consultation with all the states concerned.

3. Construction of the Multipurpose Water Resources Facility

There are thirty dams and ten barrages either already in existence or under construction. Among these dams, seven have been constructed or are under construction, strictly speaking, for dual purposes. To meet the water demands in the future, it is proposed in the plan to construct forty-seven dams and barrages as well as nine diversion facilities over a period of two decades. Among these dams and barrages, twenty-four are recommended to be constructed for multipurpose use. For this reason, it will be necessary to establish a legal and/or institutional system for the promotion of development of multipurpose water resource facilities, not only from the viewpoint of making optimum and efficient use of the limited water resources but also for the purpose of ensuring equity among project beneficiaries and taxpayers.

The legal/institutional system for the development of multipurpose facilities should be considered from the following viewpoints:

It is necessary:

(1) to establish a planning system and procedures for coordination among the agencies concerned;

(2) to strengthen the functions of the coordination agency as well as to designate the implementation agency;

(3) to prepare a rule and/or standard for equitable cost allocation and operation/maintenance.

It is worth considering the establishment of a new body for implementation and management of multipurpose facilities as well as other large-scale dam facilities, either on a regional basis or nationwide, in order to construct rapidly a large number of water resources facilities.

II. Integrated Planning and Organization

1. Integrated Planning and Organization at the Federal Level

For the purpose of meeting water demands and needs in the future, water resources development and management from now on will require a federal administration system capable of formulating the national water policy and water resources master plans, coordinating the water-related activities of a number of agencies, and assisting the state governments in carrying out integrated water resources management. None of the existing councils and committees is endowed with the expertise to formulate a national water policy or the responsibility to coordinate the water resources administration, which are being undertaken by the federal and state governments and local authorities. A number of source facilities will be constructed based on a certain schedule, and the operation of all facilities should be centrally controlled under the proposed Regional Water Demand and Supply Balance Program. Furthermore, multipurpose, interstate and international projects will be planned all over the nation in the future. For the purpose of detailed planning, construction and management of the above-mentioned projects, a new statutory body should be set up.

In order to cope with future needs, the following recommendations for planning, coordination and implementation should be considered. It is necessary:

(1) to set up a new central agency (Federal Water Resources Division) in charge of planning and coordination; and

(2) to establish a National Water Resources Council and a permanent interdepartmental National Water Resources Committee for formulation of a national water policy and coordination of the water-oriented programs of all government agencies.

2. Integrated Water Resources Management at the State Level

With the development of urban and rural areas, the river utilization ratio (demand/surface run-off) is projected to increase from 4 percent in 1980 to 9 percent in 2000. Due to the increase in water demand under the constraints of the restricted water resources, the balance between demand and supply will be tightened in the future, leading to competition among various water use purposes and sometimes, in the case of severe drought, to conflicts of interest. Increasing water demand, on the other hand, will lead to increasing water discharge into the river. With regard to the legal system for river management, the Waters Enactments were made several decades ago. According to these laws, it seems that it is unnecessary for the governmental agencies to take legal procedures to use river water. Instead, institutional arrangements such as holding *ad hoc* committees have so far been utilized for coordination. However, it is anticipated in the future that there will be no integrated legal system for river management nor any authoritative agency to manage the river and water resources in a continuous and integrated manner.

In order to cope with the abovementioned problems, it is recommended that:

(1) a concept be formulated whereby a single agency could appropriately review and wholly control the river water use activities, not only by private users but also by governmental agencies;

(2) a legal and/or institutional system be established for the river maintenance flow, clarifying the effects of establishing such a legal system, its procedure, the responsible agency and so forth;

(3) some legal and/or institutional system be established for the integrated river basin plan;

(4) a coordination system (a State Water Resources Committee) be provided among all the agencies concerned with a river basin (or a group of river basins) with regard to the review and preparation of the river basin plan, authorization of the river maintenance flow, formulation of the integrated water pollution abatement and comprehensive flood mitigation program and water use coordination during drought.

III. Groundwater Exploitation and Management

It is anticipated that the demand for groundwater in 2000 will increase more than four times that of the present. Eighty percent of the groundwater demand is estimated to be for domestic use and a large portion of the remainder would be for industrial use. It is also worth studying the possibility of utilizing groundwater for agricultural use in some areas. In the recommended plan, the safe yield of the ground-water is assumed to be 8 percent of the potential yield. However, with the anticipated rapid increase of groundwater exploitation, adverse effects such as reduced yield in existing wells, ground subsidence and sea water intrusion may occur if overexploited. Although there are a few provisions in the Geological Survey Act (notification system) and the Environmental Quality Act (prevention of groundwater pollution), a legal and/or institutional system for managing and controlling the groundwater is not yet established.

In order to control adequately and to develop the groundwater resources in an orderly and efficient manner, it is recommended that:
(1) a registration system (which leads to order or advice for improvement) be established or a permission system in the groundwater-restricted areas designated by the state government; and
(2) an integrated survey and exploitation system be established for planning and coordination by all the agencies concerned.

IV. Integrated Water Pollution Abatement

As far as the condition of water pollution in 2000 is concerned, it is expected that most rivers on the west coast of Peninsular Malaysia will no longer be clean if only the existing waste water treatment system is utilized. To cope with the water pollution anticipated in the future, it is proposed in the recommended plan that the limit of Biological Oxygen Demand (BOD) concentration to be attained in 2000 be set at 5 mg/l. In order to achieve this goal, recommendations include the improvement of the purification system in palm oil mills, rubber factories and animal husbandry, as well as the development of the public sewerage system. With reference to water pollution abatement, the Environmental Quality Act (water pollution control), the Local Government Act (water pollution control in the local authority area) and the Street, Drainage and Building Act (public sewerage system) were enacted for their respective purposes, while the Water Enactments of several states were revised to include the provision on the prohibition of pollution of rivers. However, the common goal of the desirable environmental quality standard of the river water, where all the agencies and those concerned are expected to make efforts, is not yet established. Furthermore, a legal/institutional system and approach, especially at the enforcement level, among all those concerned is not yet provided.

For the purpose of ensuring the integrated approach by utilizing the

existing laws for water pollution abatement, it is recommended that:
(1) the desired environmental quality standard for the river water be established where all those concerned are expected to endeavor to attain the goal; and
(2) a coordination/consultation system be set up for enforcement of respective functions on water pollution abatement among all the agencies concerned, including not only those at the federal level but also those at the regional/local level.

V. Integrated Flood Mitigation System

In Peninsular Malaysia, flood-prone areas where maximum floods are recorded cover approximately 15,300 km^2, which is 11.5 percent of the total land mass. It is recommended that 3,500 km^2 of the flood-prone areas be protected by such structural measures as channel improvement, bypass flood-ways, polders and flood mitigation dams. Recognizing some limitations and inefficiency in promoting only structural measures, nonstructural measures such as restriction of development, change in land use and guidance/restriction of building are also recommended. The nonstructural measures are preliminarily planned in five river basins, leading to the restriction of development of areas of approximately 830 km^2. In addition, a flood forecasting and warning system are also recommended in the plan. With reference to the restriction of development in the flood-prone areas, several laws can be cited, for example, the Waters Enactments (prohibition of building in the vicinity of the river and declared flood channel), National Land Code (alienation of land), Town and Country Planning Act (development control by allocating land to specific purposes), Forest Enactment (reserved forest system) and Land Conservation Act (watershed management in hill land and control of silt and erosion). Thus, various kinds of legal systems have already been provided at a fairly good level in terms of land use restriction in flood-prone areas and watershed management. Nevertheless, some deficiencies could be found in the present legal/institutional system to promote integrated flood mitigation measures; for example, among enforcement of various laws, and among structural and nonstructural measures.

For these purposes, the following measures are recommended:
(1) establishing an integrated planning system by the priority river basin, including not only a set of structural measures but also nonstructural measures;
(2) providing a coordination system among all the agencies con-

cerned which would be responsible for the implementation of flood mitigation projects, river management, forest management, town and country planning, land use control, flood relief, resettlement projects and so on;

(3) preparing the guideline/rule for effective guidance of the people who are residing or going to settle in flood-prone areas.

(4) setting up a forest planning system at the national and regional levels in conjunction with those of water resources development and management.

VI. Financial System

For the purpose of promoting water resources development, it is necessary to consider the equitable financial burden among the beneficiaries and taxpayers, investment from the viewpoint of balanced development of the whole nation, strengthening of federal financial aid and proper financial/accounting procedures.

For these purposes, the following are recommended:

(1) setting up standards for cost allocation for the construction and maintenance of multipurpose water resources facilities for the purpose of promoting equity among project beneficiaries and taxpayers;

(2) establishing that the criteria for water supply grant and loan systems will be investigated and definitely presented from the viewpoint of balanced development of the whole nation;

(3) establishing the criteria for charging domestic and industrial water rates as well as irrigation and drainage rates, not only for the purpose of ensuring sound management of accounting and promoting, if necessary, the uniformity and equity among the states and the people, but also taking into consideration the ability of the water users to pay;

(4) setting up such federal financial aid as grants and special loans for water supply projects, construction of high-cost water resources facilities, regional development in the dam reservoir area in case of necessity, sewerage projects, urban drainage projects and so on, taking into consideration the financial ability of the state governments and local authorities;

(5) setting up generally accepted commercial accounting principles and practices through the adoption of the State Water Supply Fund Act by all the state governments.

VII. Recommendations

In consideration of the elements stated above, the following points are recommended in drafting a national water resources code in Malaysia:

(1) fundamental principles and policy statement, responsibilities of those concerned and coordination with other public policies;

(2) detailed functions of water-related agencies at federal, state and local levels, especially for the purpose of planning coordination and integrated river management;

(3) a long-term and integrated water resources development planning system;

(4) procedures and criteria for preparing and coordinating interstate water resources development and the construction of multipurpose facilities;

(5) setting up the implementation body for the construction of large-scale dams;

(6) preparation of the guidelines and determination of such basic rules as the river maintenance flow and the desired environmental quality standard of the river water;

(7) a coordination system such as a water resources council/committee at the national level and at the regional level;

(8) measures and procedures for mitigating adverse effects on the natural environment and living conditions of the affected;

(9) special financial aid systems to rapidly promote water resources development and management.

Coastal Zone Management and Law

A Review of Coastal Zone Legislation in Malaysia

Nik Abdul Rashid Majid

Malaysia is a federation of thirteen states, eleven of which are situated on the Malay Peninsula and two on the island of Borneo. The two regions are separated by the South China Sea. It has an area of 333,403 sq. km and a coastline of approximately 3,400 km. Since it is situated in the middle of Southeast Asia, it occupies a focal position in the region, commanding one of the major sea lanes of the world, the Straits of Malacca.

The Malaysian Constitution provides that land is a state matter, and, according to Section 5 of the National Land Code 1965, land includes inland waters. The Constitution is silent as to who has jurisdiction over the sea and the ocean. However, Section 3 of the Continental Shelf Act 1966 (Act 83) declares that all rights with respect to the exploration of the continental shelf and the exploitation of its natural resources are vested in and exercisable by the federal government.

The importance of the coastal zone to the lives of human beings is unquestionable. The largest concentration of population of Malaysia lies on the coasts. Major cities and industrial areas of Malaysia are located along the coasts or on lowlands close to the coastal zones. To improve the quality of life, we need to have legislation protecting the lives of millions of people living in the coastal areas.

To date, we have no less than twenty pieces of legislation governing various aspects of the environment, mostly relating to the control and regulation of waste materials and the exploitation of natural resources. But that is not enough. We need more. At the same time we need more effective and efficient enforcement.

I. Coastal Zone Legislation

There is no such thing as coastal zone legislation *per se*. This paper will attempt to review legislation affecting coastal zones.

1. The Exclusive Economic Zone

Like other nations, developed or developing, Malaysia in 1975 staked a claim for an "exclusive economic zone" extending 320 km into the ocean. By such a claim, Malaysia exercises sovereign rights to the renewable and nonrenewable resources that lie within the zone. This right, however, does not extend to other rights, such as the right of navigation, in which case the twelve-mile territorial sea limit still prevails.

As a result of this claim, PETRONAS, a state-owned petroleum company, was formed to exploit petroleum and natural gas within the "exclusive economic zone."

2. Continental Shelf Act 1966 (Act 83)

This Act vested the right to explore and to exploit the continental shelf in the Malaysian government. Exploring, prospecting or boring operations for minerals and petroleum in the seabed or subsoil is prohibited except under license (Section 4). Section 5 extends the civil and criminal law of the land to the continental shelf, and any act committed within the zone is punishable as if it were committed on the land.

3. Environmental Quality Act 1974

As the name implies, this act relates to the prevention, abatement and control of pollution, and enhancement of the environment. For purposes of the coastal zone, Sections 25–27 are of special relevance.

Section 25 prohibits, except under license, any person from emitting, discharging or depositing any wastes into any inland waters, directly or indirectly through access to any waters. The prohibition extends to an act of placing any waste in a position where it falls, descends, drains, evaporates or is washed or blown off or percolates into any waters.

Sections 26 and 27 prohibit any person from discharging or spilling any oil or mixture containing oil into Malaysian waters or any part of the sea outside the territorial waters of Malaysia, if such discharge or spill would result in its being spread or washed into Malaysian waters.

Section 28 provides special defenses for the act if it is done for the purpose of securing the safety of the vessel, or saving human life, if reasonable care has been taken to prevent spillage or leakage; or if, in the operation for the refining of oil, the effluent produced could not reasonably be practicable to dispose anywhere except into Malaysian waters.

4. Fisheries Act 1963 (Act 210)

This act regulates and controls the catching of fish both inland and offshore. It prohibits the use of any poisonous or explosive substance with intent to stupefy, poison or kill fish without a license.

5. Waters Enactment (Cap. 146)

This is a state legislation that deals exclusively with waters relating to rivers and streams. It regulates and controls the use of rivers and streams, and imposes rigid prohibitions against the unauthorized use of rivers, and the alteration or diversion of river banks and river courses. Felling of trees into rivers is prohibited. So is the act of discharging or emitting any deposit or wastes into any river. The object is to prevent the blockage of river waters and pollution of these waters.

6. Merchant Shipping Ordinance No. 70, 1952

This ordinance regulates and controls merchant ships plying between ports within the territorial boundaries. There are only two sections relevant to coastal zones, namely, the prohibitions on discharging wastes and human corpses into the sea within the territorial limits.

II. Law vs. Enforcement

In brief, we have reviewed the various laws that regulate and control the use of land, rivers and waterways, and the ocean—all for the benefit of mankind. However, the existence of legislation is one thing, and the enforcement of the laws is another.

Consumer associations and environmental societies the world over have claimed that more and more damage has been done to the environment, to the extent that the industrial world is no longer a safe place to live.

We need to strike a balance between development on the one hand and preservation on the other. But more often than not, indiscriminate exploitation of natural resources by a few, coupled with lack of enforcement or nonenforcement by the government, leads to unnecessary inconvenience to the greater majority of the population.

III. Harmonizing of the Laws

At present, not all laws are uniform and harmonized. Each state has its own legislation relating to matters within the jurisdiction of the state. It is submitted that Act 76 of the Federal Constitution should be invoked to make state laws uniform. The National Land Code is the child of this Article. The following laws need to be updated, revised and harmonized: Waters Enactment (Cap. 146), River Rights Enactment (F.M.S. Cap. 201), Merchant Shipping Ordinance No. 70 (1952), Mining Enactment (Cap. 147), Mineral Ores Enactment (Cap. 148) and a host of other legislation relating to the control of the environment. Only with uniform legislation can the Department of the Environment, which is a federal department, enforce proper control over environmental quality.

Coastal Zone Management in Asia and the Pacific

Nobuo Kumamoto

Coastal zone protection is one of the most urgent environmental concerns in Asia and the Pacific area today. It covers marine pollution, wetland protection, coral reef ecosystems, coastal zone resources, mangrove forest management, aquatic resources exploitation, beach mining, offshore oil exploration, fisheries and land use projects for recreational facilities, housing and industrial activities along the seacoast. Problems in the coastal zone are found in four areas: the upper river, to the lower river, to marine water and to coastal land.

I. Land Soil Erosion in the Upper River Area

The upper river-related problems are quite closely concerned with land soil erosion, which may cause floods in the mouths of rivers and change the environmental vegetation and the physical condition of the coastal zone. Erosion in mountain areas has become a serious problem in recent years, not only in Asia but in other parts of the world. The problem in Asia, however, is quite serious, and different in its character from other parts of the world. This is because the forest-cutting or wood-burning process in Asian nations is more rapid and radical than any we have ever had before in history, and causes very serious environmental hazards. For example, the government of Indonesia has decided to regulate and gradually to forbid cutting trees and shipping them abroad, in order to protect the forests. These are natural and wise countermeasures against a trend toward diminishing green forests, but this wise change of policy will bring economic risks to the country as well, because timber prices are closely related to gross national income, and raw material is still a main element in supporting a balanced budget in these developing nations.

This is, of course, the main cause of land erosion problems in several forest preservation areas. The cutting and shipping of trees may satisfy the economic needs and demands of the people in the regions where economic development is an urgent policy goal. The burning of forests may make fields available for planting, mainly of biomass vegetation such as cassava, which is turned into tapioca from which alcohol is produced, as, for example, in the northeast part of Thailand. Cutting and burning forest, however, causes serious land erosion when the rainy season starts, and brings thousands of tons of eroded soil to the lower parts of rivers. Good examples may be seen in the mouths of the Mekong in Vietnam, of the Irrawaddy in Burma and of the Chao Phraya River in Thailand. In addition, there are many other examples along the long coastlines of Asian nations, such as the Solo River on Java; the Kampar, Inderagiri and Asahan Rivers in Sumatra; the Seruyan, Sampit and Rajang Rivers in Borneo; the Cagayan River in the Philippines; and the Stitang and Kaladan Rivers in Burma.

Such development along the mouths of rivers by the accumulation of eroded soil brought from the upper parts of rivers is a quite natural process of evolution of the land. It is also important, however, to prevent floods and extreme changes of coastlines.

In order to prevent erosion of soil along the rivers, tree planting and forest preservation are adopted as partial solutions in several countries. Thus control and management of river water in Asia relate to coastal zone protection. In addition, a good supply of trees and forests along rivers supply plentiful fishery products in the mouths of rivers. For this reason as well, we must find a systematic way of preserving forest projects in Asian nations.

II. Lower-River Water Pollution

The second problem of coastal zone protection relates to the lower river areas. This clearly is closely concerned with polluted water, which is discharged from human habitats such as cities, towns and villages. It is also concerned with discharged water, polluted by chemical substances for agriculture. Thus, the second type of problem is water pollution itself, which has been considered one of the most serious pollution problems in present years. Obviously, river water, polluted by water that is discharged from human habitats or from agricultural fields, flows into the ocean and pollutes marine water along the coastal area.

In order to keep such water pollution from cities and agricultural fields, several countries have adopted countermeasures through sanitary legislation for the building of sewage systems, as in Thailand, or establishing environmental standards and surveillance systems, as in countries such as Japan and the United States.

We may find several patterns of these problems, such as urban, industrial and agricultural water pollution. We may then classify the characteristics of water pollution under such categories as pollution due to noxious substances, organic pollution and pollution due to other causes such as petroleum. Depending upon these characteristic differences, we may adopt countermeasures against water pollution (Environment Agency 1977).

As one example, we have seen serious water pollution in the Surabaya River, Indonesia, in 1975, 1976 and 1977, because of sugar refineries and other industries producing sodium glutamate, alcohol, pesticides, textiles, leather, metal, paper or various chemicals. The Agano River and the Minamata Bay area in Japan are also good examples of serious water pollution from chemical factories and mining. Another experience with water pollution control is seen in Singapore, which has achieved the provision of a sewage treatment works. In some countries, such as Thailand or Singapore, water pollution control has been combined with policies on public health. Legislation for water pollution control in these areas is an urgent problem.

Declared general policy on the environment in the National Environmental Policy Act of 1969 in the United States should be considered in this case. As to countermeasures against water pollution, those setting up effluent standards, implementation programs and enforcement procedures in the United States, which appeared in the Act Relating to Coastal Zone Management of 1977 (Hawaii) and the Federal Coastal Zone Management Act of 1972, should be considered, as well as water pollution control measures under the Water Pollution Control Law (Law No. 138 of 1970) in Japan (Schoenbaum 1982).

One model of keeping coastal water clean may be seen in California, where the State Water Quality Control Boards and the Department of Fish and Game adopted a coastal plan requiring an adequate treatment system to receive all wastes released into the ocean. The plan also includes a $100 million oil-spill liability fund financed by a two-cent per barrel tax on oil entering California, to provide for the clean-up of accidental spills and for prompt payment of damages and clean-up costs.

California requires that all municipal and industrial waste discharge shall be upgraded to meet the goals and standards of the Federal Water Pollution Control Act and to comply with the California Water

Code. The ultimate goal is the removal of all pollutants from waste discharges (California Coastal Plan 1975).

In order to protect clean water in the cities and in the ocean, the Japanese experience is worth considering. Japan has two main statutes: the Water Pollution Control Law and the Marine Pollution Prevention Law of 1970, in addition to the Law Concerning Special Measures for Conservation of the Environment of the Seto Inland Sea (Law No. 110, 1973). The former includes the establishment of effluent standards, the enforcement process, strong restrictions on the construction of facilities, strong control of water pollution and compensation for damages. The statue also includes penal provisions for violators of this law. In addition, the steady progress of sewage system construction in major cities in Japan should be counted as a substantial reason for the achievement of clean water in rivers. Although we still have serious water pollution in bay areas in coastal zones, some major rivers now are recovering enough that salmon and other fish are gradually appearing again.

The latter is expected to prevent marine pollution by controlling the discharge into the ocean of oil and wastes from ships and offshore facilities by securing appropriate disposal of waste oil and by taking measures for the prevention of marine pollution. As to conservation of the environment of the Inland Sea water, basic and local plans for the conservation and their implementation for effective measures can be seen in the Law Concerning Special Measures for Conservation of the Environment of the Seto Inland Sea, which provides special measures in connection with restrictions on the installment of specified facilities. Japan, however, has no specified act concerning coastal zone protection, although a model for "The Basic Law for Conservation of the Seashore" in 1976 has been proposed by citizen groups which have been promoting the right of access to the beach.

Singapore's experience in preventing marine water pollution is a good example of this case, for the principle of water pollution control adopted there is to remove pollution at its source. Namely, all land-based sources of marine pollution, such as trade effluent, domestic sewage and sullage waste water, are collected by an extensive network of sewers and conveyed to sewage treatment works for treatment before discharge into the sea.

Basic international cooperation for preventing marine water pollution has been promoted by the International Convention for the Prevention of Pollution of the Sea by Oil in 1954 (amended 1962 and 1969). As of 1983 many countries in Asia and the Pacific, such as New Zealands, Papua New Guinea, the Philippines, Republic of Korea, United

States, Vanuatu, Australia, Bangladesh, Fiji, India, Japan, Maldives and Singapore in addition to countries relating to this area such as the Netherlands, USSR, Great Britain and Northern Ireland and France have joined this International Convention. In order to achieve the goals of this Convention, implementation should be strongly promoted by adopting concerned domestic legislations.

Singapore, as an example, has achieved it through passing the Prevention of Pollution of the Sea Act (No. 3 of 1971) and the Regulations made under the Port of Singapore Authority Act. Measures adopted in these acts show us examples to be implemented in such legislations:

(a) Any discharge oil or a mixture containing oil into local waters from a vessel or from any place on land or from any apparatus used for transferring oil from or to any vessel is made a criminal offense. The offense is one of strict liability in which there is no need to establish fault, although the Act itself provides for several defenses to the offender;

(b) Dumping of refuse, garbage, waste-matter, trade effluent and substances of a dangerous or obnoxious nature from a vessel into Singapore waters is punishable;

(c) Recovery of the cost of removal of refuse, garbage and waste matter discharged from a vessel is ordered to its owner;

(d) Owners or operators of oil refineries and oil terminals are required to store detergents and equipment to deal with oil pollution. Regulations under the Prevention of Pollution of the Sea Act require every company listed in the Regulations to keep a stock of readily usable dispersants. The company is required to provide the dispersants and help in combatting the pollution in the event of an incident resulting in pollution of the sea by oil.

(e) Regulations under the Act stated above prohibit the pollution of port waters by ashes, solid ballast, sludge or any other matter.

(f) As to facilities to enable vessels to discharge or deposit oil residues, refuse and other waste matter, the Port Authority has the power under the Act for providing them and for requiring every vessel to make use of such facilities.

III. Marine Water

Marine pollution obviously has a close connection with the life of marine habitats along the coastal zone area. Marine habitats in Southeast Asian waters have a special character; namely, their types are unique and diverse. They include coral and mangrove resources and other marine life and vegetation. These natural resources are, characteristically, easily destroyed by human activities such as fishing, waste and sewage disposal and recreational activities, as well as industrial development. If we cannot properly manage and control these activities in coastal zone areas, environmental degradation and resource depletion can easily result in those areas.

1. Marine Water Pollution

The marine water problems are closely related to lower-river problems. These are mainly caused by accidental spills of petroleum. In order to prevent such spills, establishing surveillance and enforcement systems has been considered most effective.

2. Mangrove and Coral Reefs

As to mangrove and coral protection programs, the experience in the Philippines is worth citing. The Philippines adopted mangrove, coral and marine park programs in 1977, when a National Mangrove Committee was created, composed of representatives from the Ministry of Natural Resources and consultants from the Office of the Minister and the Marine Science Center at the University of the Philippines. Since the Philippines is an archipelago, it is therefore quite rich in marine life and vegetation such as mangrove and coral. The programs for protecting mangrove and coral consisted of intensive investigations of the state of mangrove and coral resources. The investigations concluded that unwise use or overexploitation, in spite of a standing ban on coral gathering which took effect as early as 1973, caused serious damage to the natural coastal zone. Thus the government issued Presidential Decree 1219, which prohibits gathering, harvesting, collecting or exportation of ordinary corals. The countermeasures for protecting marine resources resulted in the coral and mangrove management programs being geared toward increasing the productivity of local fishermen.

3. Marine Parks

A marine park is also suggested as a tool for protecting the marine environment. There are such marine park projects in Apo Island and Reef in Mindoro; Sumilon Island in Cebu; the Panglao-Balicasag area in Bohol; and Somreo in Batangas in the Philippines. These were launched in order to protect and to conserve numerous habitats and ecosystems in the marine environment. The marine park project is also expected to be an educational measure for people who may be ignorant of marine life. Necessary facilities for this purpose are expected to be built (California Coastal Plan 1975).

4. Coastal Water

As to coastal water quality, the California Coastal Plan suggests several categories: waste discharges, heated and cooled discharges and oil and toxic spills. Generally speaking, California adopted a comprehensive ocean water quality research and regulatory program, based on the project carried out by the State Water Resources Control Board and other state and local agencies. This program includes empirical studies of the condition of marine living resources, assessment of damage from various activities and evaluation and appropriate control of all potentially hazardous discharges and development affecting the marine environment. The program is closely coordinated with the marine living resources management program. Then it is reviewed, evaluated and reported annually by the Coastal Zone Agency to the Governor and the Legislature.

a. Heated and Cooled Discharges
California has faced the fact that a certain amount of sea water is needed to cool power plants on the coast. Additional use of sea water, especially for major heating and cooling systems in energy facilities, causes the same type of problem along the coast. Because of heated discharges from these power plants and facilities, some kinds of marine species will leave or die off. On the other hand, other native species and aquaculture operations may be enhanced by warmer temperatures.

Therefore, in order to avoid the adverse effects of thermal impact on environmentally sensitive or highly scenic areas, as identified in the Coastal Plan or by the State Water Resources Control Board, the Department of Fish and Game, the Department of Parks and Recreation, the State Land Commission or other appropriate public agencies, California adopted the following criteria for permitting thermal discharges:

(1) The best available technology and mitigation measures have been incorporated to prevent oil leaks and spills;

(2) Adequate plans, personnel and equipment exist from the project's inception to guarantee prompt reporting, abatement, containment and clean-up of any discharges from such a facility or related operation;

(3) The facilities are consistent with Coastal Plan energy policies;
(4) There is no alternative location that would result in less environmental damage.

In order to ensure the success of these policies, California empowered the State Water Resources Control Board or other public agencies to promote research, to execute enforcement processes and to initiate a liability procedure.

The State of California has several other countermeasures and policies to protect the coastal zone, especially coastal waters, estuaries and wetlands (California Coastal Plan 1977).

IV. Methods for Coastal Land Management

As for the coastal land problem, the important roles of the Coastal Commission of California and the Coastal Management Program of Guam may be cited.

1. Coastal Commission of California

This agency consists of one State Commission and six Regional Commissions, established by passage of a citizen initiative in the election of November 1972.

The duties of the Coastal Commission are enumerated as follows:
(1) to prepare a "comprehensive, coordinated, enforceable plan for the orderly, long-range conservation and management of the natural resources of the coastal zone," and
(2) during the planning period, to regulate development in coastal waters and in a 1,000-yard shoreline permit area to ensure that by proper development the plan being prepared is not undercut.

The role of the Coastal Commission is, as indicated in its Plan 162, to promote a comprehensive plan of preserving natural resources in harmony with use of the coastal zone area. According to the plan, such natural resources include the following:

- wetlands and estuaries;
- tide pools;
- coastal streams vital to andromous fish runs and continued sand supply to the coast;
- natural areas that should be preserved for future scientific study, education and public enjoyment;
- habitats of rare and endangered species of animals and plants;
- agricultural (including grazing) and forestry lands;

- mineral deposits;
- clean air;
- sandy beaches and dunes;
- recreational lands and waters; and
- highly scenic areas and coastal land forms.

2. Guam Coastal Plan

Like many other islands in the Pacific region, Guam has long stretches of beach, which are considered as precious resources, especially in light of the island's tremendous recreational growth along the seashore. Such development and improvement of seashore activities lie mainly in the examination of existing land uses adjacent to coastal waters. Thus, the Guam Bureau of Planning evaluates the existing coastal land uses in order to ascertain how each sector is fulfilling its role in satisfying those activities (Government of Guam 1977). This evaluation will serve as a guide to the future preservation, improvement or development of the coastal lands. According to the coastal management program of Guam, seashore activities are divided into the following categories: residential areas, archaeological sites, agriculture, aquaculture, urban renewal, dredging, landfill and the marine transportation network. Depending upon the kind of activity, policies, designs and regulations are diverse.

V. Special Concerns

1. Scenic Beauty

The California Coastal Commission has a policy of making the use of coastal land areas compatible with scenic beauty. Of course, to protect the scenic beauty of the coastline is one of the main targets of coastal zone protection. For instance, the National Trust movement in England, which collects funds and purchases scenic coastal land, is sometimes cited as a good example of the important movement for coastal zone protection. We may also see an example of preserving scenic beauty in the land use planning program of the island of Guam, which includes recreation, parks, fishing and other uses.

The "Access to the Beach" movement in Japan is another example of preserving the citizen's right to protect the coastal zone area. It is based on a motivation to keep the scenic beauty of the coastal zone.

The spirit of these movements is also applicable to preservation of scenic beauty along the extensive coastal zones of Asia and the Pacific area.

2. Public Access to the Beach

As for public access to the coast, California sets forth this right in its Constitution. This does not mean, however, that it is enforced, and that no part of the coast is fenced off from the public. The Coastal Plan, therefore, proposes that existing legal rights of public access to the coast be enforced and that reasonable requirements for public access to the beach be established in new developments along the coast (California Coastal Plan 1977).

In Japan, a proposal for the Fundamental Act for Seashore Protection, which includes the right of access to the beach, was proposed by citizens' movements in 1976 (Kumamoto 1983). It has, however, not yet been actually considered in the Diet.

3. Energy Production

Another important problem along the coastal zone relates to energy production. Although we know that saving or reducing energy consumption is the most important problem in recent years, we still need energy production to maintain our standard of living at present and in the future. In the Asian area people require not only that present standards of living be maintained, but that they be raised. From this standpoint, energy facilities, including those for petroleum production and refining, should be considered in the coastal plan as well. Naturally, this problem is different from country to country. For example, the situation in Japan is very serious in locating those facilities along the coastal area. Several court cases in Japan indicate the hardship of storing petroleum or liquefied natural gas along the coastal zone. The Mizushima case in Japan in 1974 involved accidental spills of petroleum from tanks installed along the coast, which caused serious sea water pollution in the Seto Inland Sea. The 1979 cases of the Okinawa central terminal station construction and the Himeji liquid natural gas base reclamation also demonstrate the difficulty of selecting bases for these facilities. We may learn that a general and comprehensive plan for locating petroleum preparation bases, and for safety, should be carefully standardized and applied beforehand in order to avoid such accidents and litigation.

VI. Conclusions

We have seen that the types and quality of the problems of CZM are diverse and complicated. In addition, we may see a similarity in the problems before us, such as clean water or protection of aquatic resources of each country. The attitude toward land use for industrial activities of the countries in the region, however, is not so simple that we can set standards for improving and maintaining good environments, and apply them equally to all these nations.

In addition, the domestic problems in the region differ from country to country. Some countries really need affirmative policies for economic growth and development, while others are required to stress preservation of the natural beauty of the coastal zone rather than to emphasize economic development. However, through our surveys and discussions at our conferences, we may find common goals, tasks and interests in the future in order to protect our environment. For this purpose, we need to meet at least every two years somewhere in Asia or the Pacific to exchange ideas and information and to foster international cooperation among our Asian and Pacific colleagues. Our goal is still far away, but it is not beyond our ability to achieve.

References

Abe, Yasutaka. 1981. Land reclamation and the protection of the sea and seashore surrounding Japan. In *Environmental Law and Policy in the Pacific Basin Area*, eds. Ichirō Katō, Nobuo Kumamoto and William H. Matthews. Tokyo: University of Tokyo Press.

California Coastal Zone Conservation Commission. 1975. *California Coastal Plan*, 6.

California Coastal Zone Conservation Commission. 1977. *California Coastal Plan*, 30–43.

Environment Agency. 1977. *Quality of the Environment in Japan*, 139.

Government of Guam, Bureau of Planning. 1977. *Coastal Management Program Technical Report*, Vol. 1, 1.

Kumamoto, Nobuo. 1983. Coastal zone laws and litigation in Japan. In *Water Management and Environmental Protection in Asia and the Pacific*, eds. Ichirō Katō, Nobuo Kumamoto, William H. Matthews and R. T. M. Sutamihardja. Tokyo: University of Tokyo Press.

Schoenbaum, T. J. 1982. *Environmental Policy Law*, 639–822. New York: The Foundation Press.

Integrated Coastal Zone Development Strategies

A. Maheswaran

The present prosperity and relatively high living standard of Malaysians draw heavily on Malaysia's rich resource base, both renewable and nonrenewable, ranging from forestry, land, fossil fuels and minerals, to the most basic resource of all—water.

In addition, Malaysia has a relatively long sea frontage of about 4800 km (3000 miles) endowed with valuable marine ecosystems and resources. The special characteristics of the Malaysian coastline are clearly seen in the extensive beaches, which serve as national amenities, or mangrove swamps of 640 km (400 miles), which constitute one of the most productive ecosystems for its role in offshore commercial fishery. The Straits of Malacca is the most important fishing ground in Peninsular Malaysia. It produced about 400,000 tons of fish in 1978, while the South China Sea waters bordering the east coast produced approximately 150,000 tons.

For many years, the major environmental problem in Malaysia stemmed predominantly from the lack of development and inadequate infrastructure facilities; in short, poverty itself seemed polluting and a trap to break out of. It was thus that the country for nearly a decade and more after Merdeka (independence) opted over successive plan periods for accelerated development programs spanning mining, forestry, estate development, agriculture, land settlement and industrial development. The high rate of sustained economic development has made substantial inroads into the reserves of minerals, soils, forests and water, to an extent where a condition of near depletion may well be reached by the end of the present century.

From the Malaysian experience, it is crucial for small developing countries to protect the source of their wealth, both currently available and that of the future, on the principle that renewable resources can best be husbanded in the context of a healthy environment. In addition, these countries must be constantly vigilant; since their most basic resources are finite, at all times farsighted and enlightened resource husbandry is of paramount importance. In this process, the right balance between development and the environment has to be struck.

In recent years, there has been some serious rethinking among both developed and developing countries alike on the directions, thrust and pace of future development efforts. In many ways, these endeavors have been prompted by new perceptions of the need for the harmonization of goals and policies of economic development with those of environmental protection and improvement, to ensure a better quality of life for the people and accelerate it by coming to terms with the prospect of near depletion of resources.

It has now become increasingly clear that the problems of environmental protection are inseparable from the problems of economic development. They are in fact two sides of the same coin, two aspects of the same goal, one reinforcing and underpinning the other. It is then just a matter of prudent management that environmental protection be approached as a dimension of economic development in all its aspects, since we desire neither an immaculate and pristine environment for its own sake nor allout economic development at the other extreme which extracts a heavy price in terms of a degraded environment.

In the past, there has been a tendency to equate development with the more narrowly conceived objective of economic growth as measured by the rise in gross national product or by physical indicators alone. It is usually recognized today that high rates of economic growth, necessary and desirable as they are, do not by themselves guarantee the easing of urgent social and human problems. Indeed, in not a few countries high growth rates were accompanied by increasing unemployment, rising disparities in incomes both between groups and between regions and the deterioration of the social and cultural quality of life. A new emphasis is thus coming to be placed on the attainment of social and cultural goals as part of the development process. The recognition of environmental issues in developing countries is an aspect of this widdening of the development concept. It is part of a more integrated or unified approach to the development objectives and in the Malaysian context timely, as we have entered the Fourth Malaysia Plan.

Such an enlightened perception of the role of environmental management in the context of nation building is particularly relevant to developing countries like Malaysia, dependent on natural resources for the generation of economic activities. The economic growth, progress and well-being of a nation depend largely on adequate resource availability as well as the systematic development and use of these resources, both renewable and nonrenewable. However, the capacity of these resources as part of the whole ecological system is not unlimited. In effect, there are limits to growth in a sense. Much will depend on the prudent management of these resources and the extent to which extraction and distribution impacts on the environment, which in turn has a bearing on productivity. The capacity of the environment to generate essential renewable resources must be maintained, restored or improved, as otherwise, negative side effects on the environment will result with the pay-off from the hoped-for development being significantly less than the optimum.

Malaysia, compared to most developing countries, can be considered as fortunate in that it has seemingly abundant resources. All these have experienced rapid growth rates and in the course of development, various environmental problems have arisen.

I. Strategy for Environmental Management

In view of the interaction that exists between resource development and environmental quality, environmental management is understood to mean prudent or optimal use, maintenance and enhancement of both the quantity and quality of our natural resources. As the prospects for a long-run abundant supply of natural resources are weak, and technological innovations are inadequate, discrete and unpredictable, the developing countries have to take a serious look at their resource limitations, especially renewable resources, and tailor their development efforts suitably. This does not imply sacrificing development itself. What it does imply, however, is that the patterns of resource development and resource use have to be restructured by adopting policies of resource management which are innovative and imaginative, and which focus on employment and efficiently organized productive activities. Resource development, therefore, has to be approached on an integrated basis, treating environment as an important parameter in order to bring maximum economic and social benefits to improve the quality of life. Essentially it should aim at:

(1) minimizing wastes in the process of resource development and utilization of wastes;

(2) developing appropriate technology for management and control of wastes;

(3) limiting the environmental problems.

Since development of natural resources itself is a continuous process which involves intentional changes to the environment through the various activities, it must therefore be accompanied by conscious effort in guiding these environmental changes, so that economic growth can be sustained to provide an increasingly better standard of living, not only in the material sense but also in the value of life itself. The essential task of guiding this change must be carried out through a proper long-term management of the resources, to maintain an equilibrium between the modes of resources and the rising demands while staying within environmental needs. It simply means a farsighted view by the users of our resources so that we can continue to use them or even improve their yield for a long time to come.

As for the Malaysian experience, Malaysia has a three-tier system of government—federal, state and the local authorities—with each level having legislative and administrative competence in specific fields and, through their actions, having potential for impacting on the environment. Resource management is currently being carried out in this country, both at the federal and state level, by the various departments responsible for the development of the respective resources. Therefore, the task of environmental management has to be shared. State governments and local authorities, in view of their legislative and administrative competence in specific fields, have a considerable role to play in solving environmental problems. Through effective coordination and willing cooperation they could contribute considerably towards effective performance in environmental protection and management, so that available resources of manpower and funds are deployed to good purpose and duplication of efforts is avoided.

In this context, the government has pledged to undertake the leadership role in the overall management of man's relationship with the environment. It has responded to this task favorably by passing the Environmental Quality Act of 1974, followed by the establishment of the Environment Division under the Ministry of Science, Technology and Environment. The policy of the government in administering the Act rests on two factors. The first is that Malaysia is a developing country and essentially must pursue a policy of economic growth. The second is that Malaysia's economy, today and for a long time to come, depends on the renewable resource sectors and these, for a small country like ours, are limited, fragile and in urgent need of comprehensive protection and sustained production. Malaysia's overall environmental policy therefore takes account of the following factors:

(1) the impact that population growth and man's activities in resource development, industrialization and urbanization have on the environment;

(2) the critical importance of maintaining the quality of the environ-

ment relative to the needs of the population, particularly in regard to the productive capacity of the country's land resources in agriculture, forestry, fisheries and water;

(3) the need to maintain a healthy environment for human habitation;

(4) the need to preserve the country's unique and diverse natural heritage, which contributes to the quality of life; and

(5) the interdependence of social, cultural, economic, biological and physical factors in determining the ecology of man.

In light of these factors, the responsibilities for environmental management fall under four basic tasks:

(1) environmental assessment, which includes monitoring, research and review;

(2) planning;

(3) controlling; and

(4) decision making in such areas as resource allocation, land use, economic and industrial development and planning.

The above elements underpin and reinforce each other in the strategy of the government in terms of the overall structure, content and thrust of the environment program. The first and most essential task is, logically, environmental assessment, which seeks to examine, assess and evaluate the environmental conditions prevailing in various localities through the air and water quality monitoring program, baseline studies and source emission inventory surveys, which are being currently undertaken by the Environment Division of the Ministry of Science, Technology and Environment. These activities are geared not only to provide the fundamental inputs for development planning, but are also expected to be useful in themselves for the formulation of the pollution control program. The data on standards of environmental quality which are being generated by these activities will provide feedback information in environmental management to help influence the future course of development.

II. Existing Environmental Control

Environmental problems are not solved by remedial measures but by a combination of proper environmental planning and pollution control, involving an integrated approach of both preventive and restorative measures. Logically, it would be sensible to work out a proper environmental plan to be carried out within the general "planning" framework before any pollution control work is done. However, in the Malaysian context, due to the necessary gestation period required to evolve a sound plan (data collection, resources, trained manpower and so forth) and the urgency of antipollution measures, a simultaneous approach is not only desirable but also inescapable.

Therefore, pollution control has been the "punch-line" activity in the Environment Division's program for environmental conservation and enhancement for environmental quality. Important as they are for controlling existing and future environmental problems, these measures must, however, be planned and designed within the framework of the growth targets implicit in the development plan, and take into due account administrative procedures at both the federal and state levels.

In the final analysis, these control measures must be consistent and workable within the framework of the Federal Constitution, insofar as it concerns the relationship between the Federation and the States. With this constitutional framework, the Environment Division is adopting a two-step approach involving (1) statutory control and (2) nonstatutory control.

The choice of these control measures and their application would depend significantly on the areas to be controlled. The statutory control is adopted in areas which are expressly within the ambit of the Environmental Quality Act 1974, or more precisely in those matters which are specified in the Federal or Concurrent Lists. Nonstatutory control, on the other hand, is applied in areas where the existing responsibilities are shared by various government agencies and in those areas which are within the competence of the state governments. It will be noted that matters such as land, agriculture, forestry, mining, soil erosion, drainage and irrigation, which are fundamentally important in environmental management, are categorically under the State and Concurrent Lists, and it is in these areas that the nonstatutory control must be directed with great care to avoid undue administrative conflicts.

The legal controls are being effectively instituted through the various regulations, which have been drawn up on the advice of the Environmental Quality Council in accordance with the Environmental Quality Act 1974. They are, among others:

(1) Environmental Quality (prescribed premises) (crude palm oil) Regulations, 1977;
(2) Environmental Quality (prescribed premises) (raw natural rubber) Regulations, 1978;
(3) Sewage and Industrial Effluents Regulations, 1979;
(4) The Clean Air Regulations, 1978.

These regulations are directed principally against industrial pollution in the form of discharges and emissions which damage our common property resources, namely, land, air and water. However, they are by no means the complete answer in themselves in tackling the whole catalogue of problems. For example, they will not be able to deal with those problems arising from the development of land and natural resources, which are equally as serious as pollution from industrial sources. Nevertheless, these regulations constitute positive steps towards the control of pollution from point sources.

Under these regulations, control is effected through the establishment of criteria or standards for the reduction of pollutants, enforced by both legal and administrative methods including "resource charges." With the enforcement of these regulations it is estimated that a total of 820 licensed premises (sources) and more than 7000 nonlicensed premises are subject to these regulatory measures. The fundamental reason for this approach is to induce a polluter to install antipollution devices and to absorb the social cost for the use of resources. The imposition of "resource charges" in particular provides scope for each polluter to make his decision, which in the aggregate will keep the cost of pollution control as low as possible.

It is evident from the above that although action could be initiated by the Environment Division, it is unrealistic to expect it to be involved with the detailed procedures and the control mechanism for coping with various environment-related matters (e.g., use of pesticides, mining discharges). Further, it is only logical for the implementing agencies to take heed of the environmental safeguards in the course of the implementation of their various projects.

III. Environmental Planning

As has already been pointed out, the environmental problems arising as the result of development of Malaysia's land and natural resources are more complex, and can only be overcome through an integrated approach entailing advance or forward planning in the environmentally related activities in terms of the long-term conservation of environmental assets. It means that while preparing as best we can to cope with those situations which it is too late to avoid, we should focus on emerging problems by striving to head them off by timely action before they assume serious or crisis proportions. For this purpose, it is important to ensure that an environmental consciousness pervades the decision makers and planners in both the public and private sector, so that the imperatives of environmental protection are built into the development projects and the need for costly and time-consuming remedial measures is obviated.

The machinery and the commitment to planning already exist, and what is needed is the development of an enlarged planning methodology so that an environmental dimension could be incorporated in a systematic way in development planning right from the start. The integration of the environmental dimension with resource management would require a broader elaboration of development goals encompassing qualitative aspects as well, rather than a mere increase in gross national product. Generally speaking, the optimal development process should be one which sets, as one of its main objectives, the satisfaction by present and future generations of their basic requirements without transgressing the outer limts of the biosphere's tolerance of man's activities. There is a delicate balance here and it demands very careful consideration. For such rational management to be achieved, methods must be developed to deal more adequately with the full social and environmental—and not just economic—costs and benefits of development-related activities.

It is necessary to find techniques for quantifying the impacts, both favorable and unfavorable, of development projects on the environment, so that the society can choose projects with a fuller knowledge of their social costs and benefits in the light of a number of options generated. All too often the social costs of various projects are ignored or receive short shrift in the initial appraisal, especially in the context of a laissez-faire economy, so that society's recognition for what they are of many of the environmental disruptions resulting from these projects comes at too late a stage to permit effective and timely remedial action. It is important that the social costs should be ascertained to the maximum extent possible before undertaking development projects, so that society can carefully assess whether they are still worthwhile, whether some of the costs could not be minimized through careful design of the project and whether some of the costs could not be avoided or at least deferred through adoption of alternatives.

In this context, the Environment Division under the Ministry of Science, Technology and Environment has undertaken the leadership role in providing the necessary instruments of control. It has responded to this task positively by preparing several guidelines which are intended to help state governments and other agencies to incorporate environmental consideration into their development plans. The most important guidelines are:

(1) zoning and siting of industries;

(2) environmental impact assessment;

(3) selection of sites for solid waste disposal and management of sites; and

(4) prevention of erosion and siltation.

The usefulness of zoning is self-evident. Without it, environmental problems can grow to unmanageable proportions. The main advantages can be summarized as follows:

1. *Isolation of residual pollutants and their impact.* The Malaysian approach in regulatory control of pollution is largely based on the best practicable means (B.P.M.) concept with provisions for gradual integration with the air quality management concept. The B.P.M. draws its strength from considerations of technical feasibility and economic viability. Therefore, the installation of in-plant control equipment and adoption of control measures would limit the discharge of pollutants to a certain level but not necessarily totally eliminate it, and as much as 5 percent to 10 percent of the "residual pollutants" might still be discharged into the environment from each polluting source. The provision of buffer zones would fulfill the purpose of isolating the people from the impact areas.

2. *Reduced cost of control measures.* As the degree of control becomes more stringent, the cost increases exponentially. If the polluting source could be located well away from populated areas, control measures need not be as stringent as would otherwise be necessary. In the ultimate analysis pollution control cost would be borne by the consumers, hence the reduction or control cost would reduce the burden on the people and the country as a whole.

3. *More efficient and effective infrastructure planning.* The provision of various zones for housing, buffer and compatible industries would help to lower implementation costs in planning infrastructure facilities such as commuting routes, sanitary services, centralized treatment system for industries, water and electricity supplies, water recycling plants and so forth.

Under the proposed Environmental Impact Assessment (EIA) procedure, which is currently being refined by the Division of Environment for submission to the Cabinet Committee on Investment, projects with high potential impact would be required to have an assessment made and submitted to the Ministry for review. Initiators of the project would be required to submit the various environmental and pollution impacts which can be foreseen and quantified so that steps may be taken in advance to plan and control or mitigate their environmental consequences.

The advantages of the Environmental Impact Assessment are self-evident. While it is reckoned that the primary goal of the environmental impact assessment is to determine the impact of a project on the surrounding environment, it also serves the following purposes:

(1) The findings of an impact assessment may be utilized in selecting a site for a project, where the resulting adverse environmental impact and the associated cost of implementing control measures to reduce the impact will be minimized, and the hoped-for benefits maximized.

(2) With regard to an existing facility, the EIA will help to determine the actual need and extent of control required.

(3) The disclosure of the environmental consequences of an activity may be made to government agencies and the public, if and when necessary.

The guidelines for selection of sites for solid waste disposal and management of the site are intended to help the various local authorities to avoid haphazard selection and management of waste disposal sites without taking environmental factors into consideration.

The problems of soil erosion and siltation can only be overcome by employing suitable controls and preventive measures, especially at the planning stage of a project, whether for agriculture, mining, housing, road construction or logging. The guidelines for prevention of erosion and siltation contain well-defined and precise specifications in terms of preventive measures to control siltation, such as silt traps and other appropriate control structures.

IV. Implementation of Strategy

As for putting the strategy to work, here the need for a pragmatic, systematic, graduated and coordinated approach, not just at the level of the environmental protection agency but all environment-related agencies, including the research institutions and universities, cannot be overemphasized.

It must be recognized, particularly in the context of developing countries, that environmental control regulations, however skillfully formulated and drafted in themselves, constitute no magic wand to cure the environmental ills of society overnight or even in a relatively short time span. An immense amount of hard work, to ensure primarily that the standards set are realistic in terms of protecting the environment, that the technology for treatment is either available or can be developed readily and that the treatment involved is cost effective in the sense of being within the means of the industry concerned, has to be backed up by systematic and sustained enforcement to get across the message that the authorities mean business.

It can be stated without fear of contradiction that the success stories to date in Malaysia in bringing environmental pollution woes to manageable proportions are in the main due to the pragmatic, systematic and businesslike approach consistently adopted by the Environment Division, backed up at the same time by an uncompromising, firm, yet fair approach in enforcing the regulations which it has a mandate to enforce in the public interest.

The good working relationships built up over an extended period of time with the research institutions in Malaysia and all five universities, along with a whole spectrum of public sector agencies, both at the federal and state levels, have stood us in good stead.

V. Conclusion

Assaults on the environment are many and varied, arising from the wide range of activities in a rapidly developing economy. While the costs of measures and programs addressed to the improvement and protection of the environment are fairly apparent to people at large and to the affected groups in particular, their far-reaching benefits, which often spread beyond the sectors where environmental control was initially introduced, are not so clearly seen or appreciated. The result of this is that benefits from environmental measures are understated.

The developing countries in practice find it difficult to make inroads into the traditional methodology and approach of project evaluation adopted by development planners and decision makers. The lack of systematic studies to demonstrate clearly, in a comprehensive and quantitative manner, the assessment of benefits accruing from environmental measures, and the constraints imposed by competing policy priorities and alternative claims on resources, have led to the expediency of all too often ignoring the environmental dimension in resource management. These countries, therefore, need some assurance and perhaps conclusive proof that environmental management, far from being a handicap, can actually be a plus factor in any sound resource management program in helping to ensure its success. It should in fact become evident that the environmental protection approach is a resource management concept, while economic development is generally pursued as a resource use concept, and that the whole objective of integrating environmental planning with development is to absorb the resource management ideas into the process of planning for resource use.

In Malaysia, the Environment Division is making an all-out effort to get this message across through the promotion of environmental education. The quarterly magazine *Sekitar* published by the Environment Division is yet another step in terms of our strategy to promote environmental education to key target groups.

Trends in International Cooperation in Research and Training in Coastal Zone Management

Mohd. Ibrahim b. Hj. Mohamad

The concept of Coastal Zone Management (CMZ) is "to preserve, protect, develop and where possible to enhance the resources of the coastal zone." The coastal zone in turn is defined as the region bounded by shorelands, estuaries, nearshore oceans, large lakes and enclosed seas. Both these definitions are based on criteria for the U.S. Coastal Zone Management Act of 1972 (CZMA).

By necessity in dealing with trends, the impending ocean regime deliberated by the 158 member states of the United Nations Conference on the Law of the Seas (UNCLOS) will play an important role in shaping the nature of international cooperation and obligation in the conduct of research and training. Relevant articles of this international legal regime are based on the Informal Composite Negotiating text/ Revision I (RICNT).

In order to recognize the trends of the future, it is necessary to look back into developments that led to the present status of international cooperation in the coastal zone.

I. Present Status of Coastal Zone Management

The uses of the coastal zone fall into six basic categories: (1) living space and recreation; (2) industrial and commercial activity; (3) waste disposal; (4) food production; (5) natural preserves; and (6) special government uses.

The roots of many nations are in coastal zones. Population centers, availability of cooling water, offshore oil and gas deposits, oil refineries, energy processing facilities, recreation, even disposal sites have been conveniently sited in this region. Pressures brought about by the conflicting demands on coastal uses both onshore and offshore have created awareness of the importance of the region. Realization that the processes of the ocean, air-sea interaction and its effects on world climate, necessitate concerted efforts to preserve and manage the coastal zone. Oceanic processes know no political boundaries. Therefore, coastal zone management is by necessity global or regional in nature. Article 197 of the RICNT clearly reflects the desire of the world community for this policy (UN Law of the Sea 1979):

> States shall cooperate on a global basis and, as appropriate, on a regional basis, directly or through competent international organizations, global or regional, in formulating and elaborating international rules, standards and recommendations, practices and procedures consistent with this convention for the protection and preservation of marine environment taking into account characteristic regional features.

Attainment of international cooperation in CZM is difficult to achieve. However, the conviction of the world community is clearly shown by the large number of articles at the RICNT specifying the global and/or regional approaches to CZM.

International cooperation in research and training has been successfully demonstrated by the various programs of the Intergovernmental Oceanographic Commission (IOC), such as the International Decade of Ocean Exploration (IDOE) within the framework of the Long-term and Expanded Programme of Oceanic Exploration and Research (LEPOR). Sixteen programs on environmental forecasting, five on the quality of the marine environment and nine on the nonliving resources of the sea were carried out under IDOE. One of the main criteria of participation in IDOE programs was that projects must be multinational in nature (Roll 1979). Global Investigations of Pollution in the Marine Environment (GIPME) is a result of coordination and cooperation of various United Nations agencies such as IMCO/FAO/ UNESCO/WMO/WHO/IAEA/UN/UNEP through the Group of Experts on Long-term Scientific Policy and Planning (GELTSPAP).

At present, more than sixty regional and international organizations are established to deal with the various aspects of coastal zone use, development, protection and preservation (Alexander 1977). These organizations represent varying degrees of success in implementation of their programs due to cross-cutting of national interests in the utilization of coastal zone resources.

As pointed out by Clingan (1977), in certain areas, cooperation on a multinational basis can be successful because of common national interests, for instance in pollution. However, in exploration of resources, the interests balanced are national in scope rather than regional in common.

Problems that affect the true achievement of international cooperation in research and training are many. The following discussion may be of value in determining the trends of coastal zone management efforts.

Membership of the IOC increased from 40 states in 1960 to 103 nations in 1979. With this tremendous increase it became necessary for the objective of IOC to be expanded to contain enhanced utilization of the ocean and its resources for the benefit of mankind, besides the original enhancement of knowledge of oceanic processes among its members. This trend in marine science research clearly illustrates the shift in emphasis from purely scientific research to the application of scientific results to the utilization of oceanic resources for the benefit of all nations.

There is a large differential in terms of scientific knowledge, technology and sophistication in marine scientific research between the developed and the developing nations. This difference in standards prohibits close cooperation in terms of joint research in the coastal zone.

Faby (1979) pointed out that lack of coherence among the CZM programs of the United Nations Environment Programme (UNEP) is basically due to the following reasons:

(1) UN agencies have primarily sectoral responsibilities;
(2) the global mandate of UN agencies determine to what extent important resources can be channelled to regional programs;
(3) national interests.

Other obstacles to setting up a purely international accord in CZM involve matters such as lack of intercalibration of results and standardization of methods. Atwood (1979) also concluded that the lack of funds is another hindrance. He pointed out that most UN organizations only coordinate planning and provide funding for workshops and regional meetings. There is not sufficient funding for actual programs.

Data confidentiality also undermines true internationalism in coastal zone management. It is easy to imagine this aspect of coastal zone management, as national interest may dictate prudence to avoid liability in pollution cases, or such data may enhance national interests in negotiations towards harvesting of marine resources.

The "consent regime" of marine scientific research has alarmed the scientific community of nations developed in marine sciences. Clingan (1979) observed that this regime is hardly liberal. Ample opportunities for cooperation are detailed in the RICNT but proper guidelines are absent.

How will the present shortcomings pave the way for future international cooperation in research and training in CZM?

II. Trends in Research

Present international cooperation in research on CZM has primarily been based upon the protection and preservation of the coastal zone. The nature of most projects deals with determination of baseline data, and prevention of pollution and monitoring, aimed primarily at the ecology and protection of the coastal zone. Sadly lacking is research aimed at development and enhancement of this region. With the realization of the importance of coastal zones, the motivation of marine research is no longer purely scientific but clearly stresses the application of scientific results to the utilization of oceanic resources for the benefit of all nations. This new element, as observed by Roll (1979), necessarily affects the determination of IOC's goals, which have to be adjusted to include utilization aspects and needs of all nations.

The future of the coastal zone will not merely involve its conservation and preservation. As utilization of the coastal zone becomes necessary, especially to the developing countries, trends in future research will be towards development with the minimum detrimental effect to the ecology of the coastal zones.

Whereas collection of baseline monitoring data to understand the forcing function in an ecosystem was predominant in the '60s and '70s, real-time or near real-time data is important to enable predictions of future phenomena. This is of absolute necessity to safeguard property and investment in the coastal zone. Such programs as the Integrated Global Ocean Station Systems (IGOSS), Ocean Data Acquisition System (ODAS) and tsunami warning systems in the Pacific (ITSU) will be further expanded to achieve some parallel to the present network of meteorological monitoring stations.

In the area of marine pollution, the trends in international cooperation are illustrated by the following objectives of the Marine Pollution Monitoring Program (MARPOLMON): (1) providing early warning of significant environmental changes to induce consideration of protective measures, and (2) enhancing qualitative knowledge of the marine environment and its dynamic balance as a basis of managing marine resources. Both these criteria further illustrate the trends toward gathering predictive knowledge in research in the CZM.

Two future trust areas in research are: (1) the principle of optimum participation oriented towards practical goals of interest and providing benefits to a great number of states; (2) sophisticated research which may not be of immediate interest to developing countries but promises important scientific progress in special fields (Roll 1979). Clearly both these trust areas emphasize the need for international cooperation in research in the CZM. International cooperation is essential to overcome some of the legalities of the "consent regime" on scientific research in the Exclusive Economic Zone.

The key to successful management of the CZM is international cooperation and coordination in resource-oriented projects to benefit a large proportion of member states. To obtain such a state of cooperation among member states, real partnership must be developed between marine scientists both from nations advanced in oceanography and from those nations which lack the scientific personnel and infrastructure. This requires understanding from developed states when instituting research programs. Priorities of research, considering limited funds and facilities and the national interest, are frequently different.

Only when the marine science capacities of almost all nations have been raised to a reasonably competent level will international research in coastal zone management lead to results that are beneficial to all mankind. This will require concerted efforts in training and education in marine science on a multinational basis.

III. Trends in Education: Conclusion

International cooperation in training and education in coastal zone management can be modeled on the concept and objectives of the Training, Educational and Mutual Assistance Program (TEMA) of the IOC and as well as activities by the Marine Science Division of the United Nations Educational, Scientific and Cultural Organization (UNESCO).

While local institutions develop marine science education within their boundaries, an international organization that coordinates and accelerates training and education programs towards a higher scientific and technological standard in all member states in the field of marine science is necessary, and is fulfilled by TEMA. Several recommendations and decisions derived through the Working Committee for TEMA in 1971, 1973, 1975 and 1977 are aimed towards the objective of enhancing marine science education, as listed below:

- training of marine science administrators;

- strengthening of educational and research institutions in developing countries;
- development of a well-balanced program at different levels;
- introduction of marine science elements in the curricula of primary and secondary schools;
- translation of marine science texts and production of annotated bibliographies pertaining to marine science education;
- participation in oceanic cruises and participation of young foreign scientists in research and training projects of developing countries;
- setting up of regional training centers;
- program of work and budget for TEMA.

The IOC Voluntary Assistance Program (IOC-VAP) constitutes a supplementary source of support to achieve these objectives.

Implementation of the above strategies can be shown by the development of marine science curricula in the university and nonuniversity areas. One such development is the Marine Affairs/Ocean Policy/ Marine Law and Ocean Policy Programs flourishing in university curricula. These programs take two forms: (1) training of marine lawyers, economists, analysts, planners and managers who can handle the new task of environmental protection and management of marine coastal resources; and (2) training marine scientists and engineers so that they can deal with the new challenges which involve policy considerations as well as scientific factors.

The Division of Marine Sciences of UNESCO is also playing an active role in the development of national and regional infrastructures in marine science. Two such programs in the West Pacific region include the strengthening of the Ocean Research and Development Institute of the Republic of Korea and development of marine science education in Thailand. A more general program of scientist exchange, fellowships, study and travel grants, advice on manpower, training and research, development of new projects, provision of books, equipment and the Open University Program are also provided by UNESCO.

Achievement of academic and technical competence at the professional level must also be accompanied by parallel development of subprofessionals and technicians in this field. Such programs as that of the Japanese International Cooperation Agency in technician training is an effort to parallel development at this level.

The introduction of elements of marine sciences in school curricula is currently being tried by the University of Hawaii. The University of Rhode Island has a somewhat similar program of short duration to introduce the problems and complexities of the marine environment to school children. Judging from recommendations of various workshops pertaining to coastal zone management, these programs will comprise some of the most significant trends in education and training in coastal zone management.

References

Alexander, Lewis M. 1977. *Regional Arrangements in Ocean Affairs.* Kingston R. I.: University of Rhode Island.
Atwood, Donald K. 1979. The International Oceanographic and 10 CARIBE. In *Proceedings of the Symposium on Marine Regionalism*, ed. Lawrence Juda, 109–177. Galilee, Rhode Island.
Clingan, Thomas A., Jr. 1979. UNCLOS III and future of regional arrangements. In *Proceedings of the Symposium on Marine Regionalism*, ed. Lawrence Juda, 14–22. Galilee, Rhode Island.
Faby, Jean Claude. 1979. The United Nations Environmental Programme and Regionalism. In *Proceedings of the Symposium on Marine Regionalism*, ed. Lawrence Juda, 94–100. Galilee, Rhode Island.
Harger, J. R. E. 1982. UNESCO Activities in Marine Sciences. Paper presented at the Sea Grant Seminar Workshop 25–28 May 1982, Universiti Pertanian Malaysia, Kuala Trengganu, Malaysia.
Hawaii Coastal Zone News. Course Probes Ocean Future, 5:5 September, 1980.
Pravidic, Velimir. 1981. GESAMP: The first dozen years. Geneva: UNEP.
Roll, Hans Ulrich. 1979. A focus for ocean research. Intergovernmental Oceanographic Commission technical series 20.
Storer, J. 1979. FAO and marine regionalism. In *Proceedings of the Symposium on Marine Regionalism*, ed. Lawrence Juda, 90–94. Galilee, Rhode Island.
United Nations Educational, Scientific and Cultural Organization, Division of Marine Science. Marin F-37 (also IOC/WESTPAC – II/8) Paris, 4 August 1981.
United Nations Third Conference on the Law of the Sea; Revised Informal Composite Negotiating text for the Eighth Session. Reproduced from UN DOC A/Conf. 62/WP.10/Rev. I, 1979.
United States Department of Commerce. 1978. *U.S. Ocean Policy in the 1970s; Status and Issues.* Washington, D. C.: U. S. Government Printing Office.

The Marine Environment and the Coastal Zone

Impact on the Marine Environment of Harvesting of Coastal Zone Resources
A Thailand Case

Twesukdi Piyakarnchana

The impact of harvesting of coastal zone resources in Thailand can be concentrated on three main subjects: the fisheries, the mangrove forests and tin mining resources. The utilization of some of these resources by the fisheries and tin mining in the coastal zone areas has been practiced for many decades. However, its impacts on the marine environments have not been too severe until recently.

The coastline of Thailand is about 1600 miles long and borders two important oceans of the world, the Gulf of Thailand of the Pacific Ocean and the Andaman Sea of the Indian Ocean. The Gulf of Thailand, in the past, has been one of the richest in marine living resources of the world. There are many rivers which drain large amounts of plant nutrients such as nitrate, phosphate and others into the Gulf. On the Andaman coastal zone, besides the fisheries resources, there are many tin mines and the richest mangrove forests.

I. Harvesting of Demersal Fish Resources

Thailand was ranked by the Food and Agricultural Organization (FAO) in 1977 to be tenth among the top largest marine fishing countries of the world. The total catch annually was 1.48×10^6 tons (FAO 1977). However, the fisheries wealth in the Gulf of Thailand region has declined since 1965. This is due mostly to the overexploitation and mismanagement of the marine living resources. It is also claimed that the deterioration of the marine environment might be one cause of such a decline in the catch (Tanapong and Boonyapiwat 1981). It is estimated that about 30–40 percent of the total fish catch comes from outside of Thai waters. Thus, with the increasing cost of petroleum fuels and the proclamation of the Exclusive Economic Zone (EEZ) to

200 nautical miles of Thailand's neighboring countries, the total catch of marine fishes has decreased sharply.

However, the average amounts of fish caught in Thai waters by the Fisheries Research Vessel No. 2 in 1963 were 231.6 kg/hr, and in 1977, 47.3 kg/hr. The decreasing ratio is about 4.8 to 1. Surprisingly enough these figures are equal to the increasing ratio (4.7 to 1) of the total fish catch in tons: 198,190 in 1963 and 921,671 in 1977. These increasing amounts are due to the expansion of the fishing grounds and also to the increasing number of trawlers, which is about 2.7 times within 14 years. The highest increase in numbers of trawlers, however, occurred within a short period of the first five years from introduction of this catching method into Thailand waters. It also coincided with signs of overexploitation of the demersal fish stocks in the Gulf region.

It was estimated that the maximum sustainable yield from the demersal fish resources was about 686,640 metric tons (Boonyubol 1979). Thus, it is clearly indicated that the amount of the catch in 1977, which reached 921,671 tons, is far above the previous estimate. It is very difficult to bring the stock back to the normal condition under the present fishery management program.

II. Harvesting of the Mangrove Forest and Intertidal Mud Flats

The total mangrove forest of Thailand is about 312,714.4 ha, or about 3,127 km^2. About 80 percent of these forests is located on the coastline of the Andaman Sea and the rest is on the Gulf of Thailand. Thailand uses the wood resources from its mangrove forests as firewood and charcoal, timber, construction materials and fish traps.

The statistics in 1972 indicated that about 876,000 m^3 of mangrove were harvested. However, the production decreased to about 750,000 m^3 in 1975 (Piyakarnchana 1979). It was estimated that 30 percent of the mangrove forests was destroyed within the last decade (1970–1980) (Sabhasri 1979).

The intertidal mud flats of the mangrove forest and its vicinity are used for fish and shrimp farms. The areas which were utilized for these purposes in 1980 were 26,036.32 ha. They produced about 8,063.07 metric tons. The impacts of the mariculture on the mangrove forests are very great. The farmers usually clear the trees before they start to rear the shrimps or fish in the impoundments.

The intertidal and subtidal mud flats on the outermost edge of the mangrove forests are used for fish and mollusc farming. The statistics for 1980 show that 300 ha were used for horse mussel farms, 630 ha for oysters, 500 ha for cockles and 2,625 ha for green mussels. The total production of the bivalves in 1957 was 59,900 metric tons and in 1978, 111,673 metric tons (Fisheries Statistics 1978, 1980). It is interesting to note the highest production was in 1971 (292,805 metric tons) and the green mussel was the major one (214,593 tons). The lowest production between 1971 and 1978 was in 1974 (52,103 metric tons).

The factor that caused the mollusc production to decrease is mainly the deterioration of the environment, especially by the industrial wastes from the Mae Klong River. It was reported that during 1973–1974, the cockle and shrimp farmers lost about U.S. $1.5 million by sugar mills discharging wastes into the river (Ratasuk 1973).

III. Tin Mining along the Coastal Zone

Thailand is one of the few tin producing countries. It started to mine the tin on land in 1907. The mining from the sea, however, was begun only recently. Tin production from the sea has increased every year; in 1978, for example, it reached about 18,180 tons (Ajolaphuti 1979).

On the Andaman coastline where tin is extracted, the government had already permitted a concession area of about 427,000 ha in 1977. The mining areas, however, are about 21.6 percent and the price of tin was 410 million baht (U.S. $20.5 million) (Suthas Na Ayudhaya 1979).

The environmental impacts from strip mining on the sea floor and also from the discharge of tailings have been described by many authors (Baram et al. 1978). The geomorphological damages alone can be clearly shown by looking at the excavating capacity of one of the dredgers in Phang Nga Bay, Southern Thailand. It has an excavation capacity of 77,000 m^3 per month or 0.77 million m^3 per year for a 10-month operation period. The tailings are spread into marine habitats and are believed to cause severe destruction to marine life, especially to the coral reefs.

IV. Attempts to Protect the Coastal Marine Environment

1. General Policy on the Protection of Marine Environment

In order to protect and to minimize the increasing deterioration of the marine environment, the Cabinet, on the advice of the National Environment Board, set up a policy on the marine environment on 3 February 1981 (Sanidwong 1981). This policy covers the best and wisest use of marine resources, the development of coastal areas with less adverse impacts on the marine resources and marine ecosystems, the conservation of the marine ecosystem and marine life and the conservation of the marine environment, for example, the islands and sea floors with natural beauty.

The policy is also concerned with conservation of the mangrove forests. It covers measures to control the effective use of the mangrove forests by minimizing the adverse impact on the environment, and stresses reforestation of the destroyed mangrove forests. A third concern is aimed at controlling, protecting and preserving the sea water quality.

It is expected that with the strong implementation of this policy, the severe deterioration of the marine environment will be cured. It is also hoped that with the restoration of marine water quality, the marine life will be less harmed.

2. Formulating a Better Management for Marine Fisheries

In order to prevent the continually decreasing trends of the fishery resources, the Department of Fisheries, Ministry of Agriculture and Cooperatives, has proposed the marine fisheries development program in the Fifth Five-year Economic and Social Development Plan, which is now in the implementation stage (1982–1986).

This development plan is expected to increase the amount of fish catch from 1,350,000 tons in 1982 to 1,400,000 tons in 1986 (Sithimong 1981). It also laid down the master plans for the management of the marine fisheries in Thai waters, and the development of coastal mariculture. It will strictly control the overexploitation of the fishery stocks.

It is interesting to note here that the Fisheries Department intends to amend the laws on controlling the numbers of fishing boats, and reducing the fish meal plants.

3. Introducing New Techniques for Mangrove Forest Management

In recent years, the deep sea fisheries in Thailand have declined sharply. There are at least two reasons; namely, the expansion of the Exclusive Economic Zone of its neighbor countries to 200 nautical miles, and the oil shortage since 1973. Many fishermen have now turned to nearshore harvesting and practicing mariculture. This will lead to intense destruction of the mangrove forests. It was estimated that at least 2 to 3 percent of the mangrove forest has been destroyed annually.

In order to preserve these most valuable mangrove forests, the new and practicable management methods such as the silvi-fishery practice should be used. The longer term leasing period to ensure long benefits to the mangrove planters must also be granted. The strip cutting technique, which has proved to be the most practical one in Thailand, must be used. In order to have more effective reforestation of the mangrove forests, the Department of Forestry should closely cooperate with the private sector.

V. Conclusion

The harvesting of the coastal zone resources in Thailand has had a severe impact on the marine environment. The decline in the amount of fish catch in the Gulf of Thailand is caused mainly by the overexploitation of the fish stocks and also by environmental pollution. It is a good example of rapid development with little planning. The destruction of the mangrove forests also has an adverse impact, not only on the fisheries but also on the consumption of fuel wood by the people. The deterioration of the environment by the tin mining and tailings is met with strong resistance from the local people whose island home is a tourist resource. More and thorough studies are needed on pollution prevention techniques for tin mining wastes.

The government is working together with the private sector in order to protect the living marine resources. They are exploring new and practical management techniques which can be used both by the policy makers and also at the implementing levels. It is hoped that with this cooperation, coastal marine resources in Thailand will be restored.

References

Ajolaphuti, C. 1979. Resources from the sea: Present and future utilization. Proceedings of the first seminar on marine science, 28–30 May 1979, 93–101. National Research Council of Thailand.

Baram, M., W. Lee and D. Rice. 1978. *Marine Mining of the Continental Shelf*. Cambridge, Mass.: Ballinger.

Boonyubol, M. 1979. Demersal fish resources in the Gulf of Thailand. Proceedings of the first seminar on marine science, 28–30 May 1979, 190. National Research Council of Thailand (Abstract).

Department of Fisheries. 1979, 1980. *Fisheries Statistics.*

Food and Agricultural Organization. 1977. Yearbook of Fishery Statistics, Vol. 44.

Piyakarnchana, T. 1979. Environmental pollution in Thailand with special emphasis on marine pollution. Proceedings of the 2nd symposium on our environment, 14–16 November, 1979, 322–331. Institute of Natural Sciences, College of Graduate Studies, Nanyang University, Singapore.

Rabanal, H.R., U. Pongsuwana, A. Saraya and W. Poochareon. 1977. The shellfish of Thailand: Present status and prospects.

Ratasuk, S. 1973. The Problem of Mae Klong Pollution. Visawakam Sar., June 1973, 1–12.

Sanidwong, K. 1981. Policy on the conservation of marine environments. Proceedings of the second seminar on the water quality and the quality of living resources in Thai waters, 35–43. National Research Council of Thailand.

Sithimong, A. 1981. The development of marine fisheries in the fifth five-year economic and social development plan (1982–1986). Proceedings of the second seminar on the water quality of living resources in Thai waters, 44–56. National Research Council of Thailand.

Suthas Na Ayudhaya, P. 1979. History of the activities and the policy on the utilization of science and technology for marine mineral development resources. Proceedings of the first seminar on marine science, 28–30 May 1979, 54–61. National Research Council.

Tanapong, C. and C. Boonyapiwat. 1981. Result of otter board trawl catches in the Inner Gulf of Thailand, during the year 1979–1980. Proceedings of the second seminar on water quality and the quality of living resources in Thai waters, 196–207. National Research Council of Thailand.

Environmental Trade-Offs in Mangrove Forest Management

P. B. L. Srivastava

In the region of the Association of South East Asian Nations (ASEAN), where most of the countries are maritime nations having long shorelines, mangrove swamp vegetation forms an important component of the coastal zone. Any plan to use the coastal resources judiciously and to manage them scientifically has to take into consideration the presence of luxuriant, well-developed and highly productive mangrove forests on the sheltered coasts. They not only provide a variety of commercially important renewable products, but also play an extremely important role in maintaining marine productivity, building and stabilizing the shoreline, acting as a buffer against wild storms and providing other amenities to the local people. In fact, the real significance of the mangrove forests lies in their influence on the adjoining hinterland and the adjacent seas, and their impact on the socioeconomic conditions of the people dependent upon them for their livelihood. However, being an ecotone between land and water, these are unique and fragile ecosystems developed under peculiar hydrodynamic and sedimentation conditions. At the same time, because of our continued multiplicity of demands, there are several conflicting interests in the utilization of mangrove environments. Many of these competing uses involve irreversible changes that irretrievably alter functioning of these natural systems. As a result, the fragile mangrove ecosystem has been subjected to enormous stresses. In recent years, contamination of coastal waters and surface layers of the ocean, precisely where the biological productivity is greatest, has increased many times over. It has threatened the stability of a clean and productive mangrove environment.

This paper briefly reviews our knowledge of management of mangrove forests, environmental ill effects caused by their overexploitation, changes in land-use patterns and problems caused by pollutants.

105

I. Mangrove Forests in the ASEAN Region

Mangrove forests find probably the optimum site conditions for development in the ASEAN countries. According to Walsh (1974), there are five basic requirements for extensive mangal development:

(1) *Tropical temperatures.* Well-developed mangals are found only along coastal areas where the average temperature of the coldest month is higher than 20°C and the seasonal temperature range does not exceed 50°C.

(2) *Fine-grained alluvium.* Mangrove forests are best developed along deltaic coasts or in estuaries where soft mud composed of fine silt and clay rich in organic matter is available for growth of seedlings. Volcanic soils are highly productive of mangroves (Macnae 1968).

(3) *Shores free of strong wave and tidal action.* Mangroves develop best along the protected shores and estuaries because strong waves and tidal action uproot seedlings and carry away soft mud. This is the main reason for the absence of mangrove on the east coast of Malaysia.

(4) *Salt water.* Though mangroves are facultative halophytes they find the best conditions for growth and development in saline water along the sea coasts.

(5) *Large tidal range.* A wide, near-horizontal tidal range is a prerequisite for extensive growth of mangroves where natural succession leads to the development of distinct communities resulting in a climatic climax formation (Watson 1928; Richards 1952).

The above five factors determine the occurrence of mangroves, species composition and the area occupied by mangal. Jennings and Bird (1967) list six environmental factors which affect geomorphological characteristies in estuaries and, therefore, flora and fauna: acidity, wave energy, tidal conditions, sedimentation, mineralogy and neotectonic effects.

It appears that all the abovementioned factors are favorably present in the ASEAN region. It is therefore not surprising to find that mangrove forests in this region rank among the best of such forests in the world in terms of number of species and quality of crop.

Gomez (1980) has compiled data indicating that there are about 4.8 million ha of mangrove forests in the ASEAN region. Indonesia, with an area of about 3.6 million ha, has the largest area in mangrove swamps and constitutes about 75 percent of the total for ASEAN countries. Malaysia comes next with 13.6 percent, while Thailand and the Philippines have about 6.5 percent and 4.6 percent, respectively.

Table 1. Mangrove Forests in the ASEAN Region

Country	Land Area (km²)	Area in Mangrove Forest (ha)	Percentage of Land Area in Mangrove
Indonesia	1,903,650	3,618,100*	1.9
Malaysia	333,652	644,035	2.0
Philippines	300,838	220,242	0.7
Singapore	615	3,209	2.9
Thailand	514,000	312,700	0.6

* Slightly under estimated; later reports indicate area in Kalimantan higher by 30,000 hectares.
Source: Gomez 1980.

In the island republic of Singapore, only small patches of mangrove swamp are left due to the very fast pace of industrial development, and those that are left are in a very degraded condition. The area is only about 1 percent of the total mangrove in the ASEAN region. Table 1 presents the extent of mangrove forests in the region.

In Malaysia, out of 644,035 ha of mangrove forests, 105,076 ha are located in the Peninsula, 96 percent of which are on the west coast. About 39 percent of the total mangrove forests in the Peninsula is situated in the state of Perak, 25 percent in Johore, 22 percent in Selangor and 9 percent in Kedah. However, the area in mangrove forests is only 1.5 percent of the total forest area. Even in the mangrove-rich states of Perak, Johore, Selangor and Kedah, they form only 4.0 percent, 4.6 percent, 9.6 percent and 2.4 percent, respectively, of the total forested land (Tang et al. 1981). In Sarawak, mangrove forests cover an area of 173,600 ha, and in Sabah, mangrove swamp vegetation is spread over an area of 365,345 ha.

Luxuriant evergreen vegetation, forming an almost continuous cover, occurs in these mangals. A large number of plant species, ranging from lower plants like algae to ferns and orchids, and pure communities of *Rhizophora* and *Bruguiera* spp. have been reported (Johnson 1979; Gan 1982; Sahavacharin 1979). These species develop into distinct communities and niches. The mangrove species may occur in the open sea front where the ground is submerged twice a day, to the ecotone belt between inland forest and swamp communities where saline water reaches rarely, only during the high tides, depending upon the position of the species on the successional gradient. Along the rivers, however, mangrove species may reach 30–40 km upstream. The same diversity is observed in the faunal species composition (Sarekumar 1974). Gomez (1980) has reproduced the tables listing the plant and animal species in mangrove forests of ASEAN countries.

In terms of growth potential, in the well-managed forest of Matang

Table 2. Growth Potential of *Rhizophora apiculata* in Matang
Mangrove Reserve

Age (years)	Density (stems/ha)	Diameter (cm)	Height (m)
15	3236	8.28	12.3
19/20	2107	9.65	16.9
25	1321	13.90	17.1
29/30	830	17.45	26.3

Source: Tay and Srivastava 1982.

Mangrove Reserve, *Rhizophora apiculata*, economically the most important species, can attain the dimensions shown in Table 2.

The current and future wood yields from this area have been projected by Haron (1980).

Until recently, the value of mangrove forests was assessed in terms of forestry products—rather, wood products—since they have been managed by the foresters with the sole objective of producing maximum fuel wood (including charcoal) and poles on a sustained basis. During the last few decades mangrove wood has been chipped for the export market. It is believed that the management objective would remain the same in the near future, although other agencies like environmentalists and those involved in fisheries development, having a stake in the productivity and stability of the mangrove ecosystem, have started asserting themselves in more definite terms.

The precision of management of these forests, however, varies greatly in different ASEAN countries and even in different states/regions of the same country. It is mainly dependent upon the availability of staff, population pressure and demand for mangrove products. Although the management of mangrove forests is simpler compared to that of inland forests, there are a number of problems that have yet to be solved. Current management systems and their problems were discussed earlier by Noakes (1952), Dixon (1959) and Mohd. Darus (1969); and recently by Haron (1980), Tang et al. (1981), Srivastava (1980, 1982), Tay and Srivastava (1982), Srivastava and Singh (1980) and Saw (1981).

In the Matang Mangrove Reserve, the best-managed mangroves in Malaysia, a clear felling system on a thirty-year rotation is currently followed. Until recently there were three thinnings, first at the age of 15–19 years with a 1.22-m stick, second at 20–24 years with a 1.83-m stick and third at 25–29 years with a 2.13-m stick. In the current working plan, the third thinning has been abolished. The areas poor in regeneration are planted with *Rhizophora apiculata* at 1.22 × 1.22-m and *R. mucronata* at 1.83 × 1.83-m spacing. The areas prone to invasion by the weed fern (*Acrostichum* spp.), which inhibits natural regeneration, are recommended to be planted immediately after felling. In Klang and Johore a twenty-five-year and twenty-year rotation without any intermediate thinnings is followed, respectively. In Sarawak, the Wood Chip Company follows a twenty-five-year rotation and in Sabah the minimum girth system is followed. The current management system of mangrove forests in the Philippines and in Indonesia has been described by Burbridge and Koesobiono (1980) and Feurdeliz (1980).

II. Utilization Pattern of Mangrove Products

The utilization pattern of the products derived from mangrove ecosystems is well documented, particularly at the component level. Besides the major products in the form of wood and fish, there are numerous other uses, such as thatching material, homesteads, recreation areas, salt ponds, wildlife sanctuaries and medicinal plants, to which the mangrove forests are put by the people in and around the coastal zone (de la Cruz 1979).

The most obvious renewable product of the mangrove ecosystem is timber. Mangrove wood yields an excellent quality of charcoal, and poles are extensively used as pilings in the construction industry and for fishing stakes. Together with its use as firewood, mangrove timber is a good source of renewable energy for the local people, particularly where the use of gas is not yet popular (Yudodibroto 1982). The earnings from these products are substantial. The estimated total annual value of forest products from Matang mangrove is about U.S. $9 million (Haron and Cheah 1979). In fact, on an area basis, a hectare of mangrove forest yields a higher amount of revenue than the inland forest. According to Tang et al. (1981), mangrove forests (at approximately U.S. $3,300/ha for firewood and U.S. $9,000/ha for charcoal on a thirty-year rotation (leaving aside the value of poles extracted in thinnings) yield more than inland forest (at U.S. $5,000/ha for logs on a sixty-year rotation). In Riau province of Indonesia, during 1973–1976, the annual production of 23,259 tons of charcoal and 24,305 m^3 of firewood was achieved (Yudodibroto 1982). Abdullah Sani (1978) and Razali Kader (1980) have quoted the revenue and quantity of forest products from Matang Mangrove Reserve, while Burbridge and Koesoebiono (1980) have given the figures for Indonesia, and Feurdeliz (1980) for the Philippines.

Besides the above forest products, there are two others that have high potential in terms of socioeconomic benefits to the local people. During the last two decades, mangrove wood has been increasingly converted into chips, mainly for the export market. This has not only generated employment potential but also foreign exchange earnings. The practice is common in East Malaysia, Indonesia and Papua New Guinea. In 1981 the Sarawak Wood Chip Company exported 11,003.50 tons of mangrove chips with a revenue of M$222,007.00 (Report of Forest Conference 1982). The Jaya Chip Company in Sabah exported more than 6000 metric tons of chips in 1980 (Phillips 1980). Figures for an earlier period from Sabah have been quoted by Liew et al. (1977). Another cash product from the mangrove ecosystem is the manufacture of alcohol from the inflorescence of the nipa palm. Other local uses of this palm have been described by Fong (1980). In addition, mangrove bark is still an important source of tannin, despite its gradual replacement by synthetic chemicals (de la Cruz 1979).

Another direct product of equal or even more importance from the mangrove ecosystem is marine animals that inhabit the channels and streams which crisscross the mangrove swamp, rivers and estuaries. These include a variety of fish, prawns, molluscs, crabs and cockles. Not much information is available about the actual harvest from the mangrove forests and adjoining shallow seas and estuaries, mainly because much of the capture is for direct consumption and not for sale. However, Pollard (cited by Chong 1979) has given examples from the United States and Australia. Tang and his coworkers (1981) have reproduced a table showing total landings of prawns, cockles, crabs, fish and others in Peninsular Malaysia in 1978. According to Nafis Ahmad (1980), 7 million and 9 million kg of fish were caught from Sunderban mangroves in Bangladesh during 1978 and 1979, respectively. The relationship between the mangrove vegetation and fisheries resources is discussed in Section IV-I.

III. Environmental Stresses

In discussing the environmental trade-off in the mangrove ecosystem, all activities have been included that in any way change the natural environment, resulting in degradation of the existing biotopic conditions. It is an established fact that with an increase in population and with a faster pace of development in the ASEAN region in recent decades, there has been a tremendous increase of activities in the coastal zone. As a result, this fragile ecosystem has been put to enormous stresses, almost to the point of complete removal of mangrove vegetation in some localities, and endangering and injuring its existence in others. It may be assumed that the trend will continue in the near future. Some of the most important threatening activities are discussed below.

1. Overexploitation

Since mangrove forests have diverse uses, the area of exploitation has increased multifold in recent years due to continued multiplicity in demands for its products. In East Kalimantan, a company has been licensed to exploit 85,000 ha of mangroves for wood chips (Soegiarto 1980). A total of about 217,000 ha of Indonesian mangrove forests is being commercially exploited for wood products, producing about 250,000 m³/year, which may be increased to 3 million m³/year in the near future (Wiroatmodjo and Judi 1979). In the Philippines, mangrove areas declined from 418,990 ha to 249,138 ha during the period from 1967 to 1976, or by approximately 16,741 ha annually. The rate of decline has been abated. From 1977 to 1978, the area was further reduced by 2439 ha. Another scale of exploitation is indicated by an example from the Philippines. Although mangrove areas constitute only 1.9 percent of the total Philippine forest area and contain only 0.46 percent of the standing timber volume, they provide 25 percent of the nation's charcoal and 31 percent of the firewood (Hegerl 1980). In Malaysia, large areas have been earmarked for the wood chip companies: 21,173 ha to Sarawak and about 80,000 ha to Sabah. Both companies have large annual coupes to run at the maximum capacity and fulfill the export commitments. The overexploitation of mangrove forests has created many problems, some of which are mentioned below.

a. Deterioration in Quality of Crop

It has been commonly observed that the species composition and forest structures change in the residual stands after clear felling. In many situations, less important species like *Bruguiera parviflora* may predominate in the potential *Rhizophora* stands. Attempts are made to eradicate this species during thinnings. But in the areas where thinning is not practiced, it may completely replace *Rhizophora* and be the cause of low final yields (Srivastava 1980). According to Librero (1980), as much as 50 percent of exploited mangrove areas have what he called "reproduction brush." Another serious problem in the clear-felled areas is the invasion by a weed fern (*Acrostichum* spp.), particularly in drier areas. A large acreage of the species in Malaysia has degraded many potentially productive areas due to its dense growth, which completely inhibits natural regeneration of economically important species (Mohd. Darus 1969). So far, no satisfactory technique has evolved to eradicate this weed. Lately in Matang Reserve, experiments are in progress on chemical control of this weed (Gan 1980). It is hoped that a thorough investigation will be undertaken to study the effect of these chemicals on marine fauna before they are used on a large scale.

b. Poor Natural Regeneration
In the past, when the size of the annual coupe was not large, most of the area was regenerated naturally after the slash resulting from clear-felling had decomposed (Noakes 1952). According to Tang et al. (1981), during the period 1970–1979, more than 75 percent of the annual coupe required planting in the Matang Reserve. Similarly, Phillips (1980) reported extensive bare areas after logging for chips in Sabah. Feurdeliz (1980) and Burbridge and Koesobiono (1980) have discussed the problem of getting natural regeneration in the Philippines and in Indonesian mangrove forests. The causes of failure of regeneration are yet to be identified. On the other hand, all the problems associated with artificial planting including the high cost, availability of seeds, labor and so forth have yet to be solved.

c. Low Yield From Final Fellings
Tang and his coworkers (1981) have reported a decline in yield in the second rotation in the well-managed forests of Matang Reserve. Information of this nature is not available from other ASEAN countries, probably because the silviculture and management have not been of long enough duration to have another rotation. The actual trade-off is perhaps the loss in site productivity due to more intensive harvesting, which leads to lower productivity. However, the cause or causes of this decline needs immediate investigation, which may be helpful in the improvement of management techniques in other mangrove areas.

d. Fisheries Resources
Enough evidence, it appears, has been collected to show a close relationship between marine productivity and mangrove forests wherever they occur. This relationship between the two components of the ecosystem may be manifested in different forms. A number of fish, prawns, crabs and others may depend to a lesser or greater extent upon the vegetation for their food. The calm and sheltered atmosphere in the mangrove forests may provide spawning grounds for larval and

postlarval stages of many varieties. In addition, a number of marine fish may enter the mangrove environment during high tides and feed on the rich fauna present there. A few examples will illustrate these relationships. Leh and Sasekumar (1980) observed that the food of penaeid prawns consisted of 12–36 percent of plant matter, of which 11–62 percent was mangrove-derived. Foo and Fong (1980) collected 110 species of fish from Mengkabang estuary in Sabah. It was noted by Suntaratok et al. (1976), Frith et al. (1976) and Chensri et al. (1976) that the horseshoe crab spawns in the mid-flat area at Cholburi Province, and that the fry of seabass and milkfish and larvae of shrimps are abundant in the mangrove forests in the Andaman Sea coastal province and at Prachaub, Khirikhan Province. Sasekumar (1978) recorded some thirty species of fishes and several species of prawn in rivers and creeks which drain the mangroves. Their gut content showed mangrove-derived detritus and mangrove-dwelling invertebrates. Similarly, he recorded 38 percent to 82 percent of mangrove leaf detritus in some fish inhabiting mangrove waters. Chong (cited in Sasekumar 1978) recorded 40 percent of the diet consisting of mangrove leaf detritus in *Liza melinoptera*. Carnivorous fish like the barbel eel (*Plotosus canius*) were solely dependent on snails inhabiting mangrove forests. Sasekumar and Thong (1980) noted that eleven species of fish entered the mangrove forest with tidal waters to consume resident invertebrates.

Chong (cited in Sasekumar 1980) clearly showed the importance of mangrove forests in prawn fishery development both as a diet material and as nursery grounds. According to him, 50,987 metric tons of prawns out of the total of 54,584 metric tons were collected from the west coast of Peninsular Malaysia where mangrove forests form an almost continuous belt. In Sabah over 63,000 tons of prawns valued at more than M$32 million were landed in 1977. These were caught mainly from mangrove habitats (Foo and Wong 1980). Prawns constituted 12 percent of total marine fisheries landed in Peninsular Malaysia in 1977, but in terms of monetary value they contributed M$360 million of the total of M$810 million for all marine fisheries; that is, about 44 percent (Chong, cited in Sasekumar 1980). According to Krishnamurthy and Jeyaseelan (1980), prawn production in Pichavaram mangrove was 110 kg/ha/year whereas in the adjacent Vellar estuary (which is devoid of mangroves), it was only 20/kg/ha/year. In addition, about 400 tons of penaeid prawns were harvested from adjacent coastal waters, of which 74 percent of the catch was those which used mangrove as nursery grounds. In Indonesia Martosubroto and Naamin (1977) showed a close relationship between prawn landing and mangrove forests. Fredericks and Lampe (1980) quoted an interesting example of the prawn's dependence on sheltered lagoon-mangrove environments in Mexico, while Yusof (1978) implied the same was true in Sabah.

On the basis of ecological and socioeconomic realities, it appears that the mangrove ecosystem is an important fisheries resource base. These examples emphasize the point that utmost care should be taken to manage the mangrove ecosystem.

2. Changes in Land Use Patterns

Mangrove forest lands have been put to a variety of uses, at times resulting in complete destruction of vegetation and of the aquatic environment. This is one of the most serious threats to the maintenance of the mangrove environment in the natural and productive state. There is no doubt that some of these alternative uses have generated employment potential and other social benefits, but at the same time, conversion and removal of mangrove forests may adversely affect the communities traditionally dependent on them. The status and economic benefits of these conversion projects have not been evaluated critically in a majority of the cases.

a. Rice Fields

Large areas of mangrove forests have been converted to paddy fields and other cash crop plantations, such as coconut and palm oil. In fact, Ponnamperma (1980), of the International Rice Research Institute (IRRI), presented a strong case for the conversion of mangrove forests into rice fields. In Peninsular Malaysia, a total of 10,563.9 ha was excised for agricultural purposes during the period 1955–1980 and another 6342.1 ha have been earmarked (Razani 1982). During 1967–1978, 172,291 ha (41 percent) of the Philippine mangrove forest were converted into agricultural lands, salt production, industrial sites, human settlements and, in particular, fish ponds. In Indonesia, almost 20,000 ha of tidal forests were reclaimed from 1969 to 1974. In the five years which followed, an additional 500,000 ha were converted into rice fields, fish ponds and other food production areas (Soegiarto 1980). Present government policies are likely to result in the reclamation of another 1,000,000 ha of mangroves for growing salt-tolerant rice varieties (Hegerl 1980). Similarly, large areas of mangrove forests have been converted into rice fields in Thailand, despite the fact that the yield is low (Krishnamara, cited in Fredericks and Lampe 1980).

b. Fish Ponds

One of the most important alternative uses of the mangrove environment has been the conversion of large areas into fish ponds. In Peninsular Malaysia, for example, a total of 528.8 ha of mangrove forests has been converted into aquaculture and another 5434.2 ha are earmarked for the same purpose (Razani 1982). However, the Philippines provides the best (or worst) example of excision of mangrove for development of fish ponds. According to Feurdeliz (1980), in 1952 the fish pond area in the Philippines was only 88,072 ha; by 1972 it was already 174,101 ha. It has stabilized at about 176,000 ha. In 1978, however, the National Mangrove Committee reported 2795 applicants for fish ponds covering an area of 52,393 ha, which was about 21 percent of the remaining mangrove forest in the Philippines. It was ironic, however, that despite the large area already converted to fish ponds, aquaculture yield was only 10 percent of the total fish catch in the Philippines. This fact, coupled with other technical and socioeconomic problems, including pollution, associated with fish pond culture both in the Philippines and in Indonesia, has generated doubts about the usefulness of a single system of resource development by destroying a complex ecosystem (Wiratno 1980). However, conversion of mangrove forests into fish ponds has been going on in other ASEAN countries, too, such as Singapore (Hegerl 1980) and Thailand (Christensen 1979).

c. Mining

In most of the ASEAN countries except in Thailand (and, of course, Singapore), mining activities are confined largely to the hinterland. At one site in Thailand, a yield of 60 kg of tin (with a value of U.S.$64,100/ ha) was obtained per 0.16 ha. With replanting of mangroves placed at a cost of U.S.$104/ha, no objection was raised to the mining operation (Christensen 1979). According to Burbridge (1980), however, if external costs caused by increased turbidity, siltation, loss of fuel wood and charcoal, or the decrease in primary productivity of estuaries, are imposed upon direct users of mangrove or people who harvest fish and other products supported by the mangrove ecosystem, the benefit from this may be considerably reduced. Further, increased mining activities in the hinterland may cause a problem of siltation in estuarine rivers which may adversely affect the mangrove environment. Other alternative uses of mangrove lands include salt farming, clearance for human settlements, expansion of port facilities and establishment of industries.

In spite of the changes in land use patterns in the mangrove ecosystem, extremely few attempts have been made to compare the socioeconomic benefits of different land uses. Gomez (1980) quotes an interesting exercise by Christensen (1979) in Thailand. On the basis of annual income per hectare, he noted that the best land use was intensive shrimp farming. The yield from mangrove plantations was also high, and charcoal production exceeded shrimp farming and rice cultivation; however, it ranked low in employment potential. More of this type of investigation, including environmental impact studies, are needed to justify an alternative land use of the mangrove ecosystem.

3. Pollutants

The mangrove ecosystem is also threatened by various kinds of pollutants, such as agroindustrial waste products, oil pollution, pesticides and herbicides, heavy metals, domestic sewage, husbandry waste products and even physical pollutants. The waste products from agro-based industries may cause considerable pollution in rivers draining into mangrove forests. In Malaysia, the effluents are produced from a procession of palm oil and natural rubber on a large scale and from copra and pineapple on a smaller scale. Seow (1976), in a study of Sungei Puloh (Malaysia), noticed that downstream pollution from agricultural waste extended over a distance of 2 to 3 km. No pelagic fauna were found at the outfall, but at a distance of 2 km downstream several species of fish and penaeid prawn were abundant. Kaur (1978) claimed that toxicity of effluents may be the cause of low production in polluted rivers. In Thailand effluents from sugar refinery mills resulted in a loss of about U.S.$3.2 million in cockle farms. Razor clam beds were also adversely affected. According to Piyakarnchana (1980), pollution from a canning factory, sugar mills and distillery plants along Pramburi River in Thailand left many organisms dead. Ramamurthy (1980) reported considerable damage to marine fauna from the agricultural pollutants received from paddy fields, sugar processing plants and small-scale coir-making industries on the southwest coast of India. According to him, commercially important prawn landings were considerably decreased. Juvenile and larval forms of many shrimp species suffered a heavy mortality of up to 75 percent for a period of twelve to fifteen days. Although most of these agro-based effluents are biodegradable, they have a high biological oxygen demand, which is probably inimical to many species of aquatic fauna. However, serious attempts are being made to treat the palm-oil effluent and convert it into useful products, with some notable success (*New Straits Times* 18 August 1982).

The oil can be a dangerous source of pollution to the mangrove environment in three ways: if the swamps become a source of exploration, production and storage; if refineries are located nearby; and if oil spills occur during the transportation of crude and refined petroleum. In the ASEAN countries, probably only the Thailand mangrove swamps have been explored for petroleum. Hardjosuwarno (1980) monitored the pollution effects of an oil refinery in the Donan River (South Central Java) during 1977-1978. It was noticed that mangrove species belonging to genera *Rhizophora, Ceriops, Aegiceros* and *Sonneratia* started dying during April–May 1977. By August of that year, twelve mangrove species were dead. The molluscs and crustacean fauna declined both in number of species and population size. However, the greatest threat to the mangrove environment in the ASEAN region is posed by oil spills and ship casualties. Sasekumar (1980) has reproduced the list of ship casualties from 1975 to 1980.

According to Ross (1974), 100,000 ha (36 percent) of mangrove forests were defoliated and destroyed in Vietnam during the recent war. It resulted in increased erosion and slow regeneration capacity (partly due to lack of seeds from defoliated trees). According to some workers, it might be the cause of the decline in marine fishery off Vietnam (Sasekumar 1978).

Although pesticides are being used at an increasing rate in Southeast Asian countries, not much information is available about their concentration in mangrove waters. Soegiarto (1980) reports that Indonesia uses more than 2000 tons of pesticides annually, while Malaysia imported about 2827 tons in 1977 (Sasekumar 1980).

IV. Future Research, Management and Conservation

The importance of the mangrove forests in maintaining productivity and environmental balance along the coasts wherever they occur, has, it appears, been fully realized. However, much remains to be done to maintain this fragile ecosystem in a productive state without deterioration of the quality of the crop and avoiding, as far as possible, irreversible adverse consequences. In the author's opinion, the following aspects need the immediate attention of those entrusted with the management of this ecosystem.

1. Sustained Yield Management

One way to avoid deterioration in the quality of the mangrove environment is to maintain the forests at productive levels by judicious management. This is probably the best way to justify the maintenance of mangroves as forest ecosystems. However, as emphasized by Srivastava (1982), even in the best managed mangrove forests of Matang Reserve, there are a number of problems, such as the number and timing of thinnings, rotation age and so forth, which need to be worked out. In other areas, particularly those contracted to the wood chip companies in Sarawak and Sabah, the problem appears to be even more serious. To the author's knowledge, the silviculture system being followed there is still tentative and the problem of getting adequate regeneration in the residual stands by natural and artificial means is serious. If a proper technique of obtaining regeneration is not evolved for these areas, a large tract of mangrove forests may be completely destroyed or may greatly and progressively deteriorate in quality. This would, in fact, be inviting claims by other agencies to alternative uses of these areas. This holds true for most of the mangrove forests in the ASEAN region.

2. Role of Mangrove Forests in Marine Productivity

More intensive studies are needed to establish the links between fish resources and mangrove vegetation. It is still not established whether the relationship between the two components is facultative or obligate except probably in the case of prawns.

3. Impact of Pollutants

So far very little is known about the effect of various pollutants on the survival of mangrove seedlings and growth of mangrove trees, and particularly on marine faunal life in the mangrove zone. Research on these aspects has to be intensified to get a clearer picture, particularly of the toxic level in edible products and the tolerance level both of the flora and fauna in the mangrove belt.

4. Alternative Uses of Mangrove Lands

The people depending for their livelihood on the stability of the mangrove ecosystem, either as subsistence fishermen or working in any venture related to mangrove wood utilization (such as loggers, boatmen, charcoal kiln attendants and so on) are the ones most threatened by the overexploitation, alternative land uses and pollution threats in this ecosystem. However, very little information is available on their mode of life, economic dependence on mangrove ecosystem products and environmental stresses.

A comprehensive study must be started to determine the socioeconomic and environmental effects of land use patterns in the mangrove zone before these forests are cleared and put to other uses.

5. Conservation of the Mangrove Ecosystem

The coasts in general, including those covered with mangrove forests, particularly in maritime countries of ASEAN, are areas of high activity. For some purpose or other, practically all the mangrove forests have been disturbed by man's activities. However, the degree of disturbance may vary from area to area in different countries in response to demands from this ecosystem, from a total "hands-off" (rarely found) to "unwise management," through more or less "sustained yield" situations. It may be assumed that it is not possible to completely stop all management activities in the mangrove forests. The alternative is to preserve certain areas which are typical representatives of each type in different localities, which would serve as gene pools and provide natural conditions for research and education (Ong 1982).

Note

The author wishes to thank Professor Abdul Manap Ahmad, Dean, Faculty of Forestry, Universiti Pertanian Malaysia, for permission to present this paper, and to Mr. Doraisingam Manikam for interesting comments.

References

Abdullah Sani b. Shafie. 1978. Effect of logging on the natural regeneration of *Rhizophora* spp. under the current silvicultural practices in Matang Mangrove Reserve, Perak. B.S. (For.) project.

Burbridge, P. R. 1980. The management and planning of mangrove resources in Asia. Paper presented at the Asian Symposium on Mangrove Environment: Research and Management, 25–29 August, Kuala Lumpur, Malaysia.

Burbridge, P. R. and Koesoebiono. 1980. Management of mangrove exploitation in Indonesia. Paper presented at the Asian Symposium on Mangrove Environment: Research and Management, 25–29 August, Kuala Lumpur, Malaysia.

Chensri, C., T. Lekholaryut and B. Tiensongrusmee. 1976. Abundance of post-larval penaeids at Klong Wan, Prachuab Khirikhan Province. In Proceedings of the First National Seminar on Mangrove Ecology, Phuket, Thailand.

Chong, V. C. 1980. Mangrove and prawns—with special reference to Malaysia. In T. A. Sasekumar, *Status Report on Mangrove Ecosystems in Southeast Asia and the Impact of Pollution*. FAO/UNEP Pub. No. SCS/80/WP/94b.

Christensen, B. 1979. Mangrove resources: Their management and utilization for forestry, fishery and agriculture near Khlung, Chantaburi Province, Thailand. Bangkok: Report to the Government of Thailand.

de la Cruz, A. A. 1979. The functions of mangroves. In *Proceedings of a Symposium on Mangrove and Estuarine Vegetation*, eds. Srivastava et al., BIOTROP Special Bulletin No. 10, 125–138.

Dixon, R. G. 1959. A working plan for Matang Mangrove Reserve, Perak. Forestry Department Publication.

Feurdeliz, M. L. 1980. Issues and research programmes on the management, conservation and utilization of mangrove forests in the Philippines. Paper presented at the Asian Symposium on Mangrove Environment: Research and Management, 25–29 August, Kuala Lumpur, Malaysia.

Fong, F. W. 1980. Nipa Swamps—a neglected mangrove resource. Paper presented at the Asian Symposium on Mangrove Environment: Research and Management, 25–29 August, Kuala Lumpur, Malaysia.

Foo, H. T. and J. T. S. Wong. 1980. Mangrove swamps and fisheries in Sabah. In *Proceedings in Tropical Ecology and Development*, ed. J. I. Furtado, 1157–1161.

Fredericks, L. J. and H. Lampe. 1980. Socio-economic aspects of mangrove systems in Asia. A keynote speech at the Asian Symposium on Mangrove Environment: Research and Management, 25–29 August, Kuala Lumpur, Malaysia.

Frith, D. W., R. Tantanasiriwong and O. Bhatia. 1976. Zonation and abundance of macrofauna on a mangrove shore, Phuket Islands, Southern Thailand. *Phuket Marine Biological Center Research Bulletin*.

Gan Boon Keong. 1982. The role of *Acrostichum aureum* in the natural regeneration of mangrove trees, especially *Rhizophora* species in Malaysia. B. S. (For.) Project Report.

Gomez, E. D. 1980. *The Present State of Mangrove Ecosystems in Southeast Asia and the Impact of Pollution*. FAO/UNEP Publication No. SCS/80/WP/94.

Hardjosuwarno, S. 1980. Biological monitoring in the Cilacap refinery area. Paper presented at the Asian Symposium on Mangrove Environment: Research and Management, 25–29 August, Kuala Lumpur, Malaysia.

Haron bin Haji Abu Hassan. 1980. A working plan for the Matang Mangrove Forest Reserve, Perak. Forest Department Publication.

Haron bin Haji Abu Hassan and L. C. Cheah. 1979. Sustained yield management of the mangrove forest of Peninsular Malaysia with special reference to Matang Reserve. Paper presented at the 7th Malaysian Forestry Conference, 24–28 September 1979, Penang, Malaysia.

Hegerl, E. J. 1980. Developing a conservation strategy for the mangrove ecosystems in Asia and Oceania. A keynote address at the Asian Symposium on Mangrove Environment: Research and Management, 25–29 August, Kuala Lumpur, Malaysia.

MANGROVE FOREST MANAGEMENT 121

Jennings, J. N. and C. F. Bird. 1967. Regional geomorphological character-istics of some Australian estuaries. In *Estuaries*, ed. G. H. Lauf, 131–138.
Johnson, A. 1979. The algae of Singapore mangroves. In *Proceedings of a Symposium on Mangrove and Estuarine Vegetation in Southeast Asia*, eds. Srivastava et al., BIOTROP *Special Bulletin* No. 10, 45–50.
Kaur, B. 1978. The effect of palm oil and rubber effluent on the primary product of phytoplankton at Sungei Puloh. B.Sc. (hon.) thesis, University of Malaya.
Krishnamurthy, K. and M. J. P. Jeysaleen. 1980. The impact of Pichavaram mangrove ecosystem upon coastal natural resources: A case study from Southern India. Paper presented at the Asian Symposium on Mangrove Environment: Research and Management, 25–29 August, Kuala Lumpur, Malaysia.
Leh, C. M. U. and A. Sasekumar. 1980. Feeding ecology of prawns in shallow waters adjoining mangrove shores. Paper presented at the Asian Sympo-sium on Mangrove Environment: Research and Management, 25–29 August, Kuala Lumpur, Malaysia.
Librero, A. R. 1980. Mangrove management in the Philippines. Paper pres-ented at the Second International Symposium on the Biology and Manage-ment of Mangroves and Tropical Shallow Water Communities, 20 July–2 August, Port Moresby, Papua New Guinea.
Liew That Chin, Mohd. Nor Diah and Y. C. Wong. 1977. Mangrove exploita-tion and regeneration in Sabah. In *A New Era in Malaysian Forestry*, eds. Sastri, Srivastava and Abdul Manap, 95–110.
Macnae, W. 1968. A general account of the fauna and flora of mangroves, swamps and forests in the Indo-West-Pacific region. *Advances in Marine Biology* 6:73–270.
Martosubroto, P. and N. Naamin. 1977. Relationship between tidal forests (mangroves) and commercial shrimp production in Indonesia. *Marine Research in Indonesia* 18:81–86.
Mohd. Darus Hj. Mahmud. 1969. A Working Plan for Matang Mangrove Reserve, Perak. Forestry Department Publication.
Nafis Ahmad. 1980. Some aspects of economic resources of Sunderbau mangrove forests of Bangladesh. Paper presented at the Asian Symposium on Mangrove Environment: Research and Management, 25–29 August, Kuala Lumpur, Malaysia.
New Straits Times, 18 August 1982.
Noakes, D. S. P. 1952. A Working Plan for Matang Mangrove Reserve, Perak. Forestry Department Publication.
Ong, J. E. 1982. Malaysia mangroves: A strategy for conservation through relational use. *Proceedings of the IVth Annual Seminar by the Malaysian Society of Marine Sciences*, 5–9.
Phillips, C. 1980. Conservation and rehabilitation of Sabah mangroves. Paper presented at the Asian Symposium on Mangrove Environment: Research and Management, 25–29 August, Kuala Lumpur, Malaysia.
Piyakarnchana, T. 1980. *Status Report on Research and Monitoring of the*

Impact of Pollution on Mangrove Ecosystems and Its Productivity in Thailand. FAO/UNEP Publication No. SCS/80/WP/94.

Ponnamperma, P. N. 1980. Mangrove lands of South and Southeast Asia as potential rice lands. Paper presented at the Asian Symposium on Mangrove Environment: Research and Management, 25–29 August, Kuala Lumpur, Malaysia.

Ramamurthy, V. D. 1980. The effect of agriculture pollutants on fish and fish production in the mangrove swamps of Southwest coast of India. Paper presented at Asian Symposium on Mangrove Environment: Research and Management, 25–29 August, Kuala Lumpur, Malaysia.

Razali Abdul Kader. 1980. Utilization of mangrove trees in Peninsular Malaysia. In *Proceedings of a Workshop on Mangrove and Estuarine Vegetation*, eds. Srivastava and Razali Kader, 49–63.

Razani, U. 1982. The role of mangrove forests in the management of the coastal zone. Paper presented at the Workshop on Ecological Basis for Regional Resource Utilization in the Humid Tropics, 18–22 January, Universiti Pertanian Malaysia, Serdang, Malaysia.

Report of the Annual Forest Department Conference. 1982. Rajang Mangroves, Sarawak, 16 May 1982.

Richards, P. W. 1952. *Tropical Rain Forests. An Ecological Study.* Cambridge: Cambridge University Press.

Ross, P. 1974. The effects of herbicides on the mangrove of South Vietnam. In *The Effects of Herbicides on South Vietnam, Part B. Working Paper.* Washington, D. C.: National Academy of Science-National Research Council.

Sahavacharin, O. 1979. Some orchids found in mangrove forests of Thailand. In *Proceedings of a Symposium on Mangrove and Estuarine Vegetation*, eds. Srivastava et al., BIOTROP *Special Bulletin* No. 10, 51–60.

Sasekumar, A. 1974. Distribution of macrofauna on a Malayan mangrove shore. *Animal Ecology* 43:51–69.

Sasekumar, A. 1978. The value of the mangrove ecosystem and its pollution problems. In *V FAO/SIDA Workshop on Aquatic Pollution in Relation to Protection of Living Resources.* FAO Publication.

Sasekumar, A. and K.L. Thong. 1980. Predation of mangrove fauna by marine fishes at high tide. Paper presented at the Asian Symposium on Mangrove Environment: Research and Management, 25–29 August, Kuala Lumpur, Malaysia.

Saw Leng Guan. 1981. Progress of crop: Composition, density and growth of *Rhizophora* dominated stands before first thinning in Matang Mangrove Reserve, Perak. B.Sc. (For.) Research Project Report.

Seow, R. C. W. 1976. The effect of a mixed organic effluent on the distribution of pelagic macrofauna at Sungei Puloh with special reference to water quality. B.Sc. (hon.) Thesis, University of Malaya.

Soegiarto, A. 1980. Country report on research and monitoring of impact of pollution on mangrove and its productivity in Indonesia. Discussion paper presented at FAO/UNEP Expert Consultation Meeting on Impact of Pollution on the Mangrove Ecosystem and its Productivity in Southeast Asia. Manila, Philippines.

Srivastava, P. B. L. 1980. Research proposals for mangrove vegetation in Malaysia. In *Proceedings of a Workshop on Mangrove and Estuarine Vegetation*, eds. Srivastava and Razali Abdul Kader, 64–75.

Srivastava, P. B. L. 1982. Present status of mangrove forest management. Paper presented at the Seminar on Recent Advances in Marine Sciences, 27 March, Universiti Pertanian Malaysia, Serdang, Malaysia.

Srivastava, P. B. L. and H. Singh. 1980. Composition and distribution pattern of natural regeneration after second thinning in Matang Mangrove Reserve, Perak. Paper presented at the Asian Symposium on Mangrove Environment: Research and Management, 25–29 August, Kuala Lumpur, Malaysia.

Suntarotok, V., C. Rachitprinya and S. Tongmes. 1976. Collection of milkfish frys (*Chanos chanos*) on the seashore of Prachnap Khirikhan Province of Thailand. In *Proceedings of the First National Seminar on Mangrove Ecology*, Phuket, Thailand.

Tang, H. T., H. A. H. Haron and E. K. Cheah. 1981. Mangrove forests of Peninsular Malaysia—a review of management and research objectives and priorities. *Malaysian Forestry* 44(1):77–86.

Tay, S. P. and P. B. L. Srivastava. 1982. Crop composition and density after thinnings and before final felling in the Matang Mangrove Reserve, Perak. *Pertanika* 5(1):95–104.

Walsh, G. E. 1974. Mangroves: A review. In *Ecology of Halophytes*, eds. Reimold and Queen, 51–172.

Watson, J. G. 1928. Mangrove forests of the Malay Peninsula. *Malaysian Forestry* Rec. 6.

Wiratno. 1980. Some aspects of brackish-water pond operation in Central Java, Indonesia. In *Proceedings on Tropical Ecology and Development*, ed. J. I. Furtado, 1071–1076. Kuala Lumpur: ISTE.

Wiroatmodjo, P. and D. M. Judi. 1979. Management of tidal forests in Indonesia. In *Proceedings of a Seminar on Ecosystem of Hutan Mangrove*, Jakarta, 191–198.

Yudodibroto, H. 1982. A case of energy supply from mangrove forests. In *Tropical Forest—Source of Energy through Optimization and Diversification*, eds. Srivastava et al., 245–249.

Yusof Nair. 1977. An appraisal of economic potential of mangrove swamps in Sabah. M.S. Thesis, Universiti Pertanian Malaysia.

Coastal Zone Productivity

Ong Jin Eong

The ultimate organic productivity of any system is, in the final analysis, based on its primary productivity. A perspective on this may be gained by examination of a global map of primary productivity. One such map is that compiled by Leith (1964) and later presented, after computerization, as the so-called Seattle Productivity Map (Leith 1975a). Leith and Whittaker (1975) also give a good account and perspective of the global primary productivity of the biosphere.

I. Analysis of Global Primary Productivity

Leith (1975a, 1975b) gave a figure of 176.9 $\times$ 10^9 metric tons (t) of dry matter per year for global primary productivity. Of this total, the productivity of the continents (land area of 149 $\times$ 10^6 km^2) is 121.7 $\times$ 10^9t and that for oceans is 55 $\times$ 10^9t. The figure quoted for the oceans is essentially that of Koblentz-Mishke et al. (1970). This work is based on some 7,000 observations, mainly from chlorophyll and radioactive carbon-14 measurements. Ryther (1969) divided the oceans into provinces based on their level of primary production: open ocean, coastal zone and upwelling areas. Although upwelling areas consist of only 0.1 percent of the total ocean area, it accounts for about 1 percent of the primary productivity. Coastal zones which account for about 9.9 percent of the total ocean area account for about 18 percent of the total primary productivity. This difference in productivity in different oceanic provinces is magnified at the fish production level. Here Ryther (1969) estimated that almost all the fish production of the oceans comes from upwelling (12 $\times$ 10^7t fresh weight) and coastal areas (12 $\times$ 10^7t). Fish production in the oceanic province is almost two orders of magnitude lower than the upwelling and coastal provinces. This is because of

125

the shorter food chains (one and a half trophic levels in upwelling areas, three trophic levels in coastal areas and five trophic levels in oceanic areas) and hence greater efficiencies of the upwelling and coastal areas. All the figures just quoted above are subject to debate. The main argument about the primary productivity estimates centers around the radioactive carbon-14 method of estimating primary productivity and the high variations obtained in chlorophyll measurements (e.g., see Sieburth 1979). Although the radioactive carbon-14 method is rapid enough to allow many more observations to be made than by other methods, there are a number of deficiencies. The main ones are:

(1) The unnatural enclosure of water in small glass containers can result in productivity being inhibited through depletion of nutrients and accumulation of toxic products (especially with long incubation periods).

(2) The inevitable presence of small zooplankton (practically impossible to remove from the water sample) results in phytoplankton being grazed and thus giving an underestimate of primary productivity.

(3) Complications in the correction for respiration (phytoplankton and nonphytoplankton, e.g., bacteria) due to differences in dark and light respiration. In the case of phytoplankton, photorespiration complicates the picture. With bacteria, light inhibition of bacteria is reported to be the problem (Lavoie 1975, quoted in Sieburth 1979). Again, these result in underestimates.

(4) Most of the observations measure only particulate primary productivity but it has been demonstrated that dissolved organic productivity can be very significant (Antia et al. 1963; Fogg et al. 1965; Helleburst 1965; Williams and Yentsch 1976). The earlier works show that losses could be up to about 50 percent although the more recent work of Williams and Yentsch (1976) gives figures of 0 percent to 6 percent.

(5) In coastal and especially tropical coastal waters total carbon dioxide is low and if the figure of 90 mg 1^{-1} for temperate oceanic waters is taken, an underestimate will result.

Sieburth (1977, 1979) contends that since the dissolved organic carbon in the open ocean is much greater than one would anticipate from primary productivity measurements, and high levels of bacterioplankton (free living bacteria in the 0.2 to 1.0-μm size range) that have been measured (Sorokin 1971; Sieburth et al. 1977) require this higher concentration of organic carbon to explain their abundance, the present estimate of primary productivity is a gross underestimate (see Sieburth 1977 for further discussions).

Apart from what has been stated so far, the estimates of primary productivity of the oceans do not include highly productive communities like seagrasses, corals and mangroves. This further compounds the argument of an underestimate.

Most of us will find it hard to argue that ocean primary productivity has been underestimated rather than overestimated. The controversy is the degree of underestimate. Bunt (1975) quoted theoretical limits ranging from 10 to 488 × 10^9t C yr^{-1} (metric tons of carbon per year), approximately equivalent to 22 to 1084 × 10^9t dry matter yr^{1-}. Finenko (1978) gave a range of 12 to 155t C yr^{-1} (equivalent to about 27 to 344t dry matter yr^{-1}). It would appear that the Koblentz-Mishke et al. (1970) figures of 55 × 10^9t dry matter yr^{-1} could be underestimated by anywhere from a factor of about two to more than an order of magnitude (up to 20x). Which figure we pick is, at this stage, a matter of conjecture.

II. Coastal Productivity in the Straits of Malacca (Malaysia)

1. Primary

Moving from the general to the more specific, we may look at the productivity picture of the Straits of Malacca (Malaysian side). Productivity data available for this approximately six million ha of coastal zone are scant. The Koblentz-Mishke figure of primary productivity in the Straits of Malacca given in Finenko (1978) is between 0.15 to 0.25 g C m^{-2} day^{-1}. The total fish weight of fish landings for the area in 1978 was 410,770 tons (Malaysian Ministry of Agriculture 1979). From the fish landing statistics of previous years, this figure appears to be just above the sustainable yield (size of fish caught has tended to decrease). Using 10 percent as a figure for conversion from fresh weight to organic carbon, and a factor of two to convert sustainable yield to fish production (Gulland 1970), the estimated fish productivity is equivalent to 0.00375 g C $m^{-2}day^{-1}$. If we assume that the conversion process involves two trophic levels (phytoplankton-zooplankton fish) and an efficiency of between 10 percent and 15 percent in the conversion from one trophic level to the next, then the estimated primary production is just able to support the fish production. On the other hand, if we were to assume that three trophic levels are involved, as Ryther (1969) suggested for coastal waters, then there is a shortfall of some 5x.

Chlorophyll A estimates of waters around Penang (Chua et al. 1980) ranged from about 2 to 8 mg chlorophyll A l^{-1}. Considering the high turbidity of these waters (Chua et al. 1980) primary productivity would be confined to the first meter or so of water. Using these figures and the 3.7 g C per g chlorophyll A hr^{-1} conversion figure of Ryther and Yentsch (1957) the primary production of waters around Penang would be between 0.09–0.35 g C $m^{-2}day^{-1}$. The Koblenz-Mishke figure falls within this range. It is also to be noted that the waters around Penang are the richest in the Straits of Malacca (Chua and Chong 1975) so that on the average the level will be closer to the lower part of the range.

2. Mangrove Ecosystems

The Straits of Malacca has extensive fringes of mangroves. There are close to 100,000 ha of mangroves on the Malaysian side. How significantly do mangroves contribute to the coastal productivity? Small litter fall from mangroves has been estimated to be just over 10 t dry matter $ha^{-1}yr^{-1}$ (Gong et al. 1980; Ong et al. 1982). On the six million ha basis the contribution from mangrove small litter is about 0.22 g C $m^{-2}day^{-1}$. This is almost equal to the upper limit of plankton primary productivity. If we add on productivity from slash, roots and dead trees the figure can be easily doubled.

It appears quite likely, from the gross considerations discussed, that mangroves could contribute as big a role as phytoplankton to the primary productivity of the Straits of Malacca. In view of the increasing pressures to convert mangrove to alternate uses (in particular the conversion of mangroves into aquaculture ponds) the fisheries authorities should give this matter immediate and urgent attention. A correlation exists between prawn landings and mangrove areas in Peninsular Malaysia (Gedney et al. 1982) and this emphasizes the role of mangrove further. The author has recently compared the use of mangroves for forestry versus conversion to aquaculture ponds (Ong, 1982) and found that the state of the art of pond culture (of *Penaeus monodon*) in the country is such that the venture is still economically risky, although the potential exists. Significant destruction of mangroves could result in significant declines in the fisheries.

Our understanding of the mangrove ecosystem is limited, yet it is on this ecosystem that the survival of the coastal fisheries may hinge. We have only recently learned that litter productivity of mangroves in Peninsular Malaysia is among the highest of all natural ecosystems (Gong et al. 1980; Ong et al. 1982). We also know the sesarmid crabs feed directly on mangrove leaf litter (Malley, 1978; Che Rosnani

1980; Mohd. Najib 1982) and play a significant role in litter breakdown. We do not have any hard facts as to the fate of mangrove detritus (e.g., how much mangrove detritus and dissolved organic matter originating from mangroves are exported to the adjacent coastal ecosystem?). There is an urgent need for concerted research effort.

It is opportune for this Conference on Environmental Protection to make a strong and urgent plea to the various authorities concerned (mainly fisheries and forestry) to intensify their effort to understand the mangrove ecosystem in relation to fisheries. This would also be a good opportunity to urge international funding bodies to assist in understanding the fundamentals of the productivity of the mangrove ecosystem by funding research in this area.

References

Antia, N. J., C. D. McAllister, T. R. Parsons, K. Stephens and I. D. H. Strickland. 1963. Further measurements of primary production using a large-volume plastic sphere. *Limnology and Oceanography* 8:166–183.

Bunt, J. S. 1975. Primary productivity of marine ecosystems. In *Primary productivity of the biosphere*, eds. H. Leith and R. H. Whittaker, 196–183. New York: Springer-Verlag.

Che Rosnani Saad. 1980. Dynamics of nitrogen cycling in mangrove ecosystems. B.Sc. Dissertation. Universiti Sains Malaysia.

Chua, T. E., J. E. Ong and S. K. Teh. 1980. A preliminary study of the hydrobiology and fisheries of the Straits of Penang. In "The Kurishio IV," Proceedings of the Fourth C. S. K. Symposium, Tokyo, 1979, 743–788.

Chua, T. E. and B. J. Chong. 1975. Plankton distribution in the Straits of Malacca and its adjacent waters. Proceedings of the Pacific Science Association Special Symposium on Marine Sciences, December 1973, Hong Kong, 17–23.

Finenko, S. S. 1978. Production in plant populations. In *Marine Ecology*, Vol. 4, ed. O. Kinne, 13–87.

Fogg, G. E., C. Nalewajko and W. D. Watt. 1965. Extracellular products of phytoplankton photosynthesis. Proceedings of the Royal Society (London) Series B 162:517–534.

Gedney, R. H., J. M. Kapetsky and W. Kuhnhold. 1982. Training on assessment of coastal aquaculture potential in Malaysia. Manila: South China Sea Fisheries Development & Coordinating Programme SCS/GEN/42/35, January 1982.

Gong, W. K., J. E. Ong, C. H. Wong and G. Dhanarajan. 1980. Productivity of mangrove trees and its significance in a mangrove ecosystem in Malaysia. Paper presented at the UNESCO Asian Symposium on Mangrove Environment: Research and Management, Universiti Malaya, Kuala Lumpur, Malaysia, August 1980.

130 MARINE ENVIRONMENT AND COASTAL ZONE

Gulland, J. A. 1970. Food chain studies and some problems in world fisheries. In *Marine Food Chains*, ed. J.H. Steele, 296–315. Edinburgh: Oliver & Boyd.

Helleburst, J. A. 1965. Excretion of some organic compounds by marine phytoplankton. *Limnology and Oceanography* 10:192–206.

Koblentz-Mishke, O. J., V. V. Kolkovinsky and J. G. Kabanova. 1970. Plankton primary production of the world ocean. In *Scientific Exploration of the South Pacific*, ed. W. S. Wooster, 183–193. Washington D. C.: National Academy of Science.

Lavoie, D. M. 1975. Application of diffusion culture to ecological observations on marine microorganisms. M.S. thesis, University of Rhode Island.

Lieth, H. 1964. Versuch einer kartographischen Darstellung der Productivitat der Pflanzendecke auf die Erde [Cartographic representation of productivity of vegetation in the world]. *Geographisches Taschenbuch*, 1964/65, 72–80. Wiesbaden: Max Steiner Verlag.

Lieth, H. 1975a. Primary production of the major vegetation units of the world. In *Primary Productivity of the Biosphere*, eds. H. Lieth and R. H. Whittaker, 203–215. New York: Springer-Verlag.

Lieth, H. 1975b. The primary productivity in ecosystems. Comparative analysis of global patterns. In *Unifying Concepts in Ecology*, eds. W. H. Van Dobben and R. H. Lowe-McConnel. The Hague: Junk.

Lieth, H. and R. H. Whittaker (eds.). 1975. *Primary Productivity of the Biosphere*. New York: Springer-Verlag.

Malaysian Ministry of Agriculture. 1979. *Annual Fisheries Statistics*.

Malley, D. F. 1978. Degradation of mangrove leaf litter by the tropical sesarmid crab *Chiromanthes onchophorum*. *Marine Biology* 49:377–386.

Mohd. Najib Ramli. 1982. Utilization of mangrove litter and flow of phosphorus and some metals through the mangrove crab. B.Sc. dissertation, Universiti Sains Malaysia.

Ong, J. E. 1982. Aquaculture, forestry and conservation of Malaysian mangrove. *Ambio* 11:252–257.

Ong, J. E., W. K. Gong and C. H. Wong. 1982. Productivity and nutrient status of litter in managed mangrove forest. Paper presented at BIOTROP-UNESCO symposium on Mangrove Forest Ecosystem Productivity, Bogor, Indonesia, 20–22 April 1982.

Ryther, J. H. 1969. Photosynthesis and fish production in the sea. *Science* 116:72–76.

Ryther, J. H. and C. S. Yentsch. 1957. The estimation of phytoplankton production in the ocean from chlorophyll and light data. *Limnology and Oceanography* 2:281–286.

Sieburth, J. McN. 1977. International Helgoland Symposium: Governor's report on the informal session on biomass and productivity of microorganisms in planktonic ecosystems. *Helgoländer wissenschaftliche Meeresuntersuchunten* 30:697–704.

Sieburth, J. McN. 1979. *Sea Microbes*. New York: Oxford University Press.

Sieburth, J. McN., K. M. Johnson, C. M. Burney and D. M. Lavoie. 1977.

Estimation of *in situ* rates of heterotrophy using diurnal changes in dissolved organic matter and growth rates of picoplankton in diffusion culture. *Helgoländer wissenschaftliche Meeresuntersuchunten* 30:565–574.

Sorokin, Ju. I. 1971. On the role of bacteria in the productivity of tropical oceanic waters. *Internationale Revue Der Gesaunten Hydrobiologie u Hydrographie* 56: 1–48.

Williams, P. J. LaB. and C. S. Yentsch. 1976. An examination of the photosynthetic production, excretion of photosynthetic products and heterotrophic utilization of dissolved organic compounds with reference to results from a coastal subtropical sea. *Marine Biology* 35:31–40.

Human Activities and the Coastal Zone

Human and Development Pressures on the Coral Reef Ecosystem
The Malaysian Experience

M. W. R. N. De Silva

Together with the adjacent seas, the oceans make up 71 percent of the surface of the earth. Yet our knowledge of the marine environment and the plants and animals that inhabit it can be considered to be very elementary. Throughout the ages, man has used the oceans and the seas as well as their resources for his benefit. The marine environment was once regarded as an inexhaustible and invulnerable source of fish and also regarded as a dumping ground, without limits, for man's waste. However, due to pollution, overexploitation and misuse the world's seas and oceans are fast reaching a state where they will no longer be able to carry out the functions which they have performed successfully for countless generations. Among the highly productive coastal zone ecosystems, coral reefs stand out as one which has suffered heavily due to neglect and the pressure of human development.

Coral reefs are tropical shallow water ecosystems that grow on a substratum of limestone and require bright light, stable high salinities and temperatures of between 22°C and 28°C for optimum growth and establishment. They constitute perhaps the largest shallow water community of living organisms in the world's oceans.

A coral reef is an assemblage of many animals and plants, of which corals form only one of the dominant components. Associated with coral reefs are multitudes of organisms, some attached, some hiding within it and others swimming in close proximity. Therefore, a coral reef can be taken to be a very complex ecosystem. The state of equilibrium of a coral reef ecosystem, like any other, is delicately balanced on the interactions between the biotic components as well as between the biotic and abiotic components. Critical disturbances to even one vital parameter can cause an imbalance leading to the destruction of the entire community.

According to De Silva, Betterton and Smith (1980), sixty-three genera of hard corals have been reported from the Malaysian coral reefs. This places the coral reefs of Malaysia among the richest in the world in terms of species diversity. De Silva (1982), referring to the coral reefs of Peninsular Malaysia, states that:

> they are important to the fisheries and tourist industries and are breeding and nursery grounds for many marine organisms. In addition, they act as barriers which prevent sea erosion, especially in the offshore islands. Unfortunately, they do not receive the attention due to an ecosystem considered as one of the most productive of all natural ecosystems. At present, they are exploited, damaged and destroyed without any concern for their future well being.

I. Human and Development Pressures on Coral Reefs

In 1980 the coral reef working group of the International Union for Conservation of Nature and Natural Resources (IUCN) recognized twenty-four human-related activities that cause damage to coral reefs (Coral Reef Newsletter 1980). Of these, the activities which can be considered to be relevant to Malaysia are listed in Table 1 on a three-point scale of no problem, minor problem or major problem.

1. Collecting of Shells and Corals

Shells and corals are collected on a small scale by tourists. As yet they are not collected on a large scale as souvenirs or specimens, as is done in the Philippines (Wells 1982) and some parts of Indonesia and Thailand. The main areas that have been subjected to tourists and shell collections are the offshore islands in the east coast of Peninsular Malaysia and the west coast reefs, especially of the offshore islands in East Malaysia.

Corals and shells are not collected as a large-scale commercial activity in Malaysia. However, a few individuals are involved in collecting corals and shells to be sold as souvenirs. Several shell collectors are involved in collecting specimen shells for their own collections and for exchange with collectors from other parts of the world. The offshore islands on the east coast of Peninsular Malaysia, such as Pulau Tioman and the nearby islands, Pulau Kapas and the Pulau Redang Archipelago, have been subjected to close scrutiny by several groups of such shell collectors. Wood (1977) stated that the trade in shells and corals in Kota Kinabalu in East Malaysia was greater a decade ago and was

Table 1. Human Activities that Cause Damage to Coral Reefs of Malaysia

No.	Cause of Damage	Peninsular Malaysia	East Malaysia
1a	Collecting of shells and corals by tourists	1	1
b	Collecting of shells and corals for commercial purposes	1	2
2	Spear fishing	1	1
3	Collecting of aquarium reef fishes	1	1
5	Commercial fishing of reef fishes	1	1
6	Explosives used for fishing and for public works	2	1–2
7	Poisons used for fishing	0	0–1
8	Other fishing methods destructive to corals	0	1
10	Sedimentation from fresh water run-off	1–2	1–2
11a	Domestic sewage and eutrophication	0–1	0–1
b	Red tides	0	1
14	Industrial wastes	0–1	0–1
20	Dredging activities	0–1	0–1
21	Construction activities on reefs	0–1	0–1
22	Recreational impact (scuba, snorkeling, boating and anchor damage)	1	1
23	*Acanthaster* problems	1–2	1
		6	1b
	Causes Most Damage	10	6
		24	10

Code: 0 = no problem, 1 = minor problem, 2 = major problem.
Source: Coral Reef Newsletter 1980. The numbering sequence is that given in the source.

tempted to suggest that the decrease in business might be related to the difficulty in finding good specimens.

2. Spearfishing

Uncontrolled spearfishing could lead to a reduction of residential coral reef fishes such as the grouper (*Epinephelus* sp.). Although concerned spearfishermen hunt pelagic species, such as barracuda (*Sphyraena* sp.), mackerel (*Scomberomoridae*) and trevally (*Carangidae*), the inexperienced and the trigger-happy spearfishermen will hunt indiscriminately and collect the more vulnerable, inquisitive and slow-moving residential species, decimating the fish population. Although some spearfishing is carried out in East Malaysia it has not reached serious levels as in some coral reef areas in Peninsular Malaysia (Wood 1977). In Peninsular Malaysia spearfishing is carried out by some foreign tourists as well as local spearfishermen. Due to their activities fish populations of several coral reef areas in Peninsular Malaysia are under stress. These areas include the Pulau Paya and Sembilan groups of islands in the west coast, the Pulau Tioman, Pulau Tenggol, Pulau Kapas, Pulau Redang and the associated islands in the east coast. Although spearguns need to be licensed in Malaysia, the majority of spearfishermen do not conform to this regulation and carry out their activities undauntedly.

3. Collecting of Aquarium Reef Fish

Very little commercial aquarium fish collecting is done in Malaysia. However, due to the operations of even a few of these commercial ventures that cater to the local market and to a small-scale export market, several reef areas in Malaysia have come under stress. Most commercial aquaria prefer to import their marine specimens cheaply from Sri Lanka, Singapore or the Philippines rather than go out on their own to collect the specimens, because of high overhead costs. According to Lulofs (1977), collection of aquarium fish has depleted almost all Malaysian reefs of some of their most colorful small coral fish. This statement of Lulofs is true in respect to reef areas such as those in Port Dickson, Cape Rachardo, Pulau Kapas, Pulau Songsong, Pulau Paya in the west coast and a few islands off Mersing in the east coast of Peninsular Malaysia which are fairly easily accessible. It might not be true of all coral reefs of Malaysia.

Hand nets, a variety of net systems and traps as well as tranquilizers are used to capture aquarium fish. Whatever the method adopted, the reefs undergo a fair degree of damage in the form of broken corals, disturbed habitats and the removal of organisms which might be vital to the well-being of the reef. Referring to the importance to a coral reef of the cleaner wrasse (*Labroides dimidiatus*) and the barber-prawn, which clean ectoparasites and wounds of other fish, Lulofs (1977) states: "Both the wrasse and barber-prawn are desirable aquarium fish and are easily caught. But it is known that if a reef is denuded of both these species all the other fish will eventually evacuate the reef leaving it barren of fish life."

4. Commercial Fishing of Reef Fishes

Although a reasonable amount of fishing is carried out in reef areas, the methods adopted are traditional, such as the use of handlines, traps and rod and line. These fishing methods are highly selective and pose no great danger to the reef community. Wood (1977) records that "fish beating" has been reported from at least one offshore island in Sabah. In this method of catching fish large numbers of fishermen gather over a shallow reef and drive fish into nets by banging on the corals. Fortunately this type of destructive fishing is unknown in Peninsular Malaysia.

Although trawler fishing is not carried out near coral reefs as a rule, several massive nets have been found on the reefs indicating that the fishermen have allowed their boats to come too close to the reef. The damage done is extensive once a large net gets entangled on the reef.

5. Explosives Used for Fishing and Public Works

Despite the fact that the use of explosives to "catch" fish is considered illegal in Malaysia, this method of fishing is rampant, especially in the uninhabited areas, in particular the offshore islands. Lulofs (1977), Wood (1977) and De Silva (1979) have reported that damage had been caused to several Malaysian coral reefs by the use of explosives. Mathias and Langham (1978) have also indicated that heavy damage has been caused to some coral reefs in Sabah, East Malaysia, due to the use of explosives. De Silva (1981) considers the use of explosives to catch fish as one of the major causes of coral reef damage in Malaysia.

The use of explosives to "catch" fish not only kills the juvenile and adult fish together with those of no commercial value, but destroys the coral reefs that are the basis of the very resource that is being exploited (Wood 1977). The reefs damaged by explosives might not always recover to their original state as they might get covered by filamentous algae, resulting in a deflected climax as often observed. Explosives have been used to clear coral reefs to make way for piers and similar structures; however, the damage done to the reefs is generally localized.

6. Use of Poisons for Fishing

Wood (1977) reported that tuba root has been used in Sabah as a method of catching fish. The use of such poisons to catch reef fish is rather uncommon in Malaysia. Although a certain degree of damage to coral reefs could be attributed to the use of poisons, the damage is very localized and can be generally ignored.

7. Sedimentation from Fresh Water Run-off

The exposure to brackish, silt-laden fresh water run-off is probably the greatest single cause of coral reef destruction historically (Johannes 1972). Although floods leading to fresh water run-off occur naturally, occurrence in many instances can be traced to man's poor management of land. It has been observed that corals have the ability to remove sediment from their surface. This ability will be dependent on the species and the amount and type of sediment as well as the state of the corals themselves (Hubbard and Pocock 1972; Loya 1976). However, according to Edmondson (1928) and Marshall and Orr (1931), prolonged coating or burial by sediment can result in the eventual death of the reef. Loya (1976) has also indicated that there was a significant decrease in the coral species diversity and living coral cover in locations of high sedimentation and turbidity. Mathias and Langham (1978) have suggested that the damage observed in several reef areas in Sabah, East Malaysia, could probably be attributed to sedimentation. Lulofs (1977) is of the opinion that the complete loss of several reefs in the Straits of Malacca, especially those near the islands of Pulau Pangkor and Pulau Sembilan in the west coast of Peninsular Malaysia, is due to silt from poorly controlled mining, agriculture and the building industry and from dredging harbors. De Silva, Betterton and Smith (1980) have also reported coral reef damage in several islands off the east coast of Peninsular Malaysia, which might be a result of fresh water run-off and sedimentation due to agricultural development. As in many other countries, sedimentation as a result of poor land management could be a major factor causing damage to the coral reefs of Malaysia.

8. Domestic Sewage and Eutrophication

Very few coral reef areas occur along the coastline of Peninsular Malaysia (De Silva, 1982). Therefore, threats to coral reefs from domestic sewage originating from the mainland and the resulting eutrophication can be considered to be minimal. However, in many coastal towns in East Malaysia and even in some of the offshore islands of Peninsular Malaysia, such as Pulau Redang, raw domestic sewage is discharged directly into the sea. Apart from causing direct damage to the nearby coral reefs, the raw domestic sewage can lead to increased levels of nutrients in the sea and cause problems of eutrophication.

9. Red Tides

Although the "red tide" phenomenon is uncommon in Peninsular Malaysia, it has been known to have caused extensive damage to at least the reef fauna in several islands off East Malaysia. Wood (1977) had estimated that 95 percent of the fauna moved away or were killed at a reef off Pualu Gaya in Kota Kinabalu, Sabah, after a red tide which was caused by the dinoflagellate *Pyrodinium bahamense*. The conditions which encourage outbreaks of the red tide phenomenon are not precisely known, but might be related to eutrophication as a result of man's activities on land.

10. Industrial and Agricultural Waters, Dredging, Construction and Mining

At present chemical pollution as a result of industrial and agricultural waste does not appear to be a significant cause of coral reef damage in Malaysia. This is primarily due to the fact that a large proportion of the coral reefs in Malaysia occurs in areas sufficiently far away from centers of industrial and agricultural activities. However, with the intended installation of an oil refinery on the east coast of Peninsular Malaysia and with the oil refineries already in operation in other parts of Malaysia, especially in East Malaysia, problems of chronic oil pollution will become a reality. Although there is no conclusive evidence that oil floating above corals damages them (Johannes 1972), there is evidence to indicate that chronic oil pollution could interfere with the normal development and settlement of coral larvae (Loya 1975). Lulofs (1977) is of the opinion that silt resulting from the dredging of harbors, among other factors, has contributed significantly to the loss of several reefs in the Straits of Malacca, principally those around Pulau Pangkor and Pulau Sembilan islands. Large-scale coral mining in several areas in East Malaysia has been reported by Mathias and Langham (1978) and Lulofs, Langham and Mathias (1974), but up to now no coral mining is carried out in Peninsular Malaysia.

11. Recreational Impacts

The impact of recreational activities on coral reefs is beginning to be felt in Malaysia with the rapid expansion of water-based recreational activities such as scuba diving, snorkeling, wind surfing, sailing and boating. Several groups of scuba divers and snorkelers have been indulging in indiscriminate spearfishing and shell collecting, which has resulted in an appreciable degradation of Malaysian reefs in general (Lulofs 1977).

The threat to the coral reefs due to removal of reef organisms has been so great as to encourage several hotel establishments in the offshore islands on the east coast of Peninsular Malaysia to put up notices warning tourists not to remove coral reef organisms.

The coral reefs of several islands such as Pulau Paya, Pulau Lembu, Pulau Songsong and Pulau Telor in the west coast of Peninsular Malaysia and in other parts of Malaysia are routinely used as points of anchorage by fishing boats during bad weather conditions. This has resulted in heavy damage to several reefs. It is common to see large boulders of coral completely overturned and the more delicate coral broken up by anchors in such areas. Similar damage is caused by pleasure boats being anchored on coral reefs.

12. *Acanthaster* Problems

There is controversy as to the cause of the population explosion of the predator of coral, the "Crown of Thorns" starfish (*Acanthaster planci*). Some biologists attribute it to human interference with coral reef communities, while others maintain that such increases in numbers are due to natural fluctuations in their populations. Whatever the cause for their population explosion, several coral reefs in Malaysia, especially in Peninsular Malaysia, are threatened by *Acanthaster* (De Silva 1982; De Silva and Charles 1982). Surveys by the author of the coral reefs of Pulau Kapas off the east coast of Peninsular Malaysia have shown a loss of almost 40 percent of the reefs in some areas during a period of six months due to the feeding activities of *Acanthaster planci*. At least in the northern part of the east coast of Peninsular Malaysia, *Acanthaster* can be considered as one of the major causes of reef damage.

II. Conclusions

The illegal use of explosives to catch fish, and land clearance practices without effective soil erosion control measures, are among the major human and development pressures causing heavy damage to the coral reefs of Malaysia. Several other factors, such as coral mining and population explosions of *Acanthaster planci*, are responsible for the loss of reefs in specific areas. Damage to the coral reefs is also caused by anchoring of boats and tourist pressures. The possibility of chronic oil pollution becoming a problem in the near future should not be overlooked.

There is a real need to stop the degradation of the Malaysian coral reefs which are economically, biologically and aesthetically important. The initial steps to afford some degree of protection to coral reefs have been taken by the Sabah state government by including several coral reef areas within three of their National Parks: Tunku Abdul Rahman National Park, Turtle Island National Park and the Pulau Tiga National Park. Further, a group of islands in Semporna, Sabah, has been surveyed and a proposal has been made to include these islands and the coral reefs in a marine park, which might be called the Semporna Marine Park. At present there are no protected coral reef areas in Peninsular Malaysia. However, a proposal has been made by the World Wildlife Fund Malaysia to include the Pulau Redang Archipelago in the state of Trengganu in a marine national park. A survey of the Pulau Paya-Segantang group of islands off the state of Kedah has been carried out by the Faculty of Fisheries and Marine Science, Universiti Pertanian Malaysia, through a grant from the World Wildlife Fund Malaysia, and a proposal to make these islands into a marine state park is expected soon.

The declaration of marine national or state parks will help to reduce the degradation of the coral reefs in Malaysia. However, what will ultimately save the Malaysian coral reefs will be strict adherence to erosion control measures in land clearance programs to prevent silt reaching the sea and the coral reefs; constant monitoring of pollution levels; monitoring and control of *Acanthaster planci* on the coral reefs; proper education at all levels on the value of coral reefs and the need to prevent their degradation; and properly enforced legislation to prevent reef damage.

Note

The author wishes to thank Dr. Ang Kok Jee, Dean, Faculty of Fisheries and Marine Sciences, Universiti Pertanian Malaysia for encouragement, and the Faculty of Fisheries and Marine Science for support received during the preparation of this manuscript.

References

Coral Reef Newsletter No. 2, 1980. Paris: International Union for Conservation of Nature and Natural Resources.
De Silva, M.W.R.N. 1979. The threatened coral reefs of Peninsular Malaysia. *Proceedings of the 2nd Symposium on Our Environment*, 222–229. Singapore: Institute of Natural Sciences, College of Graduate Studies, Nanyang University.
De Silva, M.W.R.N. 1981. The status of coral reefs of Sri Lanka, Singapore and Malaysia. *Coral Reef Newsletter No. 3*, 34–37. Paris: International Union for the Conservation of Nature and Natural Resources.

De Silva, M.W.R.N. 1982. The status and conservation of coral reefs in Peninsular Malaysia. *Proceedings of the 4th Annual Seminar of the Malaysian Society of Marine Sciences*, 10–16. Penang: Malaysian Society of Marine Sciences.

De Silva, M.W.R.N., C. Betterton and R.A. Smith. 1980. Coral reef resources of the east coast of Peninsular Malaysia. In *Coastal Resources of East Coast Peninsular Malaysia*, eds. T.E. Chua and J.K. Charles. Penang: Universiti Sains Malaysia.

De Silva, M.W.R.N. and J.K. Charles. 1982. "Crown of Thorns" starfish (*Acanthaster planci*) infestation of coral reefs at Pulau Kapas, Trengganu. Preprint of paper presented at the 5th Annual Seminar of the Malaysian Society of Marine Sciences. Penang: Malaysian Society of Marine Sciences.

Edmondson, C.H. 1928. The ecology of a Hawaiian coral reef. *Bulletin of the Bernice P. Bishop Museum* 45:1.

Hubbard, J.A.E.B. and Y.R. Pocock. 1972. Sediment rejection by recent scleractinian corals; a key to palaeo-environmental reconstruction. *Geologische Rundschau* 61:598–626.

Johannes, R.E. 1972. Coral reefs and pollution. In *Marine Pollution and Sea Life*, ed. M. Ruivo, 364. London: Fishing News (Books) Ltd.

Loya, Y. 1975. Possible effects of water pollution on the community structure of Red Sea corals. *Marine Biology* 29:177–185.

Loya, Y. 1976. Effects of water turbidity and sedimentation of the community structure of Puerto Rican corals. *Bulletin of Marine Sciences* 26(4):450–466.

Lulofs, R.B. 1977. Conservation of the marine environment—coral reefs. *Proceedings of the 1st Annual Seminar of the Malaysian Society of Marine Sciences*, 35–49. Penang: The Malaysian Society of Marine Sciences.

Lulofs, R.B., N.P.E. Langham and J.A. Mathias. 1974. A reef survey of Pulau Gaya and associated islands. Part II. Sabah. 14–17 March 1974. Unpublished report to the Sabah National Parks Department, Kota Kinabalu, Malaysia.

Mathias, J.A. and N.P.E. Langham. 1978. Coral reefs. In *Coastal Resources of West Sabah: A preliminary investigation in relation to oil spills*, eds. T.E. Chua and J.A. Mathias. Penang: Universiti Sains Malaysia.

Marshall, S.M. and A.P. Orr. 1931. Sedimentation on Low Isles Reef and its relation to coral growth. *Scientific Report on the Great Barrier Reef Expedition 1928–29* 1(5):94–133.

Wells, S.M. 1982. International trade in corals and shells. *Abstracts of the 4th International Coral Reef Symposium*. Quezon City: University of the Philippines.

Wood, E.M. 1977. Coral reefs in Sabah: Present damage and potential dangers. *Malayan Nature Journal* 31(1):49–57.

Environmental Controls for Offshore Oil Exploration and Production in Malaysian Waters

Lee Choong Loui

The offshore exploration for and production of petroleum covers such a wide spectrum that many people may be inclined to conclude that the environment will be adversely disturbed by such activities. But is that really the case? If the answer to that question is in the affirmative, why are there not frequent reports of upsets in the marine environment or complaints of poor fish catches attributable to such offshore operations? Is it because of the efforts taken to protect the environment in the offshore area of operation that few upsets or complaints, if any, are reported? The oil industry generally appreciates the physical environment it operates in and takes every reasonable measure to ensure that its operations have minimal impact. What then are the measures taken?

A brief introduction to petroleum activities in Malaysia is in order at this point to serve as background for this subject. The exploration for and production of crude oil began in Miri, Sarawak, in 1910. The production then was from land based reservoirs. The search for oil in offshore waters did not start until the fifties in Sarawak (Fay 1976). From then on, exploration activities increased over the years and spread to other parts of Malaysia. Their success is gauged by the numerous production platforms located off the shores of Peninsular Malaysia, Sabah and Sarawak today. Malaysia is involved in the production not only of crude oil but also of liquefied natural gas (LNG). The LNG project at Bitulu is expected to come onstream in early 1983.

While exploration and production activities were initially confined to Sarawak and Sabah, exploration programs in the seventies revealed potential sources of crude oil and gas off the east coast of Peninsular Malaysia, especially Trengganu. Today about 120,000 barrels of oil per day are being produced offshore Trengganu. In addition to the ten existing production platforms, three new ones will be installed before the end of the year. Construction is also underway to have a crude oil terminal onshore between Paka and Kerteh in Trengganu. All crude oil produced offshore Trengganu will eventually be pumped via subsea pipeline to this terminal for processing; the bulk of it will subsequently be exported.

Downstream projects are in the pipeline to enhance the value of this base stock. The offshore activities require essential support services such as the supply of food, equipment, spare parts and the like. A supply base which will provide these services is currently being constructed at Tanjung Berhala in Trengganu. It is expected to provide efficient and reliable logistics support.

Given the numerous activities necessary for the exploration for and production of crude oil, it can be seen that the potential for environmental impacts is high. A well-planned course of action must be implemented to minimize their effects on the surrounding environment.

I. Concept of Environmental Controls

Before discussing the various types of measures instituted, it is important to understand the underlying factors. These factors should revolve around:
- what the controls are for;
- why there is a need for controls;
- cost benefit; and
- cost effectiveness.

Quite often, regulatory agencies succumb to public outcries and issue stringent standards without solid scientific justification. Developing countries, because of their lack of baseline data, adopt the regulatory standards of industrialized countries which are sometimes overly stringent and not entirely appropriate for the developing countries.

From a regulatory viewpoint, environmental controls can be justified if such controls satisfy stipulated standards. But the need for such controls should be carefully evaluated. For example, if effluent is discharged into an uninhabited and nonbiological environment, will there be benefits in installing controls to attain a BOD_5 of 100 ppm? Or is such a standard absolute if the volume of effluent is negligible? The basic purpose of a control is to ensure minimal imposition of adverse effects. Therefore, environmental controls ought to not only satisfy regulatory standards but also, equally important, the physical and socioeconomic aspects of the area.

A high cost is generally attached to environmental control systems relative to the plant cost and operating expenditures. It would seem prudent that these costs be well spent and benefit the affected community directly or indirectly. As concluded at the World Industry Conference on Environment in Stockholm in 1982, environmental control should be preceded by cost-benefit analysis whenever possible, including the assessment of social and economic costs and economic and social benefits (World Industry Conference 1982). Concurrent with cost benefit application is cost effectiveness of the control. With escalation of cost so prevalent in the world today, it is highly desirable that only cost effective environmental controls are promoted.

It is believed that environmental control systems can be made more effective by considering the abovementioned qualifying factors. Regulatory agencies need not rely on units of standards to protect the environment. They can arrive at a consensus with the industries employing cost benefit and cost effectiveness techniques and still effect harmony with the environment.

II. Oil Exploration and Production Programs

An East-West Center publication on environmental planning guidelines very aptly describes the various stages of an oil exploration/production program and its associated environmental impact (EAPI 1982). Offshore exploration and production for crude oil include several steps, such as exploration, development, production and export. From the initial seismic surveys, wells are drilled to determine the presence of oil. The commercial viability of the field is then established. This is followed by the drilling of development wells followed by the production of crude. The crude can either be stored in the floating storage or brought onshore via subsea pipelines. It is finally offloaded into tankers or to nearby facilities via pipelines as base stock for downstream activities. All these phases require good logistics support for the continuous supply of food, men and equipment.

The interphasing and intertwining of so many activities involve a very complex operation. Because of the high risks and costs, countless man-hours are spent to ensure that the project runs smoothly and is not unduly delayed by accidents and external interference. Of the numerous parameters and factors, environmental considerations would be of primary importance in planning the operation of the project.

III. Environmental Controls

From the foregoing, it is obvious that exploration for and production of crude oil could impair the environment if adequate measures are not taken. Through years of experience and research, a wealth of knowledge is accumulated that can be used to minimize the impacts of these operations. Impacts on the environment can only be minimized but never eliminated, because the introduction of a new element is, by itself, a disruption to the environment. The introduction of environmental controls into a system reduces the emission and effluent discharges into the environment to the level desired.

Relatively simple methods, which are easy to maintain and operate, can be employed for environmental control. The methods so adopted address the specific issues of concern. For example, toxic substances and nonbiodegradable materials are not dumped overboard but disposed of onshore so that the surrounding marine environment is not polluted. This simple good housekeeping rule bears out the cost-benefit relationship mentioned earlier. It is also cost effective in that the cost of imposing the control is relatively low compared to the benefits gained in maintaining the environment.

With today's high petroleum prices, it makes economic sense to recover as much oil as possible and prevent unnecessary discharges. However, recovery of oil from an effluent stream is only efficient up to a certain point, beyond which further quality enhancement is not cost effective. It probably is also not cost beneficial vis-à-vis significantly improving the riches of the environment.

Water pollution resulting from crude oil exploration and production is of greater concern than air pollution. The primary contributor to air pollution is the flaring of associated gas separated out from the crude oil in the process train. Proper design of the burners ensures efficient flaring, resulting in a smokeless flare and minimal unburned hydrocarbons and other gases. To maximize its cost benefit, associated gas is currently used in generators and reinjected into the reservoir to enhance crude oil recovery. The biggest benefit will accrue when it is processed into liquefied petroleum gas and as fuel for nearby industries.

Other equally important elements in the mitigation of environmental impacts are the inherent safety and control devices in the process trains. These devices provide the base for safe operations. The good track record of the industry itself, not only in Malaysia but also internationally, speaks for the care and concerted efforts in maintaining a safe mode of operations. Failures resulting from the neglect of maintaining these safety and control systems could very well cause major damage, which not only endangers lives but also pollutes the surrounding environment. A major area of concern in such situations would be massive oil spills. The physical aspects of oil spills such as spreading, drifting and weathering have been studied extensively and well documented. The degree of impact on the environment is specific to the area affected. It is necessary to take stock of the marine resources in the surrounding environment and prioritize them. Depending on the magnitude of the oil spill, it may not be possible to protect every environmentally sensitive area except to exercise maximum protection in order of priority. Two coastal resources surveys off the coasts of Malaysia provided information on their marine resources and their relative sensitivities (USM 1978, 1980). In addition, predictions were made on trajectories of oil spill movements emanating from offshore production platforms. These data provided the bases for the development of contingency plans for oil spills from the producing areas off the coasts referred to.

IV. Regulatory Controls

Oil companies have the responsibility to minimize environmental impacts from their operations with reasonable and practical measures which are cost beneficial and cost effective. Except for references made in the Environmental Quality Act 1974, Malaysia does not as yet have marine pollution regulations. Existing regulations on air pollution and inland water pollution control the quality at source of emission and discharge (i.e., applying unit quality standards) and do not generally take into consideration the state and location of the environment into which the pollutants are discharged. Application of cost benefit and cost effective principles is limited under such regulations. It is advocated that the drafting of the marine pollution regulations evolve around the total pollutant load concept with due attention given to environmental sensitivity and socioeconomic standing. In this manner, a balance is struck between the cost of introducing environmental controls and the benefits derived from it.

Many of the production platforms in Malaysia are located some 150 miles off her coasts. From the cost benefit viewpoint, it would not be desirable for a unit standard of oil content to be imposed for effluents discharged within the Malaysian exclusive economic zone. Such imposition would also probably prove not to be cost effective. A practical approach is to have zonal standards with a decreasing degree of stringency relative to distance from shore. Where areas are known to be environmentally sensitive, stricter controls need to be imposed, depending on the biological and economic values. Of course, good baseline data on marine resources are required to exercise such controls, but that is what environmental protection and conservation are all about —knowing the resources, their biological and economic values and the appropriate preventive measures.

A set of regulations encouraging good environmental practices is preferable to the "stick by the standards" approach. It affords meaningful consultation between the regulating agency and those subject to the regulations. It will instill a sense of purpose and conviction to ensure minimal impact on the environment.

V. Conclusion

Companies involved in the exploration for and production of crude oil in Malaysian waters have a regard for the physical environment in which they operate and do provide environmental control measures to minimize the impacts. Environmental control measures ought to be simple, cost effective and easy to operate and maintain. These measures or devices should not be incorporated merely to meet stipulated standards. There should be an analysis of cost benefits and cost effectiveness in order to ensure a reasonable and balanced management of the environment. Rather than merely adhering to a set of stringent standards, a more practical approach would be to set standards appropriate to the environment with due regard to its biological and socioeconomic sensitivities.

References

Environment and Policy Institute (EAPI). 1982. *Environmental planning guidelines for offshore oil and gas development*. East-West Center, Honolulu, Hawaii.

Fay, Chris. Offshore oilfield engineering. Paper presented at Oil Symposium, Technological Association of Malaysia, May 1976.

Universiti Sains Malaysia (USM). 1978. *Coastal resources of West Sabah*. School of Biological Sciences.

Universiti Sains Malaysia. 1980. *Coastal Resources of East Coast Peninsular Malaysia*. School of Biological Sciences.

World Industry Conference on Environment. 1982. International Chamber of Commerce Document No. 210/163, April 1982.

The Effects of Stockpiling of Petroleum and Liquefied Natural Gas on Environmental Protection in the Coastal Waters of Japan

Yoshihiro Nomura

Japan owes its high economic growth in the 1960s in large part to the then abundant supply of petroleum. To achieve further economic development requires stockpiling of this important natural resource, as well as of liquefied natural gas (LNG) as one of the essential alternative energy sources. Yet this stockpiling policy is often in conflict with local interests; some disputes have already arisen between public or private entities and local residents in connection with oil or LNG stockpiling projects or accidents at storage sites.

This paper takes up three typical cases of disputes that have arisen due to conflicting interests in oil or LNG stockpiling, looking into the causes, circumstances, details and consequences, and pointing out some valuable and universal lessons that could be drawn from these cases.

The first case has to do with the most serious fuel oil leakage, which occurred at the Mitsubishi Oil refinery in the Mizushima complex, Okayama Prefecture. The dispute that arose subsequently was settled out of court. The second case is concerned with a Kinmu Bay, Okinawa Prefecture, reclamation project for a central terminal station (CTS) for oil imports. Local fishermen of the prefecture brought a suit seeking revocation of the permit for public water body reclamation in accordance with the Administrative Litigation Act; they later applied for a provisional disposition against the construction of a CTS in compliance with the civil Procedure Code. The third case refers to the suit filed by local fishermen and residents of Himeji City, Hyōgo Prefecture, seeking withdrawal of the permit for public water body reclamation for construction of an LNG terminal. Both the second and third cases are administrative lawsuits entered by local people seeking nullity and revocation of the permit for public water body reclamation for the construction of a CTS and an LNG terminal. These stockpiling-related cases may not be peculiar to Japan but common to all countries of the

151

world. Japan's current stockpiling of petroleum will also be discussed, focussing on how oil imports are stockpiled in tankers. In promoting petroleum stockpiling, attention should always be paid to environmental protection in surrounding areas and waters. It is that point which is essentially emphasized throughout this paper.

I. Fuel Oil Leakage in the Mizushima Complex

Mitsubishi Oil has a refinery located in the Mizushima complex, Kurashiki City, Okayama Prefecture, facing the Seto Inland Sea. At 9 P.M. on 18 December 1974, one of the oil storage tanks in the refinery broke down, and an enormous amount of fuel oil ran out of the tank, spreading through the Seto Inland Sea. The sea was then widely contaminated by oil spills. To date it is one of the most serious marine pollution accidents Japan has ever experienced. From the date of occurrence of the accident it was as long as eight months before an out-of-court settlement was reached between local fishermen and Mitsubishi Oil, and the refinery resumed its operation. During this period, the nation's leading newspapers, TV networks and other mass media gave prominent coverage to this accident.

1. Outline of the Accident

The accident began with breakage of one of the storage tanks in the Mitsubishi Oil Mizushima refinery. Then a vast amount of fuel oil ran out into the Seto Inland Sea where oil spills spread widely (Marine Safety Agency 1978; *Mainichi Shimbun* 1974, 1975*). To determine the cause of the tank breakage, a fact-finding committee was formed and reported results of a survey, which reads in part as follows: "...The above observations suggest that the breakage of the tank is not ascribable to any one single, simple factor, but that many complicated factors may have combined to produce the result."

Flowing out of the broken tank, the oil first spread throughout the refinery premises and then rushed into the sea. This was supposedly because the powerful spouting oil pushed down the upright staircase fitted to the tank, weighing some forty tons in all, and its foundation partially destroyed the dike. Through the wrecked section of the dike, the oil gushed out and spread through the Seto Inland Sea. The Ku-

* Issues dated 19, 20, 21, 23, 24, 25, 26, 28 and 31 December 1974; and 13 March, 11, 19, 22 and 24 June, 5 and 8 July, 19 August and 19 December 1975.

rashiki fire department estimated that the total oil leakage was about 43,000 kl, of which, according to the government's local headquarters for the accident set up in Okayama, 7,500 to 9,500 kl were flowing out into the sea. The oil spill spreading through the sea followed the following course: It reached the Straits of Shimotsui by the evening of 19 December. By noon of 20 December, it was off the port of Takamatsu, Kagawa Prefecture—somewhere near the Banno-su sandbank and Nobu Point. On 21 December, it entered the waters southeast of Shōdo Island. In the morning of 22 December, the oil reached the northern mouth of the Straits of Naruto, through which it flowed southward to the Kii-suidō channel on 23 December. The oil spill spread over the widest range from 23 December to 24 December. But it did not go westward beyond the line linking the port of Kojima with Teshima Island, Sanagishima Island and Misaki. The oil went eastward to the Straits of Naruto and reached the Kii-suidō channel just five days after it had left the port of Mizushima because there is a wind-driven current as well as a tidal current running in the Seto Inland Sea.

With the spread of the oil spill, a huge number of oil balls were cast away on the coasts of Okayama, Kagawa, Tokushima and Hyōgo prefectures, causing extensive damage to laver, young yellowtail and *wakame* seaweed farming. Offshore fisheries on the whole were also seriously damaged; the oil balls precluded local fishermen from going out to sea.

2. Steps to an Out-of-court Settlement

In fact, one of the most serious oil leakage accidents to date caused widespread fishery damage extending over four prefectures—Okayama, Kagawa, Tokushima and Hyōgo. Involved in the accident were the four prefectural federations of fishery associations, 150 fishermen's cooperative associations and some 20,000 local fishermen. Thus, compensation for grave damage inflicted on fisheries in the inland sea in the Mizushima oil spill was indeed a very complicated process.

The process consisted of long periods of negotiations (from January to May, 1975), among several parties (Mitsubishi Oil and four prefectural fishery federations), and other additional steps. Discussions were mainly focussed on the following contents of a letter of understanding which was signed by the four prefectural fishery federations and Mitsubishi Oil (Kawasaki 1975; *Mainichi Shimbun* 1974, 1975†):

† Issues dated 29 December 1974; 6, 7, 8, 14, 21, 25, 28, 30 and 31 January, 1, 3, 4, 5, 9, 12 and 20 February, 25 April, 4, 5, 8 and 19 May, 5 June, 19 and 31 July, 3 September and 20 December 1975.

(1) to get rid of the spillage oil from the Mizushima refinery, the fishermen have been committed by Mitsubishi Oil to perform sea-clearing operations on conditions that the latter is obliged to pay a *per diem* allowance, charterage and other expenses to the former. This holds true for similar operations to be conducted in the future;

(2) indemnity for damages to the fishermen due to the oil leakage is not regarded in the same light with a *per diem* allowance, charterage and other expenses to be paid by Mitsubishi Oil to the fishermen who have carried out sea-clearing operations to recover the spilled oil; and

(3) Mitsubishi Oil is held wholly responsible, at least for damages which the fishermen have suffered from the Mizushima oil spill, and the company accepts in good faith all claims advanced by the fishermen, including those for compensation for such damages.

At the final stage the fishery federations came to sign an agreement on 27 May. Through negotiations, separate or independent agreements between fishery federations and Mitsubishi Oil were sought and signed because of the diversity of their interests. The out-of-court settlement system in Japan is thus clearly observed in this oil leakage problem in the Seto Inland Sea area. This type of solution suggests several advantages, such as saving time, lower costs compared with a settlement in court and others; while disadvantages such as vague legal conclusions or others are observed as well.

3. Lessons from the Accident

The oil leakage accident at the Mizushima refinery of Mitsubishi Oil attracted public attention to the inadequacy of safety provisions and thereby furnished important lessons for future accident prevention:

(1) the importance of damage forecasting was recognized anew;

(2) each establishment should build up adequate safety provisions against accidents and reinforce a liaison/communication system so that any accident can be dealt with immediately;

(3) an organization of private businesses to prevent accidents must be set up on the local level;

(4) various bodies involved in accident prevention, both central and local, should act in concert with one another (Fire Defense Agency 1976; *Mainichi Shinbum* 1975*).

Improvement in legislation is observed as well:

---

* Issues dated 10 February and 14 June.

(1) The Law for Prevention of Disasters at Petroleum Complexes was enacted. Amid growing public interest in accident prevention at a petroleum complex, the law embodied various important lessons that could be drawn from the most serious oil leakage to date at the Mizushima refinery of Mitsubishi Oil;
(2) The Fire Services Law was partially amended.

II. Okinawa Central Terminal Station Case

1. Suit for Revocation of the Permit for Public Water Surface Reclamation for Construction of a CTS in Okinawa

This case is an administrative action brought by local fishermen of Okinawa Prefecture against the governor, seeking to overturn the permit for public water body reclamation for construction of a CTS. It was planned as part of the Okinawa industrial development program that the CTS for oil imports would be constructed at a site to be reclaimed from Kin Bay on the east coast of mainland Okinawa.

The action brought by forty-eight fishermen, who had not voted for abandonment of fishing rights, was dismissed on 4 October 1975 by the Naha District Court, which ruled the plaintiffs' "point" moot.

The District Court's decision reads as follows:

The said public road constituting a part of the land reclaimed from the public water body at issue connects Miyagijima Island with Henzajima Island and is virtually opened to the public at large. Furthermore, the said harbor facilities constructed in connection with the reclamation project under review are also actually used by local fishermen in the area. Should the land reclaimed from the public water body at issue be restored to its original state, its surrounding waters may then be significantly contaminated by earth and sand resulting from restoration work involved.

These observations suggest that it may not necessarily be physically impossible to restore the reclaimed land under consideration to its original state. Given a commonly accepted idea, however, this involves considerable legal difficulty in view of the scope of the reclaimed land in question, its structure and current state of its utilization, as well as potential socioeconomic loss and contamination of the surrounding waters resulting from restoration. This is a case where the governor should relieve the person having the right to reclamation from obligations to restore the reclaimed land at issue to its original state. The plaintiffs can no longer demand the said person to restore the reclaimed land at issue to its original state. The court rules, therefore, that the case filed by the plaintiffs seeking nullity of the permit for filling up the public water body in question has no public benefits at all (Naha District Court 1975).

In this connection, it may be interesting to examine why a need has come to be felt for building a CTS. In fact, oil tankers have become bigger and bigger in size these days, and these so-called supertankers cannot be berthed alongside the pier due to the limited depth of water, thus leading to the need to provide a CTS. In addition, the many risks involved in getting supertankers into crowded waters like the Seto Inland Sea can be avoided with the CTS, where crude oil is safely unloaded from supertankers. As for economic considerations, the CTS is also able to meet the need for storing large quantities of oil—a need that has been growing particularly since the first and second oil crises.

Regarding environmental protection, the CTS has some advantages over cargo handling at a refinery in terms of marine pollution prevention. Effluents from the refinery have adverse effects on fish and shellfish; oil-smelling fish are often found near the refinery. The CTS, however, helps greatly in abating such marine pollution.

Thus, efforts are made to go ahead with CTS construction projects to meet the abovementioned need as well as to prevent marine pollution. Yet it is also necessary for us to scientifically and philosophically consider the significance of the problem—the potential environmental effects of the CTS—raised by this case.

2. Suit for Suspension of the Construction of a CTS

As mentioned above, the administrative action brought by Okinawa fishermen seeking to overturn the permit for public water body reclamation was dismissed by the Naha District Court on 4 October 1975. Following this ruling, the governor of Okinawa Prefecture approved the completion of the Kinmu Bay reclamation project, and preparations were made for construction of a CTS for oil imports.

In protest against these developments, a total of 1250 local residents in the area filed a suit seeking suspension of the construction of a CTS for oil tankers, with their argument based on the environment right and personal rights. The Naha District Court, however, recognized no or very little probability that the CTS in question would have adverse effects on human life, body or health. And the court, seeing no reason to consider and duly weigh public interests, ruled that the plaintiffs had no claim for suspension of CTS construction work.

The court's ruling on this case, which was brought in compliance with the Civil Procedure Law seeking a provisional disposition against the construction of a CTS, contains some noteworthy points.

First, it denied the environment right as one of the specific rights in private law. Secondly, it reviewed a remedy against infringement of personal rights in two cases: one case where there is a probability that a human life may be endangered and human health damaged to a significant degree, and the other where there is a probability that human health may be damaged but not significantly. And in the latter case, it judged that consideration and weighing of public interests in various circumstances should not be avoided. Finally, it carefully examined the safety of the CTS facilities, taking into account lessons drawn from the Mizushima oil leakage.

The court's decision reads as follows:

Following the construction of the CTS under consideration, the complainants' lives, bodies or health may be damaged first of all by a fire in tanks, or radiation heat or murky smoke from burning crude oil leaked out of tanks.

It is not totally unlikely that crude oil may leak out through the broken bottom of a tank, as was the case with the Mizushima oil leakage, due to insufficient ground improvements, the poorly constructed foundation, defective welding, inadequate building inspection and imperfect maintenance and safety check-ups (including continuous observations of the subsidence of the foundation).

There is no uncertainty observed in terms of design, however, because some progress has so far been made in research or standards-making for the ground of an oil storage tank, its foundation and structure. Moreover, safety standards for oil tanks have been made considerably more stringent since the Mizushima oil leakage. (All this evidence shows that the CTS construction project at issue is quite different from the broken tank at the Mizushima refinery in terms of the improved ground and thickness of steel plates used.)

Rather, the possibility of any accident to oil tanks depends on adequate engineering work and management during construction as well as good maintenance and safety checkups on tanks. To achieve this, the first consideration should of course be the utmost efforts and care of the defendants themselves. The reality is that both Okinawa Prefecture and Yonagusuku-son Village, representing the common interests of local residents, are allowed access to the establishment of the defendants for on-the-spot surveys, inspections and testing and, if necessary, to order the defendants to curtail or temporarily stop their operation. This is in fact an effective means of monitoring and accident prevention and hence pollution control.

Thus, there is no or very little probablity that the life, body or health of the complainants living in Gushikawa City and Yonagusu-ku-son Village that face Kin Bay may be damaged by the CTS at issue. Nor does such a probability exist with the other complainants.

The complainants have no claim for suspension of the construction of the CTS in question; there is no need for considering and duly weighing public interests.

Therefore, the complainants' suit in this case is wholly unfounded (Naha District Court 1979).

III. Himeji LNG Terminal Suit

This case was originally concerned with Hyōgo Prefecture's plan to construct an LNG terminal at a site which would be reclaimed from the public water body off Shirahama-cho, Himeji City. The governor granted the permit applied for by the prefecture to fill up the public water body concerned in accordance with Article 2 of the Public Water Surface Reclamation Law. Then, a suit was brought against the governor by 5 fishermen and 141 residents of the town seeking withdrawal of this permit.

The Kobe District Court, however, turned down the plaintiffs' suit on the ground that the plaintiffs were not qualified to bring the case into litigation (Kobe District Court 1980) The following describes how this decision was handed down.

The plaintiffs, who are fishermen operating in the waters around the proposed reclamation project at issue or residents living near the said proposed reclamation project, demand withdrawal of the permit for filling up the public water body in question. The plaintiffs contend that the proposed reclamation project may have adverse environmental effects including changes in the course of tidal currents and accumulation of marine pollution, that LNG tanks to be constructed at the reclaimed land may blow up and that the air pollution in the area may be accelerated due to utilization of the reclaimed land.

The plaintiffs argue that since the possibilities of damage to local residents and fishermen, including aggravated environmental disruption, from the operation of an LNG terminal at the proposed reclamation area are examined prior to granting the reclamation permit in compliance with the provisions of the Public Water Body Reclamation Law, these provisions of the law are designed to protect the plaintiffs' individual and specific interests.

The applicable provisions of the law, however, should be regarded as abstract guidelines for accomplishing the administrative purposes to realize public interests—protection of public health and living environment—and maintain the environment at large above a certain standard.

Furthermore, such an examination should be carried out by the permit grantor from the viewpoint of general, public interests to make sure that the use of the reclaimed land is compatible with a plan based on the state's or any local public body's legislation concerning land utilization or environmental protection.

Any review made by the permit grantor pursuant to the applicable provisions of the law has for its purpose to realize public interests. It cannot be interpreted that these provisions, as the plaintiffs contend, are designed to protect the interests of local residents and fishermen, both individually and specifically, so that they would not suffer damage from environmental disruption due to reclamation or from the operation of an LNG terminal on the reclaimed land. Any other provisions of the law cannot be considered to protect such interests, either individually or specifically.

The supply of energy sources has become one of the most important problems to be solved since the first oil crisis in 1973. Awakened to the limited oil supply, people have devoted much effort to development of alternative energy sources, along with stepped-up petroleum stockpiling and energy conservation. While technologies to harness new or renewable and existing energy sources such as nuclear power, coal and solar energy are being actively developed, great hopes are laid on liquefied natural gas or LNG as one of the most potentially useful oil substitutes throughout the world. Being pollution-free clean energy, LNG is currently widely used both at home and for power generation. The action under review was brought by local people opposing the construction of a terminal for storing this LNG.

The Himeji LNG terminal suit is an administrative action, as is the case with the abovementioned CTS lawsuit. In any administrative action, the scope of an "administrative disposition" under consideration will first of all be taken up (Nomura 1981; Nomura et al. 1978). Then, "statutory interests" will be discussed as these "statutory interests" form the basis for judgment of the plaintiffs' qualifications under Article 9 of the Administrative Litigation Act. The "illegality of an administrative disposition" will not be judged until these two points are cleared. To date, there have been just a few environment-related lawsuits on which an administrative disposition was decided to be substantially illegal. In the present case, the court took up the second point —"statutory interests." In the end, the plaintiffs' suit was dismissed, reflecting considerable difficulty in winning an administrative action.

IV. National Petroleum Stockpiling

1. Stockpiling Program

In Japan, the program for stockpiling ninety days' supply of petroleum was started in fiscal 1975 by private oil concerns through government aid, and the targets fixed in this program were completely achieved at the end of fiscal 1977 (JNOC 1981). Yet a need was felt to further increase the stockpiled oil, at least to the level of the United States and Western Europe, in view of the nation's energy supply structure (as many as three-fourths of the total primary energy requirements are dependent on oil imports) and the growing instability in the Middle East oil-producing countries. To this end, the Japan National Oil Corporation (JNOC) launched a national petroleum stockpiling plan in fiscal 1978 to add up to ninety days' supply of oil in the private sector.

As of the end of July 1981, JNOC has stockpiled about 8.35 million kiloliters of petroleum; the corporation will continue building up 2.5 to 3.0 million kiloliters of oil each year and achieve the national target stockpiling of 30.0 million kiloliters by the end of fiscal 1988. On 27 December 1975, the Petroleum Stockpiling Law was enacted and announced. The law is designed to take measures necessary to stockpile petroleum against any emergency involving a serious oil shortage in Japan. This will contribute to the stability of life and the nation's economy. Currently, JNOC has proposed sites for onshore central terminal stations at nine different locations around Japan.

2. Stockpiling in Tankers

Oil imports are also stockpiled in tankers. This is a temporary measure which will continue until all oil tanks are duly constructed on land to permanently stockpile the nation's oil imports against emergency.

JNOC has had thirteen large tankers fully loaded with oil at anchor in Tachibana Bay, Nagasaki Prefecture since December 1978. In addition, seven oil tankers have been at anchor in the bays of Usuki, Tsukumi and Saeki, Oita Prefecture since May 1981. Currently, another ten tankers are at anchor in the waters west of the island of Iou. Taken together, some 8.35 million kiloliters of oil are being stockpiled offshore in a total of thirty tankers. Of course, the utmost care is being taken in safety and environmental protection measures. In this connection, the Petroleum Stockpiling Tankers Management Company was founded by all the owners of tankers loaded with oil imports for stockpiling to control them comprehensively and technically.

V. Conclusion

Prudence has always been exercised in locating petroleum and LNG storage sites, and a variety of safety and environmental protection measures have been duly taken. Yet nobody knows when or how an accident will occur. Efforts should always be made to ensure safety and to protect the environment in a simple and constructive way without relying too much on today's science and technology. Disputes over a national oil or LNG stockpiling policy are not peculiar to Japan but common to all the countries of the world. To solve various environmental problems reflected in those disputes, a mutual exchange of experiences and information among many nations of the world is of paramount importance.

References

All sources in Japanese.
Fire Defense Agency. 1976. *Guide to the law for prevention of disasters at petroleum complexes*, ed. Disaster Prevention Department. Tokyo: Zenkoku-kajo-shuppan.
Japan National Oil Corporation. 1981. *Petroleum stockpiling in tankers*. Tokyo.
Kawasaki, Ken, ed. 1975. *Marine pollution by oil spills*, 99–115. Tokyo: Jijitsūshinsha.
Kobe District Court. 1979. Shōwa 54 (1979) 11.20, 954 *Hanrei Jihō*, 17–29.
Mainichi Shimbun. December 1974; January–December 1975.
Marine Safety Agency. 1978. *A survey report on the fuel leakage from the Mizushima Refinery of Mitsubishi Oil*. 6th Regional Maritime Safety Headquarters.
Naha District Court. 1975. Shōwa 50 (1975) 10.4, 791 *Hanrei Jihō*, 17–21.

Naha District Court. 1979. Shōwa 54 (1979) 3.29, 928 *Hanrei Jihō*, 3–47.
Nomura, Yoshihiro. 1981. *Laws of environmental conservation and control*, 117–120. Tokyo: Nihon Keizai Shimbun.
Nomura, Yoshihiro, Koichi Miyazawa and Koichi Bai. 1978. *Social problems of our time*. Tokyo: Chikuma-shobō.

The Impact of Industry on Coastal Zone Resources in Thailand

Surin Setamanit

The coastal margin has only recently come to be recognized and treated as a valuable and perishable resource. It is actually a complex of unique physical resources: estuaries and lagoons, marshes, beaches and cliffs, bays and harbors, islands and spits and peninsulas.

The marine and estuarial ecosystems of the Asian and Pacific region provide a rich fishery for countries in the region as well as for other international fishing fleets. About 30 million tons of marine catches are landed in the Economic and Social Commission for Asia and the Pacific (ESCAP) region every year, which is about 40 percent of the total annual world catch. This catch will have to reach 54 million tons by the year 2000 to cope with the increase in population.

The Asian and Pacific region is also rich in a variety of minerals, containing some of the largest deposits in the world. For example, about 60 percent of the world's resources of tin are found in East Asia. Three of the world's four leading tin producers are in the ESCAP region: Malaysia, Thailand and Indonesia. An increasing proportion of the ore comes from offshore and coastal zone mining.

Mangrove forests, together with other related ecological systems, have been threatened and in many cases damaged by human activities such as land reclamation, felling of mangrove trees for firewood, charcoal and chipboard manufacture and dumping of urban and industrial wastes. Some lands were cleared for fish ponds and human settlements. Coral reefs of the region are also threatened and damaged by fishing with dynamite and other destructive means, commercial mining, siltation and recreational activities.

The seaside and coastline and the sea itself are naturally endowed with scenic beauty. With the demand for marine recreation growing with local and international tourism, pressure is increasing on many coastal zones. Swimming, boating and skin diving may sometimes be incompatible with competing alternative uses, many of which appear to have equally valid claims. In short, the region has witnessed dramatic growth in coastal zone development during the past decade, which makes the management of the coastal zone a complex and difficult task. In the face of conflicts between various uses, and long-term and short-term benefits, how and by whom will the ultimate decisions be made on the proper utilization of coastal resources?

I. The Situation in Thailand

Aquatic resources in Thailand have deteriorated greatly during the past few decades, as is the case in other countries in the same region, due to rapid urbanization and industrialization. Data indicate that major rivers that drain into the Inner Gulf of Thailand such as the Chao Phya River, the Mae Klong River and the Tha Chin River are severely polluted, mostly by the discharges of domestic sewage and industrial wastes from land-based factories. During 1971–1974, there were instances when the water in the Mae Klong River was polluted so severely and so suddenly that clam farming at Samutsongkram and Ban Laem was virtually wiped out.

Heavy metals such as lead and mercury are also found in sea water. Investigations conducted by the Department of Scientific Services during 1977–1980 revealed that the concentrations were greater in the coastal waters where there were intensive human settlement and industrial activities, varying from 0.2 ppb to 320 ppb for mercury, and from 1 ppb to 290 ppb for lead (Puangsuwan 1982).

Thailand has about 3,127.14 km^2 of mangrove forests, 80 percent of which lies along the Andaman Sea coastline (Siripong 1979). Extensive areas have been converted for other land uses and the forests are fast deteriorating due to human action. Sedimentation induced by onshore and offshore mining is believed to have aggravated the situation further. Coral reefs are also threatened by pollution and sedimentation. Damage to coral reefs results notably from oil, but also from the use of dynamite and poisons for reef fishery.

II. The Tin Mining Industry

Mining activities in Thailand have been going on from time immemorial, with tin playing a dominant role by virtue of its relative abundance and being readily exploitable in the south. Official records of the mining industry date back some seventy-five years (Aranyakanon 1981). The first tin dredge began to operate off Tungka Harbor, Phuket Island, in 1907. The activities increased gradually and extended to the other side of the island, and dredgers with a bucket-type dredge were introduced.

During the past two decades, offshore tin mining was intensified several fold, and became a major earner of foreign exchange for the Thai economy. The total value of minerals produced in 1975 was 3.1 billion baht, compared with the total value of over 13.9 billion baht in 1980, in which year the mineral exports were valued at over 14.9 billion baht in foreign exchange. Tin export accounted for about 75 percent of the total.

The Thai government also plays a limited role in offshore tin mining as a producer, by setting up an offshore mining organization in 1975, with permission to build a new bucket-type dredge of 15 cubic feet bucket capacity. The dredge was completed and put into operation in 1979.

Along with the development of large mining operations, mainly by foreign companies, the people living in the locale began to take an interest in offshore mining. A number of small boats and pontoons equipped with some rudimentary gear was constructed and put into operation, first in some coastal waters off Phuket Island and gradually moving up north to Ban Nam Kem, Ampur Ta Kua Pa in Pang-Nga Province. At that time, their number could be as high as 3,500. Sophistication moved in. These small boats and pontoons were modified, improved and equipped with more elaborate and more powerful equipment. Some of them took 3–4 million baht to construct. Some cost a great deal more, being financed by wealthy people who did not want to see foreign mining companies operating in Thai territory.

These local entrepreneurs' mining activities, which were greatly intensified after the government decided to withhold the mining right of a foreign-owned company for political reasons, were illegal at first, but later legalized by being allowed to operate under the Provincial Administration of the Pang-Nga Province. At present, tin production from thousands of these small craft, combined with those from another thirty-three standard dredges, ranks Thailand as the second largest tin producer of the world (Aranyakanon 1981).

III. Environmental Impacts

All these activities are not without cost to the natural environment.

During the Sixth Session of the ESCAP Committee on Natural Resources, a high level of concern for and understanding of environmental quality management was displayed by member countries. A preliminary evaluation of environmental impacts of both offshore and land mining showed that the problems had arisen from turbidity and sediment deposition (Suwanasing 1982). Poor mining management and inappropriate technology were probably the causes.

One aspect of the impact on natural resources which has been studied in more detail is that on land and mangrove forests. Mining in mangrove forests takes place only in three provinces: Phuket, Ranong and Pang-Nga. A total area of about 26,000 rai (2.5 rai = 1 acre) of mangrove forest has already been leased to several mining companies, but only about 5,700 rai or 0.27 percent of the total are now in operation. This has been estimated to yield about 120 million baht per annum in revenue to the government.

About 100,000 rai or 5 percent of the total area is used for other activities including salt production, fish ponds and the growing of other aquatic animals. These have been estimated to yield about 677 baht per family per annum for salt production and about 570 baht per family per year for shrimp cultivation. Around 1,108,000 rai have also been used for forestry, earning a revenue of about 38 million baht per annum. One rai of mangrove forest would yield 5695 kg of charcoal in fifteen years, valued at about 11,000 baht.

Siripong (1979) compared LANDSAT imageries taken in 1973 and 1979 and found that the change in mangrove forest area was about 1 percent. The two predominant features of the change were mining areas and human settlement. Suwanasing and Krongart (1981) surveyed 3654 rai (1.08 percent of the total area of Phuket Island) of the areas that had been mined, 2,095 of which were hinterland while the rest were mangrove forests. It was found that about one quarter of the land was not utilized or restored to its original condition. Of those which had been utilized, some were used for coconut plantations and others for farming, or subdivided into human settlements. In the case of mangrove forest area, about 25 percent has not been restored or used for other purposes.

IV. Mineral Laws

Under the Thai Mineral Laws, mining companies are required to fill up pits, winzes and shafts which are no longer in use, and to restore lands to their original condition. Local mineral resources officials are empowered to issue orders to the holders of mining leases to fulfill these requirements. But the penalty for the offense is only a fine not exceeding 2000 baht (approximately U.S. $90).

In fact, there are several clauses in the Mineral Act B.E. 2520 dealing with environmental problems which may arise from mining operations, starting from the mining plans and methods that have to be first approved by the Mineral Resources Department, to the control of slime and tailings discharges.

Section 67 of the Act empowers the Ministry of Industry to issue a ministerial regulation concerning the amount of solid matter that may be contained in such water (not to exceed 6 grams per liter at present). Failure to comply with this regulation makes one liable to a fine not exceeding 2000 baht, and the Minister has the power to revoke the leases.

The rather "un-environmental" phrases in Section 67 and Section 68 are: "When necessary, the Minister is empowered to issue a license to omit the enforcement . . . and he may prescribe any condition as he deems fit" and "By demanding the holder or holders of Prathanabats (leases) to make payment in compensation for maintenance and damages and by prescribing conditions as he deems fit when necessary, the Minister is empowered to prescribe certain public waterways as allowable for one or more Prathanabat holders to discharge slime or tailings." In 1976, the Minister did allow this for twelve canals in Ranong, seven in Pang-Nga, one river (the River Meuy, which borders Thailand and Burma) in Tak and one river (the River Yuam) in Mae Hong Son. The declaration also includes the sea as another public waterway for slime and tailings discharges (Suwanasing 1982). The compensation is set at 100 baht per rai per year of land area for the hinterland, and 40 baht per rai per year for land in the offshore area.

Understandably, these regulations were laid down to relieve some constraints from small mining companies operating upon limited leased land areas, but they provide loopholes and invite activities that cause damage to the environment, in particular the fragile coastal resources.

V. The Role of Environmental Impact Assessments

The National Environment Board (NEB) of Thailand has adopted the Environmental Impact Assessment (EIA) process as an approach to guide the planning and operation of the mining industry, so that potential environmental risks can be anticipated at the onset of the operation and corrective measures taken. The first proclamation of types and sizes of activities for which an EIA will be required was approved by the government in July 1981.

Mining companies of all sizes are required to have their EIAs completed and approved before mining operations can commence. Those that have been granted permission prior to the proclamation may proceed, but the Prime Minister, in an emergency, empowered by the Amended Improvement and Conservation of National Environmental Quality Act, may issue an order prohibiting a person from causing danger or damage or from acting in any way which will intensify the severity of environmental pollution, or issue an order that certain acts be carried out to stop or reduce the severity of the environmental pollution during the emergency.

In one case, a mining company with a prior license began to operate in Ao Pa Tong, an area of scenic beauty planned by the Tourist Authority of Thailand to be promoted into a tourist resort, which had also been approved by the government, and met with public opposition. The Prime Minister then used the abovementioned power to order the mining company to cease its operation, unless it had been at least 8 km from the line joining the upper part of the bay.

The order further states that those mining operations that have been ongoing on the west coast of Phuket Island may continue, there will be no renewal of the licenses that have expired and that if the situation is certain to cause damage to the environment, the mining operation will have to stop. All new mining leases will have to wait for the study by the NEB.

The same company moved to Karon, another scenic bay nearby, which had also been planned to become a holiday resort, and met with another public outcry. This time the Local Mineral Resources Office withheld the license to operate on technical grounds. A special task force appointed by the Mineral Resources Department recommended that the company should be allowed to try out its antipollution devices during the short period before the monsoon, since damage could not be caused and knowledge and experience gained from such a trial run would be very useful. The Science and Technology Commission appointed by the Upper House, however, recommended an in-depth environmental study before any further action. On national security grounds, the Local Administration and the Commander of Division 4 of the Army also favored discontinuing the operation.

VI. Discussion

Industries certainly have impacts upon coastal zone resources. Social and economic impacts on the positive side, such as employment generation and earning of foreign exchange are usually put aside in comparison with the adverse impacts on natural resources such as fisheries, mangrove forests, coral reefs and sea water quality. The paradox is that the mining industry, which is itself trying to exploit the natural resources of the coastal zone that everyone wants to protect, is the odd man out in most cases. Admittedly, the image of rich miners, and the past and even present evidence of the physical damage caused to the environment, play very important negative roles in the mind of the public at large. There are not many people who really wait for the outcome of the environmental studies being conducted, or who want to evaluate the improved technology that will make possible a cleaner and less damaging operation. Only a few may want to weigh the effectiveness of land rehabilitation, including the rehabilitation of mangrove forests, by planting grass and trees that will thrive on the soil of many disused mines, or the possibility of using disused mining pits as water reservoirs for public water supplies and even as fish ponds.

In technical terms, aversive risk methods are in use here. They are those of avoidance or minimization with little consideration for comparison with other risks and benefits, which may or may not benefit the public as a whole or the country in the long run. Why does someone not ask questions like—can we risk destroying a few coral reefs without really destroying all or even some of the fishes? Can we not build some artificial coral for fish to use as their nursery grounds? After all, the Japanese and many others have now moved to growing fish in cages. Are we not actually building up new mud banks, with slime and mine tailings which escape the sedimentation basins, which would soon turn into mangrove forests? After all, mangrove forests are formed on the muddy beaches of river estuaries made from the silts and sediments transported and deposited by the river water.

There are many other examples that could be cited. One such extreme case, in the United States, is that of taconite pollution of Lake Superior, the source of many concerns about water supply. Here, a certain Reserve Mining Company has been dumping for the past eighteen years into the lake each day about 670,000 tons of tailings, the residues from the grinding and magnetic separation process used to extract magnetite or iron oxide from taconite, a low grade iron ore. The fibers in the taconite rock were thought to be similar to asbestos fibers suspected of causing a high incidence of stomach cancer in Japan (the talc-dusted rice popular in Japan contains absestos contaminants). A suit was, therefore, brought against Reserve in federal court.

However, no safe level of exposure to asbestos has been established, and scientific proof is insufficient to establish whether a high incidence of cancer will result from the ingestion of asbestos fiber. Besides, Reserve contested that their tailings disposal plan had not failed, and that the tailings were not widely diffused; and, further, that the fibers in municipal water supplies were not identical to asbestos and hence could not be classified as a carcinogen.

The federal court, however, issued a shut-down order, which made sensational news. After only two days, it was stayed by a three-judge panel of the U.S. Court of Appeals for the Eighth Circuit, and the Supreme Court subsequently refused to vacate the stay. However, Reserve must switch to an on-land disposal system.

The discharge of tailings into Lake Superior will not cease for some time and the municipal water supply must at least be effectively filtered, pending the change to an on-land disposal system to be carried out by Reserve.

Two questions of overriding urgency and importance came up in this case: how clear must the scientific evidence be for a court to decide that public health is threatened?; and how great must the threat be for the court to close a plant, particularly if it happens to be of importance to the local economy?

VII. Conclusion

Industrialization is certainly one of the competing demands for coastal resources. In many cases, adverse impacts, most of which are not fully understood or may even be impossible to evaluate, usually override any positive impacts in terms of socioeconomic gains. Without fully understanding the extreme complexity of coastal zone ecology, two societies with different socioeconomic and cultural backgrounds could take greatly different attitudes toward the problems, ranging from adversative to legislative. A more rational and systematic approach to decision making that goes further than environmental impact assessment will have to be developed.

References

Aranyakanon, P. 1981. *Environment geology of offshore mining in Thailand.* Bangkok: Department of Mineral Resources (in Thai).

Kates, R.W. 1978. *Risk assessment of environmental hazards, SCOPE 8.* New York: John Wiley & Sons.

National Environment Board. 1980. *The improvement and conservation of the National Environmental Quality Act, B.E. 2518.* Bangkok.

Puangsuwan, Benja. 1982. *Analytic study of research findings—waste waters and polluted waters.* Bangkok: National Research Council Research Report No. 6.

Siripong, Absornsuda. 1979. *Ecology of Pang-Nga Bay estuaries.* Bangkok: National Research Council (in Thai).

Suwanasing, Prakmas. 1982. "Environmental problems and the mining industry," *Thailand Engineering Journal,* Year 35, Vol. 1, February.

Suwanasing, Prakmas and Chatchair Krongart. 1981. "A study of the change in environmental conditions of disused mines land areas in Phuket," *Mineral Resources Gazette,* Vol. 12, December (in Thai).

United Nations Environmental Programme. 1981. *Asia-Pacific Report 1981.* Bangkok: UNEP Regional Office for Asia and the Pacific.

Impacts of Population Pressure on Coastal Zones and Settlement Patterns in the Philippines

Hipolito C. Talavera

The environmental crisis that gripped the industrialized countries in the early 1960s has resulted in a worldwide consciousness of environmental quality. Both the developed and the developing countries became much aware of the environmental problems arising out of rapid industrialization, population growth, urbanization and natural resources degradation. The developed countries suffer from what has been called the *pollution of affluence*. On the other hand, the developing countries are threatened by the *pollution of poverty*.

The pollution of affluence is associated with high industrial productivity such as large volumes of effluents being discharged into natural waterways and the atmosphere, industrial processes that utilize toxic substances, agricultural technologies that make use of fertilizers and pesticides which cause pollution, transportation systems that produce intolerable noise and consumption patterns that create a monumental heap of solid waste.

The pollution of poverty arises out of unwise exploitation of natural resources like mines, forests and fisheries. High population growth rates and rapid urbanization in developing countries often result in improper land use, urban blight and the general deterioration of environmental quality.

The national commitment of the Republic of the Philippines to industrialization and economic development implies that it must continuously draw from its capital of natural resources in order to support its development programs. It should exploit its natural resources with deliberate care, lest it suffer the consequences of the pollution of poverty. As the country treads the path of industrialization, the character of its environmental problems would begin to resemble those associated with the pollution of affluence, unless environmental protection becomes an essential component of its economic planning, as well as of the people's daily activities.

I. Historical and Situational Overview of the Philippine Environment

Environmental management in the Philippines has three priority areas: environmental pollution control, natural resources management and environmental planning. At present, no less than twenty-two government agencies and ministries are involved in these areas. On the basis of their statutes, these individual entities have the necessary capabilities to carry out specific responsibilities in environmental protection.

Consequential to this is the inclination toward overlapping or duplication in functions and the lack of proper coordination and implementation. Common to these agencies, however, is the awareness of the deterioration of the environment together with the noble commitment to the attainment of an environmental quality conducive to a life of dignity and well-being.

The recommendation to integrate environmental programs through inter-agency coordination was conveyed to the President of the Philippines through the efforts of the Inter-agency Committee on Environmental Protection as initiated by the Ministry of Natural Resources; the United Nations Environment Programme consultant, the Hon. Jack Beale, who was commended by the Philippine Government; and the Environmental Management Program of the Ministry of Human Settlements. Accordingly, the report to the Chief Executive included a recommendation for the creation of a national coordinating agency on environmental protection.

Thus, on 18 April 1977, the proposed coordinating agency was established by virtue of Presidential Decree No. 1121, and it is now known as the National Environmental Protection Council (NEPC).

The NEPC was originally composed of thirteen member agencies: the Ministry of Natural Resources, the Ministry of Public High-ways, the Ministry of Local Governments, the Ministry of Trade and Industry, the Ministry of National Defense, the Ministry of Public Works, Transportation and Communications, the Ministry of Human Settlements, the Environmental Center of the Philippines, the Office of Budget and Management, the National Pollution Control Commission, the Energy Development Board, the National Science and Technology Authority and the Office of the President. The Ministry of Public Works, Transportation and Communications was subsequently split into two: the Ministry of Public Works and the Ministry of Transportation and Communications. And, under the recent government reorganization plan, the Ministry of Public Works and the Ministry of Public Highways were merged for effectiveness, efficiency and economy. The President himself is the chairman of the Council, and the Minister of Natural Resources functions as the Executive Officer. The top ranking officers of the other offices, in turn, serve as Council members.

To complement the creation of the NEPC, two major decrees, which are milestones in Philippine environmental history, were duly promulgated by the President on 6 June 1977 during the first National Conference on Environmental Management. These are the Philippine Environment Code (P.D. No. 1152) and the Philippine Environmental Policy Decree (P.D. No. 1151). The code, which deals with the Philippine environment in its totality, is primarily concerned with the establishment of management policies and quality standards for the different sectors in the environment.

Presidential Decree No. 1151, on the other hand, sets forth broad environmental policies for the country, namely:

(1) The creation, development and maintenance of conditions under which man and nature can thrive in productive and enjoyable harmony with each other;

(2) the fulfillment of the social, economic and other requirements of present and future generations of Filipinos; and

(3) the ensuring of the attainment of an environmental quality that is conducive to a life of dignity and well-being.

Through this law, the Government has recognized the right of every Filipino citizen to a healthy and wholesome environment. It also requires the compulsory submission of Environmental Impact Assessments for projects which significantly affect the environment. Finally, Letter of Instructions No. 549 mandated the Council to organize Inter-Agency Task Forces to study major ecological problems and to devise an administrative machinery for the installation of the EIS system.

On the enforcement of environmental protection laws, the Philippine Environment Code fully delineated the implementing jurisdictions of each agency. To answer for problems of enforcement requiring inter-agency effort, the President also created an Inter-Agency Action Council (IAAC), by Letter of Instructions No. 553, chaired by the Minister of National Defense. In turn, the IAAC has a Secretariat called the National Environmental Protection Control Action Group, with the Commissioner of the National Pollution Control Commission as the action officer.

Progress in the various aspects of environmental management can be viewed as a function of the collective endeavors of the abovementioned agencies. Furthermore, the efforts in program planning and implementation currently shared by these entities are also being complemented by increasing participation on the part of the general public.

II. Population-Environment Balance

With a population of 44 million, the Philippines is considered as the seventh most populous country in Asia and the sixteenth in the whole world. The Philippines' population growth rate of 3.10 percent in 1970 has been reduced to 2.5 percent. The decrease has been dramatic, but it is still the highest in the Association of Southeast Asian Nations region. In fact, in Asia alone the average growth rate is 1.9 percent, while the increase in the world's population is even lower—1.7 percent. China, with about a billion people (one-fourth of the earth's population), only grows at a rate of 1.6 percent. Population distribution in the Philippines is uneven, with an average people-to-land ratio of 140 persons per square kilometer.

Section 52 of the Philippine Environment Code (P.D. No. 1152) provides that in the assessment of development projects, the NEPC shall take into consideration their effect on population with a view of achieving a rational and orderly balance between man and his environment.

III. Philippine Settlement Patterns

Existing settlement patterns show that 67.6 percent of the population of the Philippines (approximately 30.0 million) lives in urban areas, while the remaining 32.4 percent (approximately 14.4 million) lives in the rural areas. At present there are 13 regional and metropolitan centers to service the regions, 27 major urban centers, 439 minor urban centers and 1043 satellite municipalities, as shown in Table 1.

Land, being an integral element in shaping the spatial dimension of any settlement, requires proper allocation and utilization with the end of conserving and protecting the public domain for future use. But with the increasing conversion of the agricultural lands for urban purposes, it is feared that the land problem of the Philippines might turn into a crisis, since the size of agricultural lands does not grow in proportion to the population. Hence the need for a coherent program which recognizes the ecological relationship of population, resources

Table 1. Distribution of Settlements by Region, Philippines

Region	Metro Center	Regional Center	Major Urban Center	Minor Urban Center	Satellite Municipalities
I	—	1	3	37	134
II	—	1	—	19	93
III	—	1	5	59	56
IV	1	—	—	—	—
IV-A	—	—	6	64	146
V	—	1	1	49	63
VI	—	1	7	49	73
VII	1	—	—	32	90
VIII	—	1	2	25	111
IX-A	—	1	—	5	26
IX-B	—	1	—	19	37
X	—	1	1	18	99
XI	—	1	1	38	41
XII	—	1	1	25	74
Total	2	11	27	439	1,043

Source: National Multi-Year Human Settlements Plan: 1978-2000

and space to ensure the proper conservation, utilization and management of the country's land resources. There should be an organized and systematic distribution in space of activities in order to maximize benefits and minimize the effects of unplanned growth.

IV. Coastal Zone

Coastal zone management is an increasingly important aspect of Philippine environmental management. The coastal zone has played a formative role in the country's traditional way of life, as well as in its economic development. Traditionally, its 18,417 kilometers of coastline and 266,608 square kilometers of marine coastal waters have provided: (1) a rich source of fish and other aquatic products, (2) a primary mode of transportation, (3) a major area of human settlement, (4) breeding grounds and habitat for Philippine wildlife and (5) a predominant feature of the country's natural beauty.

Rapid growth in population and economic activity over the last decade has intensified the use of coastal areas for such purposes as removal of wastes, reclamation activities, mining, shipping, industrial location, aquaculture/mariculture and recreation. In the planning and management of the coastal zone, the mutual impacts of such activities, as well as their impacts on the natural ecosystem, are being assessed.

Continued and optimal use of coastal resources for economically related activities requires knowledge about and maintenance of the natural processes upon which many long term uses depend. The fishery, for example, depends upon the good ecological condition of fish habitats (e.g., clean water, shelter, nutrients). One important objective of coastal zone management, therefore, is the conservation of essential life-support systems. Two such ecosystems of major concern in the Philippines are the mangrove swamps and the coral reef areas.

On the whole, proper management of the coastal zone calls for the formulation and enforcement of policies and regulations to optimize its utility while placing minimum stress on the natural environment.

V. Coastal Development: Population and Migration

With a rational approach to land use management, the development of the coastal zone and the maintenance of its environmental quality along with the preservation of unique and essential ecosystems, are compatible ends. Coastal zone policy may utilize such schemes as zoning and controlled growth in the distribution of the variety of coastal services in an efficient and environmentally sound way. Some developmental processes requiring the immediate attention of planners include: population patterns, industrial location and coastal mining.

The Philippines' archipelagic configuration of 7100 islands and 18,417-kilometer coastline make the coastal zone an integral part of the environment for the majority of Filipinos. About four-fifths of the country's provinces border on the sea. Of the 1,525 municipalities covered in the 1975 census, nearly two-thirds are coastal. The portion of the population residing in these coastal municipalities, including the Metropolitan Manila area, has been stable at approximately 65 percent for the three census years 1960, 1970 and 1975.

The desirability of coastal locations for the development of human settlements and industry subjects these areas to relatively intensive land use. Most of the country's densely populated areas are located on the coast. Seventeen of the twenty-five cities having populations of more than 100,000 in 1975 are situated on the coast. Furthermore, all of the ten largest cities, including the industrial/urban centers of Manila, Cebu, Davao and Iloilo, are coastal. The aggregate population of these ten cities alone was 4,872,352 or approximately 11 percent of the total population in 1975.

Industries are attracted to coastal locations for a variety of reasons, proximity to population centers, resources and marine transportation among them. Commonly, the costs of the environmental services supplied to industry by the coastal environment, such as water for cooling or effluent transport, are externalized. The resulting pollution of coastal locations affects fishery and aquatic organisms and the aesthetic values of beaches and bays.

VI. Endangered Coastal Resources

In 1979, adoption of the 200-mile Exclusive Economic Zone (EEZ) extended the Philippine maritime jurisdiction over a half million square kilometers of territorial waters—added to the original 1,666,300 square kilometers. Because of the nutrient cycling of mangrove and reef ecosystems, coastal waters have served as a very productive environment for aquatic life—with fifty-two fishing grounds identified.

The coastal areas are a veritable lifebelt where aquatic and terrestrial resource systems interface. Thus, in the Philippines as in most other countries, coastal zones have been natural sites for human settlements, industries and commerce, and, of course, leisure and recreation. By and large, however, these human activities have created stress points on the coastal zone ecosystem of the Philippines.

A case in point involves the mangrove forests which constitute one of the most fertile and biologically important aspects of the Philippine coastal zone ecosystem. The mangroves are not only breeding grounds and sanctuaries for many forms of aquatic life; they are also traditional sources of fuel wood. Many mangroves, however, have been converted into fishponds, while some have been reclaimed from the sea for use as mine tailings disposal areas, as well as for general site development. The National Environmental Protection Council points out that the mangrove situation in the country has become a source of worry. For one thing, according to the NEPC, only 146,143 hectares of mangrove forests have been left as a consequence of various exploitation activities.

Another cause for alarm are the country's coral reefs. These resources, which consist of 400 to 500 species, contribute as much as 15 percent to the country's total fishery output. Coral reefs are very sensitive to adverse environmental changes. When they are harmed, it takes decades for them to completely recover their beauty and utility. The NEPC has reported that because of siltation, pollution, destructive fishing methods and unregulated activities of coral collectors, only five percent of the country's coral reefs can be considered in excellent condition.

Fishing in Philippine coastal waters remains extensive. More than 60 percent of the present total fish catch comes from these waters. Happily, in general, the coastal water situation poses no alarming ecological problem as yet, although certain coastal water areas in the country are reportedly overfished.

Also included in the coastal zone ecosystem are the lakes, gulfs and bays where, aside from fish, molluscs and crustaceans thrive. It is reported that, except for Laguna de Bay in Luzon, Philippine lakes, reservoirs and other inland waters are still relatively untapped, and most of the gulfs and bays, except Manila Bay, are not yet endangered by human activities. The ecological future of these inland waters will depend, however, on the development and application of proper aquaculture technology.

A coastal zone management program is being implemented by the Government through an inter-agency committee, the Coastal Zone Management Committee. The program will hammer out a master plan for optimum coastal zone utilization without disturbing the desired harmony between man and his environment.

The Philippines and other ASEAN countries have been urged by American environmental protection experts to adopt strategies that would lessen pollution in the coastal seas, rivers and their tributaries and industrial areas. They have suggested that garbage and other wastes of the cities' populations not be thrown into the sea but dumped in reclaimed areas or lowlands where there are no houses. The American experts also suggested that all industrial firms, including mining firms in the provinces, should be required to install antipollution devices, and that city residents and the crews of ships be oriented regarding the adverse effect of water pollution on human and marine life.

VII. Conclusions: Man's Right to a Healthy Environment

One of the most remarkable achievements of the campaigns conducted by the so-called antitechnologists is that the opportunity to live in a good, wholesome environment has come to be regarded as one of man's "inalienable rights," alongside the rights to freedom, to education and to medical care. A good environment, furthermore, means conditions that are favorable to the maintenance not only of physical health, but also of certain emotional and aesthetic qualities of surroundings.

As President Ferdinand E. Marcos of the Philippines said: "Man today demands new rights: the right to clean air, the right to clean water, the right to uncluttered land, the right to a basic amount of food and food that is free from toxic substances and pollutants. Man demands that technology regenerate his depleted natural resources and dispose of wastes that constitute hazards to all. He also demands that high-pollutive products and industries be curbed, that the Dr. Strangeloves of the world, like poverty and over-population, be placed under control" (NEPC 1977a).

Such changes of attitude will certainly lead to the downgrading of certain technologies and resources and will foster the development of others that are of little significance today. Belching smokestacks, which were regarded as a sign of prosperity during the first phase of the Industrial Revolution, are now seen as evidence of poor technological management and social irresponsibility.

Except for a few remaining optimists, most people today are in agreement that the environment is in fact deteriorating. Whether it is industrial pollution, presence of toxic chemicals, occurrence of oil spills or resource depletion, environmental problems are constantly in the news. What is more alarming is that the frequency with which these problems are occurring and being reported is rising every day.

It is only natural, therefore, that a greater number of people all over the world want to learn about what is happening and perhaps do something about it. After all, skepticism regarding the existence of a problem, especially if it is based on ignorance, may very well force them into a cynicism against their will. As in many real-life situations, the old Chinese proverb that "a calamity is a time of great opportunity" is perhaps also applicable. In order to realize and appreciate the opportunity, however, people must first understand what the calamity is all about.

Legislation and international forums such as this Third AACEP Conference would be most appropriate, and in time man can make peace with Nature.

References

Bulletin Today. 6 May 1982; 8 June 1982.

National Environmental Protection Council. 1977a. *Philippine environmental management in the seventies*. Speeches delivered during the National Conference on Environmental Management, 6–7 June 1977.

National Environment Protection Council. 1977b. *Philippine Environmental Quality*. First Annual Report.

National Environmental Protection Council. 1978. *Philippine Environment*.

National Environmental Protection Council. 1981. *Philippine Environmental Laws.*

Philippine Panorama. 1 August 1982.

Assessment of Land-Based Sources of Pollution in the East Asian Seas
Preliminary Assessment Results and the Perspective for Full Assessment Exercise

Masahisa Nakamura

The preliminary assessment of land-based sources of pollution in East Asian Seas was undertaken in the context of the United Nations Environment Programme (UNEP) Regional Seas Programme: Asia. The project was designed to provide an overview of the state of environmental pollution along the coastal fronts of the region, so that it might serve as a useful basis for the future in-depth assessment of the extent of coastal pollution. A methodology for rapid assessment of pollution from domestic and industrial sources, which was proposed by the World Health Organization (WHO) in 1980, was used as a convenient tool for conducting part of this assignment.

This paper was written with respect to the above project and with two objectives in mind: The first objective was to give a brief summary of the background of the project and the results of the assessment, presenting a rough but comprehensive picture of the state of the region with respect to coastal environmental pollution from major population centers. The attempt was the first of its kind in the stated study region. The second objective was to place the forthcoming full assessment exercise in the right perspective, particularly by elaborating on some of the critical observations and potentially useful considerations in the conduct of assessment and the use of the rapid assessment methodology.

I. Background

At the first meeting of the Governing Council of the United Nations Environment Programme, held exactly one year after the UN Conference on the Human Environment in Stockholm in 1972 and six months after the inception of UNEP, a particular policy objective was set up "to detect and prevent serious threats to the health of the oceans through controlling both ocean-based and land-based sources of pollution ... ," and the Executive Director was asked to stimulate regional agreements for this purpose (UNEP 1973). In 1974, the Council singled out "regional activities" for the protection of the marine environment as an area of program concentration with specific reference to the Mediterranean. Subsequently, other regional seas, including the Caribbean, the South East Pacific, the South West Pacific, West Africa, the Red Sea and the Gulf of Aden, the areas participating in the Kuwait Action Plan and those in the East Asian seas have been included in operation or development.

The East Asian Seas Programme had its origin at the International Workshop on Marine Pollution in East Asian Waters, held in Penang in April 1976 under the sponsorship of UNEP. The workshop, attended by scientists from the region, identified priority issues and common needs, and individual projects were prepared for six sub-regions, namely, the Bay of Bengal, the Straits of Malacca, the Gulf of Thailand, the South China Sea, the Sea of Japan/Yellow Sea/East China Sea and the seas of the Eastern Archipelago.

In December 1978 at the meeting of environmental experts from the five member nations of the Association of South East Asian Nations (ASEAN)—Indonesia, Malaysia, Philippines, Singapore and Thailand —met to consider the ASEAN Subregional Environmental Programme in which the Regional Seas Programme, among others, was accorded the highest priority. After a series of consultative meetings between UNEP and ASEAN with the participation of experts from other UN agencies including the World Health Organization (WHO), the Inter-governmental Meeting on the Protection and Development of the Marine Environment and Coastal Areas of the East-Asian Region was convened by UNEP in Manila in April 1981. The meeting formally adopted the East Asian Seas Action Plan.

The Action Plan, the program details of which have now been finalized, is aimed at achieving:

(1) assessment of the state of the marine environment, including assessment of the effects of marine, coastal and other land-based activities on environmental quality, so as to assist the governments to cope properly with marine environmental problems;

(2) management of those marine and coastal development activities which may have an impact on environmental quality or on the protection and use of renewable marine resources on a sustainable basis; and

(3) development of suitable coordinating measures for the successful

implementation of the action plan, which include financial and institutional arrangements.

With the phased implementation of the Action Plan, the assessment of total pollution input to the coastal marine environment will be one of the major activities to be undertaken by the participating countries. In the course of preparing a draft action plan, WHO, a UN collaborating agency for the UNEP Regional Seas Programme, was requested to undertake a preliminary project through its Western Pacific Regional Centre for the Promotion of Environmental Planning and Applied Studies (PEPAS) to assess the overall magnitude of the pollution load in the ASEAN region, which is generated from domestic and industrial sources and has potential for being discharged into the coastal marine environment. The principal objectives of the project were:

(1) to assess, on a preliminary basis, the regional pollution load distribution profile; and

(2) to gain insight into the ways in which the full assessment exercise could be carried out most successfully.

The project produced a comprehensive report entitled "Preliminary Assessment of Land-Based Sources of Pollution in East Asian Seas" (WHO 1981). A summary presentation of the findings in the report with respect to the above two objectives resulted in this paper.

II. Preliminary Assessment Exercise and Results

1. General Scope of Work

In the Mediterranean Action Plan, assessment of the total pollution input to the Mediterranean Sea was identified as a major component of the project. Through the collaboration of six UN agencies, wide coverage of various types of pollution sources was assured and a broad-based account of the total pollution load made possible (Helmer 1977). The East Asian Seas Action Plan, although different in scale and scope from the Mediterranean Action Plan, will also include the assessment of land-based sources of pollution as a major project.

The full assessment exercise, if undertaken in a manner similar to the Mediterranean experience, would involve the following tasks:

(1) preparation of an inventory of all major sources of pollutants in coastal areas;

(2) assessment of the nature and quantity of pollutants entering the marine environment from such sources;

(3) assessment of the nature and quantity of pollutants carried into the marine environment by major rivers; and

(4) review of present waste disposal and management practices.

When establishing the pollution sources inventory, a sectorial approach could be used, as in the case of the Mediterranean project, which includes the following broad categories of pollution sources: (1) domestic sewage; (2) industrial wastes; (3) agricultural run-off; (4) river discharges; and (5) radioactive discharges.

Based upon this inventory an assessment of waste loads for each source category can be made which allows for an evaluation of its contribution to the total pollution load of the marine environment. Thus, a comprehensive account of pollution by quality, quantity and geographical distribution becomes possible.

The preliminary assessment conducted by WHO, as outlined in the previous section, was designed to cover, out of the four items listed above, only (1) domestic sewage and (2) industrial waste. Although it would be difficult to determine the exact magnitude of impact on the marine environment, airborne pollutants are also included as parts of the industrial pollution load.

2. Approach

The assessment exercise was undertaken by a team of two engineers for a total duration of approximately twelve weeks. Except for Singapore, one or both of the team members spent on the average three weeks in each of the four countries visited, in order:

(1) to identify and review the documents containing information on past pollution load assessment results; and

(2) to estimate, when reliable information is lacking, the magnitude of domestic and industrial pollution loads generated using the data obtained from appropriate sources using the rapid assessment methodology, the outline of which will be described below.

As for Singapore, a summary of information provided by the government was translated into a form consistent with that used for the other countries.

3. A Methodology for Rapid Assessment of Sources of Pollution

During the course of the work on the Mediterranean Regional Seas Action Plan, it became necessary to employ a systematic methodology to assess water and air pollution loadings generated from sources located along the coastal front, since it was an unprecedented task to compile a waste source inventory over a large geographical area. A by-product of this exercise was the compilation of a comprehensive set of pollution load factors per production unit for each of the industrial classifications. These pollution load factors, when multiplied by the annual production (in appropriate units), were determined, based on existing literature, to produce an estimate of the quantity of waste water, BOD_5 (five-day Biological Oxygen Demand), COD (Chemical Oxygen Demand), suspended solids and so forth. This comprehensive set of pollution load factors was also used, when necessary and appropriate, for this East Asian Seas preliminary assessment exercise.

Details of the assessment procedure are presented in the document entitled "Rapid Assessment of Sources of Air, Water and Land Pollution" (WHO 1982). As stated in the document, preliminary assessment of pollution loads through the use of discharge or emission factors is not a new concept. It has long been used in many developed countries where serious attempts had to be made to control environmental pollution. What is new, however, is the streamlining of the inventory procedure, as stated in the document, which enables the user to produce relatively reliable results in a very short time.

The procedure involves, in essence, two distinct tasks: data collection and computation of waste loads. The data collection task consists of several steps which include: (a) getting an overall picture of the study area, waste generating activities, their magnitudes and locations, geographical boundaries and so forth; (b) identifying proper sources of information; (c) actual visits to the sources of information; and (d) cross-checking of data collected from various sources.

The computation task consists of several steps which include: (a) assignment of unit pollution load factors to waste generating activities; (b) summarizing calculation results according to pollution load categories; and (c) establishment of pollution parameter profiles showing the contribution of the major sources. Some preliminary assessment of major environmental impacts and of the adequacy of pollution control activities may be undertaken in connection with the computation task. However, a rapid assessment exercise generally falls short of determining the need for specific remedial actions to be pursued. A detailed analysis of environmental impacts is required for such a purpose.

In carrying out these two tasks, the analyst must have a thorough understanding of the processes through which various wastes are generated and pollutant loads emitted or discharged. He must also have knowledge of the general conditions of the region under study, including socioeconomic, geophysical and climatological conditions.

4. Assessment Results

In estimating water and air pollution loads generated from coastal population and industrial activity centers in the East Asian region, the rapid assessment method outlined was applied whenever the situation warranted. That is, there were cases where more reliable past survey results were already available and there was no sense in making use of the method; or where no industrial production data were immediately available and it was not possible to make use of the method even if it would have been desirable to do so, in view of the dearth of information on the magnitude of pollution. In the latter case, some intelligent guesses had to be made on the magnitude of pollution load generated.

The assessment results are presented for water pollution, using only BOD_5; and for air pollution, the straight sum of particulates, SO_x and NO_x (sulphur oxides and nitrogen oxides) and so forth, as a measure of total pollution load. Although, as mentioned in the previous section, the rapid assessment method employed could provide other water pollution loads than BOD_5, it was not possible to present the assessment results in terms of other indicators than BOD_5 for the entire region, since BOD_5 was the only common indicator of pollution load assessment between that based on past surveys and that based on the rapid assessment methodology employed in the absence of previous studies. The same reason applies for the failure to employ COD, the most commonly accepted indicator of organic pollution in the marine environment.

Presented below is a brief account of the state of the region with respect to the amount of land-based pollution loads originating from major population centers located along the coastal fronts in each of the five countries for which the assessment was conducted.

5. Overview

a. Indonesia

The city of Jakarta and the coastal area of the Province of East Java in the vicinity of Surabaya were selected for the preliminary assessment exercise. The assessment of the liquid pollution loads in Jakarta was based mostly on previous survey results. The assessment of air pollution loads, both in Jakarta and the Surabaya region, and the liquid pollution loads in the Surabaya region, were based on the rapid assessment methodology.

The liquid pollutant discharges from Jakarta are estimated to be

43,200 tons BOD_5 per year, while the airborne pollutant load is estimated to be 872,800 tons per year. In terms of BOD_5 generated, the contribution from domestic sources (74 percent) significantly exceeds that from industrial sources (26 percent). Also, significant levels of concentration of heavy metals are reported to have been identified in some regions of Jakarta Bay.

In the Surabaya region the liquid pollutant load is estimated to be 129,700 tons BOD_5 per year, of which 58 percent is of domestic origin and 42 percent of industrial origin, while the air-borne pollutant load is 753,400 tons per year.

Food and beverage industries, textile mills and paper mills are the major sources of industrial waterborne pollutants. The airborne pollutant load arises mainly from industrial emission sources and transportation.

b. Malaysia

The assessment of air and water pollution loads from industrial sources other than rubber and palm oil mill operations depended heavily on the use of the rapid assessment method. For the four sectors of Peninsular Malaysia and East Malaysia, the estimated liquid and airborne pollutant loads are presented in Table 1. In terms of BOD_5 generated along the coastal zones, the preliminary assessment results indicate that the contribution from domestic sources is approximately twice that from industrial and agricultural sources. The recent stringent enforcement of industrial pollution control regulations, however, is said to have probably reversed the proportion of pollution load contributions from the two source types. Major industrial and agricultural pollution sources include pig farming, food and beverage industries and rubber and palm oil processing mills. The airborne pollutant load arises mainly from power stations and transportation.

As expected, in terms of the amount of waste load per unit coastal front length, the larger part of the pollution load is in the western and southern coastal regions of Peninsular Malaysia where most of the population and industrial activity centers are situated.

c. Philippines

Metropolitan Manila was the only region for which the assessment was conducted. The water pollution load assessment was based on the information provided in the Metro Manila Sewerage Master Plan already completed prior to this exercise. The rapid assessment method was also used, however, to cross-check the figures presented in the Master Plan. It was estimated that the liquid pollutant load from the

Table 1.   Liquid and Airborne Pollutant Loads in Malaysia

	Liquid pollutant load in 10^3 tons BOD_5/year	Airborne pollutant load in 10^3 tons/yr
Island of Penang	9.5	30.6
Peninsular Malaysia		
West Coast	133.8	1091.6
South Coast	10.7	78.3
East Coast	25.0	65.5
East Malaysia	30.7	90.0
Totals	209.7	1356.0

Source: WHO/PEPAS and UNEP Regional Seas Programme Activity Centre 1981.

Metro Manila area amounts to about 130,000 tons BOD_5 per year, of which approximately 75 percent is estimated to be of domestic origin. Food and beverage industries, textile mills and paper mills are the major sources of industrial liquidborne pollutants.

The assessment of air pollution loads was based solely on the rapid assessment method which had been independently carried out just before this assessment exercise. The total airborne pollutant load from fuel burning sources is estimated to be 447,000 tons per year. Apart from mobile sources, the major sources of air pollution are the four power stations.

d. Singapore

Some 400,000 m³ of domestic wastewater and 30,000 m³ of industrial wastewater (mostly organic) are discharged daily. Eighty percent of domestic wastewater is discharged from sewered areas after treatment.

The main sources of water pollution comprise domestic, industrial and farm waste. The annual water pollution load is estimated at 3,800 tons BOD_5. It is not clear, without more detailed information, whether this figure correctly reflects the order of magnitude of the pollution load generated and discharged to the marine envionment surrounding Singapore.

e. Thailand

The sources of pollution that may have a significant bearing on the coastal marine pollution in Thailand are from metropolitan Bangkok and the coastal area around the Upper Gulf in Thailand. In the Bangkok Metropolitan Authority area, the liquid pollutant load is estimated to amount to 83,000 tons BOD_5 per year, of which 93 percent is estimated to be of domestic origin. The low percentage of pollution load

Table 2. Water and Airborne Pollutant Loads from Major Coastal Agglomerations

Location	Water pollutants				Airborne pollutants from fuel burning sources						
	Total BOD$_5$ (10^3 tons/year)	Domestic (%)	Industrial (%)	Major polluting industries	Total (10^3 tons/year)	Power generation (%)	Industrial (%)	Domestic (%)	Transport (%)	Wood burning (%)	Petroleum refineries (%)
1. Manila	130.0	75	25	Food and beverage; textile; paper mills	447	30.0	8.6	negligible	61.4		
2. Jakarta	43.2	74	26	Food and beverage; textile; detergent; paper mills	545	11.7	10.9	6.2	72.2		
3. East Java	129.7	58	42	Food and beverage; textile	249	7.0	24.4	8.9	59.7		
4. Penang	9.5	64	36	Food and beverage; textile; pig farming	30.6	—	30.0	0.5	69.5		
Peninsular Malaysia 5. - West Coast	133.8	61	39	Palm oil; rubber; textile; food and beverage; pig farming	876.7	47.4	10.2	negligible	24.0	15.8	2.6
6. - South Coast	10.7	40	60	Palm oil; rubber; food and beverage; pig farming	76.9	30.6	5.9	negligible	51.8	11.6	
7. - East Coast	25.0	85	15	Palm oil; rubber; food and beverage; pig farming	65.5	—	35.1	0.5	52.8	11.6	
8. East Malaysia	30.7	66	34	Palm oil; rubber; food and beverage	65.0	7.0	34.0	0.5	53.2	5.3	
9. Bangkok[a]	83.0	93	7	Breweries; food manufacturing	304	11.6	31.2	0.4	56.8		
10. Coastal area around upper gulf, Thailand[b]	92.6	10	90	Tapioca starch; pulp and paper mills	250	65.6	14.1	0.1	20.2		

Notes: [a] The low percentage for industrial water pollution is because the majority of discharges from industrial premises are upstream of Bangkok Metropolitan Authority area and are therefore not included.
[b] The high percentage for industrial water pollution is due to the high industrial load from the East Coast.
[c] Based on 300 working days/year for industrial load and 365 days/year for domestic load.
Source: WHO/PEPAS and UNEP Regional Seas Programme Activity Centre 1981.

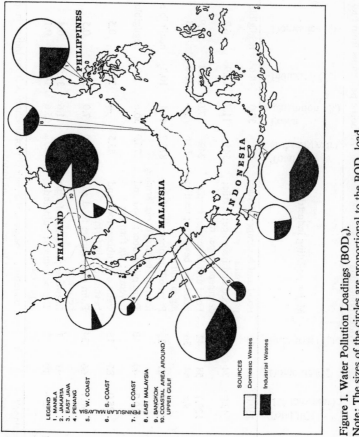

Figure 1. Water Pollution Loadings (BOD$_5$).
Note: The sizes of the circles are proportional to the BOD$_5$ load.
Source: WHO/PEPAS and UNEP Regional Seas Programme Activity Centre 1981.

contributed from industrial sources is due to the fact that the majority of discharges from industrial premises are upstream of the Bangkok Metropolitan Authority area and are therefore not included.

The airborne pollutant load is estimated to be 304,000 tons per year, of which more than half is attributed to transportation.

The liquid pollutant load from the 20-kilometer-wide coastal zone along the Upper Gulf is estimated at about 92,600 tons BOD_5 per year, while the airborne pollutant load is 265,000 tons per year. This area is highly industrialized, especially along the East Coast, and 90 percent of BOD_5 generated arises from industrial sources. A significant proportion of the airborne pollutant load in the region arises from power generation.

A tabulation of water and airborne pollutant loads from each of the major coastal agglomerations (excluding Singapore) is presented in Table 2. The airborne pollutant load given in the table refers only to that from fuel burning sources.

Figure 1 is a diagrammatic sketch indicating the proportional waste contribution to the pollution of coastal waters from the domestic and industrial sectors of the major coastal population centers.

5. Preliminary Conclusions Drawn from Assessment Results

The following are the main conclusions drawn from the results of the preliminary assessment:

(1) the Biochemical Oxygen Demand contribution from domestic sources was much greater than that from industrial sources in the majority of coastal population agglomerations surveyed;

(2) the amount of pollutant load discharged to watercourses and eventually reaching coastal marine waters is substantial. In particular, discharges of phosphates and nitrogens to the coastal marine waters ought to be quite significant since the wastes originate mainly from domestic sources as well as from such industries as food manufacturing and textile mills;

(3) published reports provide some indication of the amount of heavy metals being discharged into coastal marine waters. Although only a rough estimate can be made, the extent of heavy metal pollution along the coastal zones appears to be quite significant. There is every indication of the need for intensification of monitoring of hazardous pollutants at various locations in the standing bodies of marine water such as estuaries and bays next to large population agglomerations;

(4) the magnitude of air pollution in the major coastal population

centers is also quite severe, and it is reasonable to assume there would be measurable impacts of airborne pollutants on the coastal as well as high sea waters. The principal contribution to air pollution arises from transport and industrial sources;

(5) the relative magnitude of the estimated pollution loads obtained in this study did not always correspond in direct proportion to the population size of the cities studied. The discrepancies may be due to such factors as the types of industries in existence and their production scale, extent of provisions for waste treatment, distance from the sea coast, pattern of settlement and geographical characteristics, aside from the insufficiency of information obtained in the course of a preliminary survey.

III. Perspective for Full Assessment

As a component project of the East Asian Seas Action Plan, a much more comprehensive assessment of land-based sources of pollution is expected to be undertaken in future by the participating countries in collaboration with concerned UN agencies. The full assessment, which will involve a much longer project duration and much more manpower than those involved in the preliminary exercise, would produce much more comprehensive assessment results, which could eventually be translated into formulation of sensible environmental management policy and guidelines for protecting the marine environment from land-based sources of pollution.

The experience gained through this preliminary exercise, nonetheless, is quite valuable in that several critical observations were made regarding the conduct of the assessment and the methodology of rapid assessment procedure employed. Presented below are some of the major issues which may be usefully considered before the full assessment project is launched.

1. Definition of Land-based Sources of Pollution

The operational definition of land-based sources of pollution was given in the Mediterranean Action Plan as those from domestic and industrial sources, agricultural run-off, river discharges and radioactive discharges. The impact of air pollution transported directly through the atmosphere to the marine environment was considered separately. A similar operational definition may be employed in the case of the

East Asian Seas full assessment exercise. There are, however, a number of questions regarding the way the assessment may be carried out.

For example, there is the question of relating the waste generated on land and the waste discharged directly or indirectly to the marine environment. The countries and population agglomerations included in this assignment, with the exception of Singapore and Penang, have very limited, or completely lack, sanitary sewerage systems. Rivers and canals therefore receive the liquid wastes which may be discharged directly or indirectly, and the water in those water courses acts as the means of conveyance to the sea for disposal. It is extremely difficult to predict what waste load is received by the watercourse, how much of it actually reaches the sea or how much is destroyed through natural action in the soil and watercourse. This becomes further complicated when the question of differentiation between natural and man-made pollution arises.

Further, there is a need to clearly define a "major coastal population agglomeration" and the depth of the coastal fringe to be included in the project. These definitions are particularly important in the case of estuaries where the "major coastal population agglomeration" may be several kilometers up the river; for instance, Bangkok, where there are major sources of land-based pollution both immediately upstream and downstream of the city.

The operational definition of a coastal area has to be sufficiently flexible to make the assessment exercise practicable. At the same time, the assessment results based on such a definition ought to be sufficiently meaningful to permit the results to be easily translatable into the formulation of pollution control policy and guidelines.

2. Upgrading the Reliability of Assessment Results

In many countries, there has been little effort exerted to systematically upgrade the quality of information accumulated through various past exercises, and, therefore, consultants frequently encountered grossly conflicting data pertaining to the same subject. Further, little has been done to intercalibrate data obtained from different monitoring sites or to present data on the same subject using common units of measurement.

There is no point in carrying out an assessment which is rapid and yet grossly inaccurate. There has to be a reasonable balance. As much as possible the validity of information obtained must be ascertained through cross-checking of data from different sources so as to avoid gross misrepresentation of the actual situation, which is so likely to happen when there is a lack of reliable data.

In the absence of dependable sources of information a sample field survey may have to be carried out. Such a survey may be designed also to provide several clues to lead to the same information sought, the amount of pollution load. For example, in the case of pollution from industries the number of employees, water consumption, production output, floor space occupied and so forth, besides actual measurement of pollution loads, may be used along with the unit pollution load data obtained from other sources to extrapolate the pollution loads generated from the entire region under study.

All these activities require additional financial and manpower resources. It is quite doubtful that in any of the participating countries sufficient resources would be made available simply for this assessment exercise. However, if resources are to be mobilized for the development of a comprehensive source inventory system within each country, which could be used not only for this particular activity but for a number of other environmental assessment and management activities, these additional expenses could be fully justifiable.

3. Access to Information Sources

In many instances the data necessary for making a comprehensive assessment of land-based sources of pollution were either nonexistent or scattered among national, provincial and local government agencies dealing with environmental affairs, industrial activities, public works management, public health, agriculture and forestry, energy and so forth, as well as in governmental research institutions or research institutions affiliated with universities dealing with similar subjects. Even in the latter case, the identification of proper sources of information was quite time-consuming. Further, quite frequently either the consultants were denied access to data sources or the time it took for them to obtain access to data sources was prohibitively long.

Unlike the case where many of the countries participated in the Mediterranean Action Plan, the data base necessary for environmental assessment has not yet been fully established in most of the countries participating in the East Asian Seas Action Plan, and frequently basic reference information on regional as well as national statistics is either hard to obtain or is not sufficiently detailed to be useful for the assessment of pollution loads discharged. As environmental assessment activities require constant updating of pertinent information, the systematic generation, collection and compilation of environmental data is essential. In this respect again, the establishment in each country of a centralized system dealing with pollution source inventory appears to be a prerequisite to a meaningful assessment exercise. At least the assessment project could be regarded as a stepping stone for the establishment of such a system.

4. Rapid Pollution Load Assessment Methodology

The rapid assessment method of sources of pollution described earlier proved to be quite useful in getting a first estimate of the magnitude and quantity of pollution, particularly when there was no prior attempt to determine the magnitude of waste load generated or discharged to the surrounding environment. In the course of the preliminary assessment exercise, however, several important observations were made with regard to the proposed assessment worksheet as well as to the entire process of pollution load assessment. The following are some of the major critical observations with specific respect to the methodology.

a. Estimation of Domestic Waste Loads

Estimation of domestic waste loads, simple as it may seem, was generally quite difficult in the absence of detailed information on the condition of sanitary facilities available to households. In many instances estimates had to be made very crudely with little supporting data, particularly in the areas where no effort had yet been made for a sewerage master plan. Even more difficult was the estimation of the portion of waste load discharged through onsite treatment systems that reached a particular receiving body of water. A more refined and systematic approach may have to be devised and applied uniformly through the region to make the assessment a little more consistent with the prevailing situation.

In order to assess the magnitude of pollution loads discharged or emitted from various sources located over a vast area, a rapid assessment procedure such as the one proposed is invaluable. However, only one set of emission factors, discharge volume/production tonnage, concentrations of pollutants and so forth, are provided in the worksheet and the same figure had to be used even in cases where the prevailing operational practices appeared to be much different from one location to another or from one country to another. Further, since most basic data used in this preliminary survey were those obtained from literature applicable to countries at a more developed stage, they are not likely to reflect the situations prevailing in this region.

b. Estimation of Industrial Waste Loads

The difficulty of assessing unit pollution loads from industries can be attributed to the diversity of industries, of industrial processes and of waste treatment processes installed. While the rapid assessment worksheets are designed to help estimate waste loads based on production figures from various industrial categories, which are relatively easier to obtain, the errors attributable to differences in industrial production and waste treatment processes, and in their operational procedures, can be considered quite substantial.

It is most desirable that the participating countries review thoroughly the current set of pollution load factors, and, upon examination of additional information, refine factors at least of selected major industries contributing most to pollution of the marine environment.

c. Assessment of Special Pollutants

The assessment of the amount of heavy metals, nutrients and other trace organic and inorganic pollutants was not carried out using the rapid assessment worksheet in the preliminary exercise. Among other practical reasons, it was felt that without the availability of information on the actual measurements of pollutants at specific locations, the amount of the discharged pollutants estimated using the worksheet may be quite misleading, since the behavior of trace pollutants is known generally to be quite location-specific. For example, the concentration profiles of heavy metals are affected by a large number of factors, including the physiochemical and biological state of the area concerned. Only carefully staged monitoring programs at strategic locations can reveal the potential for less obvious but serious long-term environmental impact along the coastal zones as well as in the coastal marine waters.

In the forthcoming full assessment exercise as well, care has to be taken in relating the magnitude of pollution potential due to these special pollutants and their concentration profile in the environment. A more refined analytical framework needs to be developed for each of these special pollutants should any meaningful assessment of pollution potential from these special pollutants be established in the course of the full assessment exercise.

d. Assessment of Pollution from Small Industries

The preliminary assessment exercise placed heavy emphasis on large industrial establishments, since the information available in most regulatory agencies was for large industrial operations, and since small to marginal establishments were considered to contribute a relatively minor portion of the total amount of pollutants generated, although they were found generally to outnumber larger ones. On the other hand, while in many cases a small number of large industrial operations is responsible for the bulk of pollutants discharged to the environment, they are generally easier to control. Further, many of the small to marginal establishments have the tendency to become subsidiaries of larger establishments and deal with production of goods that involve heavily toxic or hazardous substances, discharging such pollutants to the receiving bodies. In view of the fact that the assessment of pollution must eventually lead to its effective management, the assessment of pollution from smaller industrial operations should not be overlooked in the full assessment exercise.

IV. Summary and Conclusion

The preliminary assessment of land-based sources of pollution in East Asian Seas had been undertaken in 1980 in anticipation of the implementation of the full assessment project within the context of the Action Plan for the UNEP East Asian Regional Seas Programme which was adopted in April 1981 by the ASEAN.

Through this preliminary exercise, it was possible to make a rough but comprehensive estimate of the magnitude of pollution load being discharged and adversely affecting the marine environment. However, since the project was preliminary in nature, with its sole purpose being to get an overview, no conclusive statements could be made with respect to the precise amounts of specific pollutants and their specific impacts on the coastal marine environment. Further, with the geographical as well as socioeconomic situations of one population agglomeration differing considerably from that of another and with little research information available in any of the subject countries, it was not possible to assess scientifically how much of the waste load generated within each population agglomeration actually reaches and makes adverse impacts on the coastal marine environment.

Also, in the course of carrying out the preliminary assessment a number of important observations was made both with respect to the conduct of the survey and to the use of the rapid assessment methodology. Lack of information, inadequacy of systems of information collection and compilation and other difficulties experienced in the course of the preliminary assessment suggest that for the execution of a successful assessment exercise it is essential for each country to develop a sound pollution source inventory system.

The rapid method of pollution load assessment proposed by WHO, in which a set of predetermined unit pollution load figures are to be used against industrial production figures, was found to be quite useful in cases where there is no other reliable source of information. However, it was possible to make a number of critical observations regarding the use of the method which, if appropriately refined, might be quite useful for the full assessment exercise as well.

Note

This paper, prepared for a UNEP-sponsored seminar on Regional Marine Pollution and Coastal Development Problems in Goa, India, 18–22 October 1982, is a later version of that presented at the Third Asian-American Conference on Environmental Protection, Universiti Pertanian Malaysia, 23–25 August 1982.

References

Division of Environment, Ministry of Science, Technology and Environment. 1980. The Regional Seas Programme for the East Asian Seas—ASEAN Gives Go-Ahead. *Sekitar* 2:2/3, June/September 1980. KDNO521/80.

Helmer, R. 1977. Pollutants from land-based sources in the Mediterranean. *Ambio* 6(6):312–316.

Helmer, R. 1980. The Mediterranean Action Plan—A Review of Its Research Aspects. *Progress in Water Technology* 12(1):3–15.

Nakamura, M., E. A. Drew and A. Rivera-Cordero. Some considerations in the use of rapid pollution load assessment methodology—from the experience in assessing pollution loads in the coastal zones of East Asian seas. Paper presented at the WHO South East Asia Region Inter-Country Workshop on Rapid Techniques for Environmental Assessment in Developing Countries, Asian Institute of Technology, Bangkok, Thailand, 1–5 February 1982.

Thacher, P. 1977. The Mediterranean Action Plan. *Ambio* 6(6):308–312.

UNEP. 1973. Report of the Governing Council, First Session, Geneva, 12–22 June 1973. General Assembly Official Records, 28th Session, Supplement 25 (A/9025), 37.

UNESCO. 1980. *River Input to South East Asian Seas, Final Report*, Project No. FP/0503–79–08 (2099). Paris: UNESCO.

World Health Organization. 1982. *Rapid Assessment of Sources of Air, Water and Land Pollution*, Offset Publication No. 62. WHO: Geneva.

WHO/PEPAS and UNEP Regional Seas Programme Activity Centre. 1981. *Preliminary Assessment of Land-Based Sources of Pollution in East Asian Seas, Full Report.*

Development of Coastal Zones and Its Impact on the Environment
The Singapore Experience

Henry Ong Wah Kim and Ng Cheng Siong

Traditionally, the coastal zone has served to support fishing, ports, naval bases and some leisure activities. After World War II, more demands were made on this natural resource. New pressures from education, scientific research and recreation had developed. Industries, too, required sites for power stations, more port facilities and refinery centers. Development of various kinds depleted more of this scarce coastal resource.

These pressures are increasing every year in the Association of South East Asian (ASEAN) countries. Development of the coastal zones in these countries as well as in the more developed countries has been taking place at a much greater pace than development inland. The effects of all these developments on the ecology are fairly obvious. Some habitats for plants and animals are eliminated; geographical features are marred by excavation and reclamation and the beaches of many rivers are besmirched with sewage and industrial pollutants.

The problem obviously is how to harmonize increasing and competing claims on the use of this scarce and finite coastal resource. Usually, measures of planning and control are adopted to encourage maximum utilization and minimum environmental pollution. To do this effectively, not only the planners but also the public must be made aware of the delicate position and balance on coastal zone planning, management and development, especially in the context of Singapore.

I. Development and Environmental Planning in Singapore

Historically, the early development of Singapore was focussed on trade. This was followed by rehousing of the population as part of the overall urbanization program, and recently by economic restructuring.

Part of the strategy is to develop the coastal zone to provide for extra catchment areas, industrial sites, airports and recreational activities. All these have been planned and implemented in a short space of time. To many of us, this miracle in transformation must be attributed to the foresight of the government of Singapore and the diligence of the people to make all this possible.

The need for Singapore, lacking in resources such as land, energy and water, to plan, to safeguard and to manage its coastal zone becomes essential. Since it is a small island (in 1980 its total land area was 617.8 km²), any sizable development project will necessarily involve the coast. Therefore, any discussion on coastal development will cover the overall development of the island republic.

The overall physical environmental development in Singapore was first considered in 1955. The plan covering the period 1958–1972 was approved in 1958. The central policy was urban development. However, this master plan was both conservative and lacking in aspirations. So in 1967, with the assistance of the United Nations Development Programme (UNDP) another long-range physical plan was studied. Known as the Concept Plan, this was completed in 1971 and carried projections to 1992. The Concept Plan provided the guidelines on urban and environmental development in Singapore, bearing in mind the need to create an ideal and healthy environment for social, residential, commercial, industrial and recreational activities. Also included in this plan is the development of the coastal areas surrounding Singapore. In terms of the entire economic development, coastal development was given priority, since Singapore is a small island and an important port for this region.

During the 1956–1981 period, there was a strong correlation between land area, population and gross domestic product (GDP). The trend observed is that of increasing growth. Between 1971 and 1981, the land area was increased by 32 km² through reclamation. Although by international standards the increase may not be substantial, in Singapore this increase represents 5 percent of the total land area. In the same period, the population increased from 1.4 million people in 1956 to 2.4 million in 1981. This was achieved in spite of a drop in the natural birth rate from 3.7 percent in 1956 to 1.2 percent in 1981.

As for market prices, an increase in the gross domestic product was also observed. (For example, market prices rose from $2,347 million in 1961 to $27,280 million in 1981.) However, this trend was also realized in the other countries in the ASEAN group. But, unlike its neighbors, Singapore is much more exposed to the ever-changing economic conditions in the world. As Singapore is very much dependent on external trade, in time of economic depression or recession the effect of this adverse condition is more strongly felt in Singapore than in the other countries. To insulate itself against such effects, Singapore's economic restructuring from low to high technology will perhaps help, and in the years to come, make Singapore more viable and attractive to encourage foreign investors from Europe, America and Oceania. In turn this will mean better pay and perhaps more recreation for the people, all arising from steady economic growth. The people will then be enjoying rising affluence in the future.

With rising affluence the government, as well as the people of Singapore, is much concerned about the physical environment. Although Singapore's green and clean environment is symbolic, a positive effort for Singaporeans to make Singapore a more pleasant and enjoyable place to live in is imperative, not only for ourselves but also for posterity. The concern is for the physical, social and economic aspects of the environment.

As for the social environment, Singapore's limited land space, rapid urbanization and industrialization have made their mark on the populace. In fact, every possible effort is made to offset the effects due to overcrowding, living in high-rise buildings and some undesirable Western influences. In this respect the substantial drop in birth rate, as mentioned above, will help. Otherwise, more social problems are anticipated when the population exceeds 2.5 million.

Industrial development projects will contribute to economic growth. On the other hand, they may produce an unfavorable ecological impact. Therefore, the link between industrial development and pollution must be clearly understood. In considering development of the coast, environmental issues could be considered separately or be integrated into the overall planning. In the context of Singapore, coastal development comes first, before environmental consideration. The latter has been taking a back seat primarily due to the lack of strong public opinion on this matter. The Singaporean realizes that economic development means a better chance for survival for Singapore.

II. Coastal Development and Environmental Impact

In Singapore there are a number of development projects along the coast. Some have been completed; others are still in progress. The success of these projects is now history, and is well known around the world. These developments were mostly achieved through sea reclamation and have provided the land for an airport (Changi), a bridge (Sheares), commercial and industrial sites (Marina Centre and Jurong), a recreation park (East Coast Park) and an island (Sentosa). Other facilities include Sebarok for oil recovery, and Pulau Bukom and Pulau Ayer Chawan for oil refinining. As a result the coastline has been reduced to 194 km. Reclamation of the sea as well as the marshland has increased our land area allocated for parks and open space. Damming of five rivers has provided Singapore with two additional impounding reservoirs, the Kranji Reservoir and the Western Catchment Scheme. More water is impounded at Pulau Tekong, which is the largest of the numerous islands around Singapore.

Singapore has at least forty islands in the south and at least twelve in other areas. These small islands around Singapore have also been the objects of development. About nineteen islands have been reclaimed, mostly between 1975 and 1977. The most recent industrial development project is the construction of the petrochemical complex on Pulau Ayer Merbau.

A simple qualitative impact analysis indicates that in all these developments there are more positive impacts than negative impacts. Out of twelve projects, eight have negative impacts, while all of them have some positive impacts. As a whole, these developments are beneficial to Singapore, such as the Changi airport, Pulau Bukom for oil refining and Jurong for industry.

For example the airport which was built on reclaimed land will contribute positively toward the growing tourism trade, for example, to Sentosa Island, not only for Singapore but also for this region. Also, direct benefits accrue from the airport, such as the Changi area, and in the areas of business (such as Marine Centre) and industrial air transportation. This must be a positive impact. However, the airport will increase air and noise pollution around the adjacent areas. The extent of this negative impact is not yet understood and evaluated. Loss in the coastline when the bridge was built is more than compensated for by the improved communication between the east coast of Singapore and the central commercial district. This is again beneficial to Singapore. On the other hand a very slight increase in noise and pollution level, as a result of the increased traffic over the bridge in the vicinity, is bound to be inevitable. More impounding reservoirs, such as Kranji, Pulau Tekong and Western Catchment, obtained through damming of the rivers has provided more water to Singapore. This will contribute to better health for the people of Singapore, provide water for the industries, the animals and the plants. All in all, these coastal developments have more positive impacts on the overall environment of Singapore. Obviously, if this were not so, it would be impossible to convince both the planners as well as the government which provides all the development expenditure on all these projects.

From the economic point of view, a quantitative calculation based on cost-benefit analysis would be illuminating. The cost would include the total expenditure of the project as well as the indirect cost of environmental improvement in the surrounding areas. The variation of benefits to costs would reveal the impact of these projects. However, the cost of environmental improvement is often difficult to quantify. Besides, the social cost of environmental pollution is not included in the calculation.

Another approach to environmental impact evaluation would mean working on resource allocation and depletion. However, since land in Singapore is so scarce, there is a limit to physical growth and there is not much we could do about alternatives. If any one of the natural resources were depleted, coastal zone replacement of this would be impossible.

On the other hand, the impact on the environment could also be evaluated based on the actual cost of improvement in the environment or removal of the effects due to pollution. To the environmentalist, this may be more acceptable. But to the economist, this may be a waste of time and effort. The argument against such an approach may be due to the difficulty of putting a value on these items.

III. Conclusion

In the case of Singapore, coastal development seems to be compatible at present with the overall environmental development. As a result of the coastal development, the quality of the physical environment may have been altered slightly; but other efforts in making the environment more green, clean and healthy may have offset the adverse effects due to environmental pollution. Perhaps in the future, assessment of the effects of pollution on the environment will be undertaken. The study will help us in planning for the future. Included in this exercise must be the consideration of the social cost of environmental pollution as a direct result of the coastal development.

References

Department of Statistics. *1980 Yearbook of Statistics*, Singapore.

Appendix 1
Environmental Quality Act (Malaysia)
(An Act relating to the prevention, abatement, control of pollution and enhancement of the environment, and for purposes connected therewith)

Be it enacted by the Duli Yang Maha Mulia Seri Paduka Baginda Yang di-Pertuan Agong with the advice and consent of the Dewan Negara and Dewan Rakyat in Parliament assembled, and by the authority of the same, as follows:

Part I

Preliminary

1. (1) This Act may be cited as the Environmental Quality Act, 1974 and shall apply to the whole of Malaysia.

(2) This Act shall come into force on such date as the Minister may appoint by a notification in the *Gazette* and the Minister may appoint different dates for the coming into force of different provisions of this Act and may bring all or any provisions thereof into force either in the whole of Malaysia to which the notification applies or such area as may be specified in the notification.

2. In this Act, unless the context otherwise requires—

"beneficial use" means a use of the environment or any element or segment of the environment that is conducive to public health, welfare or safety and which requires protection from the effects of wastes, discharges, emissions and deposits;

"control equipment" includes—

(a) any apparatus for collecting wastes;

(b) any automatic device used for securing the more efficient operation of any equipment;

(c) any device to indicate or record pollution or to give warning of excessive pollution; and

(d) any other device used for the purpose of limiting pollution;

"Council" means the Environmental Quality Council established under section 4;

"Director General" means the Director General of Environmental Quality referred to in section 3;

"element" in relation to the environment means any of the principal constituent parts of the environment including water, atmosphere, soil, vegetation, climate, sound, odour, aesthetics, fish and wildlife;

"environment" means the physical factors of the surroundings of the human beings including land, water, atmosphere, climate, sound, odour, taste, the biological factors of animals and plants and the social factor of aesthetics;

"industrial plant" means any plant used for the generation of power or for any industrial use or for the operation of ships, dredges, locomotives, cranes or other machines;

"Minister" means the Minister charged with the responsibility for environment protection;

"mixture containing oil" means a mixture with such oil content as may be specified by the Minister or, if such oil content is not specified, a mixture with an oil content of one hundred parts or more in one million parts of the mixture;

"monitoring programme" means all actions taken and equipment used for the purpose of detecting or measuring quantitatively or qualitatively the presence, amount or level of any substance, characteristic or effect;

"occupier" means a person in occupation or control of premises, and in relation to premises different parts of which are occupied by different persons, means the respective persons in occupation or control of each part;

"oil" means—

(a) crude oil, diesel oil, fuel oil and lubricating oil; and

(b) any other description of oil which may be prescribed by the Minister;

"owner" in relation to any premises means—

(a) the registered proprietor of the premises;

(b) the lessee of a lease including a sub-lease of the premises, whether registered or not;

(c) the agent or trustee of any of the owners described in paragraphs (a) and (b) of this definition or where such owner as described in paragraphs (a) and (b) cannot be traced or has died, his legal personal representative;

(d) the person for the time being receiving the rent of the premises whether on his own account or as agent or trustee for any other person or as receiver or who would receive if such premises were let to a tenant;

and in relation to any ship means the person registered as the owner of the ship or in the absence of registration, the person owning the ship except that in the case of a ship owned by any country and operated by a company which in that country is registered as the ship's operator, "owner" shall include such country;

"pollutant" means any substance whether liquid, solid or gaseous which directly or indirectly—

(a) alters the quality of any segment or element of the receiving environment so as to affect any beneficial use adversely; or

(b) is hazardous or potentially hazardous to health;

and includes objectionable odours, radio-activity, noise, temperature change or physical, chemical or biological change to any segment or element of the environment;

"pollution" means any direct or indirect alteration of the physical, thermal, chemical, biological or radioactive properties of any part of the environment by discharging, emitting or depositing wastes so as to affect any beneficial use adversely, to cause a condition which is hazardous or potentially hazardous to public health, safety or welfare, or to animals, birds, wildlife, fish or aquatic life or to plants or to cause a contravention of any condition, limitation or restriction to which a licence under this Act is subject;

"practicable" means reasonably practicable having regard, among other things, to local conditions and circumstances and to the current state of technical knowledge and the term "practicable means" includes the provision and the efficient maintenance of plant and the proper use thereof and the supervision by or on behalf of the occupier of any process or operation;

"premises" includes messuages, buildings, lands and hereditaments of every tenure and any machinery, plant or vehicle used in connection with any trade carried on at any premises;

"prescribed" means prescribed by or under this Act or continued in operation by this Act;

"prescribed premises" means any premises prescribed by the Minister under section 18;

"segment" in relation to the environment means any portion or portions of the environment expressed in terms of volume, space, area, quantity, quality or time or any combination thereof;

"ship" includes every description of vessel or craft or floating structure;

"soil" includes earth, sand, rock, shales, minerals and vegetation in the soil;

"trade" means any trade, business or undertaking whether ordinarily carried on at fixed premises or at varying places which results in the discharge of wastes and includes any activity prescribed to be a trade, business or undertaking for the purposes of this Act;

"waste" includes any matter prescribed to be waste and any matter, whether liquid, solid, gaseous or radioactive, which is discharged, emitted or deposited in the environment in such volume, composition or manner as to cause an alteration of the environment.

Part II

Administration

3. (1) There shall be a Director General of Environmental Quality who shall be appointed by the Minister from amongst members of the public service and whose powers, duties and functions shall be—

(a) to administer this Act and any regulations and orders made thereunder;

(b) to be responsible for and to co-ordinate all activities relating to the discharge of wastes into the environment and for preventing or controlling pollution and protecting and enhancing the quality of the environment;

(c) to recommend to the Minister the environment protection policy and classifications for the protection of any portion of the environment or any segment of the environment with respect to the uses and values, whether tangible or intangible, to be protected, the quality to be maintained, the extent to which the discharge of wastes may be permitted without detriment to the quality of the environment, long range development uses and planning and any other factors relating to the protection and enhancement of the environment;

(d) to control by the issue of licences the volume, types, constitutents and effects of wastes, discharges, emissions, deposits or other sources of emission and substances which are of danger or a potential danger to the quality of the environment or any segment of the environment;

(e) to undertake surveys and investigations as to the causes, nature, extent of pollution and as to the methods of prevention of pollution and to assist and co-operate with other persons or bodies carrying out similar surveys or investigations;

(f) to conduct, promote and co-ordinate research in relation to any aspect of pollution or the prevention thereof and to develop criteria for the protection and enhancement of the environment;

(g) to recommend to the Minister standards and criteria for the protection of beneficial uses and the maintenance of the quality of the environment having regard to the ability of the environment to absorb waste without detriment to its quality and other characteristics;

(h) to co-opt any persons or bodies to form panels of expects whom he considers capable of assisting him in relation to special problems;

(i) to publish an annual report on environmental quality not later than 30th September of the following year and such other reports and information with respect to any aspect of environmental protection;

(j) to specify methods to be adopted in taking samples and making tests for the purposes of this Act;

(k) to undertake investigations and inspections to ensure compliance with this Act or the regulations made thereunder and to investigate complaints relating to breaches of this Act or the regulations made thereunder;

(l) to provide information and education to the public regarding the protection and enhancement of the environment;

(m) to establish and maintain liaison and co-operation with each of the State Authorities in Malaysia and with other countries with respect to environment protection, pollution control and waste management;

(n) to report to the Minister upon matters concerning the protection and enhancement of the environment and upon any amendments he thinks desirable to any law affecting pollution and environment and upon any matters referred to him by the Minister; and

(o) to promote, encourage, co-ordinate and carry out planning in environmental management, waste management and pollution control.

....

Part III

Licences
10. The Director General shall be the licencing authority.

11. (1) An application for a licence or for any renewal or transfer thereof shall be made to the Director General in such form as may be prescribed and shall unless the Director General allows payment by instalments be accompained by the prescribed fee.

(2) An applicant for a licence or for the renewal or transfer thereof shall furnish in writing or otherwise such information as the Director General may consider necessary and relevant to the application.

. . . .

16. The holder of a licence shall comply in every respect with the terms and conditions thereof.

17. (1) The Minister after consultation with the Council may prescribe the fees payable in respect of a licence, any transfer or renewal thereof.

. . . .

(3) Where upon inspection it is ascertained that the pollutants or class of pollutants discharged, emitted or deposited is different from or the quantity of wastes discharged, emitted or deposited is greater than, that declared by the occupier in his application for or renewal of licence, the Director General may recover such fees as would have been payable in respect of that pollutant or class of pollutant or extra quantity of discharge, emission or deposit.

(4) In calculating the fees payable under subsection (3), the occupier shall be deemed to have discharged, emitted or deposited that pollutant or class of pollutants or that quantity of wastes for a period of six months preceding the inspection or, if the application for or renewal of licence was made less than before six months the inspection for the period beginning from the application up to the inspection.

. . . .

Part IV

Prohibition and Control of Pollution
18. (1) The Minister after consultation with the Council may by order prescribe the premises (hereinafter referred to as prescribed premises) the occupation or use of which by any person shall, unless he is the holder of a licence issued in respect of those premises, be an offence under this Act.

. . . .

20. (1) Every application to carry out any work, building, erection or alteration specified in section 19 shall be submitted to the Director General and shall be accompanied by—

(a) the plans and specifications of the proposed work, building, erection or alteration together with details of the control equipment if any to be installed;

(b) a lay-out plan indicating the site of the proposed work, building, erection or alteration which will take place in relation to the surrounding areas;

(c) the details of the trade, industry or process proposed to be carried on in such premises;

(d) descriptions of waste constituents and characteristics; and

(e) such other information which the Director General may require;

and the applicant shall pay the prescribed fee.

(2) The Director General may grant such application either subject to conditions or unconditionally and may require the licensee to provide and bear the cost of the control equipment and of a satisfactory monitoring programme:

Provided that no application shall be granted unless the applicant has obtained planning approval from the competent planning authority.

21. The Minister, after consultation with the Council, may specify the acceptable conditions for the emission, discharge or deposit of wastes or the emission of noise into any area, segment or element of the environment and may set aside any area, segment or element of the environment within which the emission, discharge or deposit is prohibited or restricted.

22. (1) No person shall, unless licenced, emit or discharge any wastes into the atmosphere in contravention of the acceptable conditions specified under section 21.

. . . .

(3) Any person who contravenes subsection (1) shall be guilty of an offence and shall be liable to a fine not exceeding ten thousand dollars or to imprisonment for a period not exceeding two years or to both and to a further fine not exceeding one thousand dollars a day for every day that the offence is continued after notice by the Director General requiring him to cease the act specified therein has been served upon him.

23. (1) No person shall, unless licenced, emit or cause or permit to be emitted any noise greater in volume, intensity or quality in contravention of the acceptable conditions specified under section 21.

. . . .

24. (1) No person shall, unless licenced, pollute or cause or permit to be polluted any soil or surface of any land in contravention of the acceptable conditions specified under section 21.

. . . .

25. (1) No person shall, unless licenced, emit, discharge or deposit any wastes into any inland waters in contravention of the acceptable conditions specified under section 21.

(2) Without limiting the generality of subsection (1), a person shall be deemed to emit, discharge or deposit wastes into inland waters if—

- (a) he places any wastes in or on any waters or in a place where it may gain access to any waters;
- (b) he places any waste in a position where it falls, descends, drains, evaporates, is washed, is blown or percolates or is likely to fall, descend, drain, evaporate or be washed, be blown or percolated into any waters, or knowingly or through his negligence, whether directly or indirectly, causes or permits any wastes to be placed in such a position; or
- (c) he causes the temperature of the receiving waters to be raised or lowered by more than the prescribed limits.

. . . .

26. (1) No person shall discharge or spill any oil or mixture containing oil into any part of the sea outside the territorial waters of Malaysia if such discharge or spill will result in oil or mixture containing oil being carried, spread or washed into Malaysian waters.

. . . .

27. (1) No person shall discharge or spill any oil or mixture containing oil into Malaysian waters.

. . . .

28. Where any person is charged for any offence under section 26 or 27 it shall be a defence to prove that such discharge or spillage was—

- (a) for the purpose of securing the safety of the vessel;
- (b) for the purpose of saving human life;
- (c) the result of damage to the vessel and that all reasonable steps were taken to prevent, to stop or to reduce the spillage;
- (d) the result of a leakage, which was not due to want of care, and that all reasonable steps have been taken to stop or reduce the leakage; or
- (e) the result of an effluent produced by operation for the refining of oil, and that all reasonable steps had been taken to eliminate oil from the effluent and that it was not reasonably practicable to dispose of the effluent otherwise than by discharging or spilling it into the Malaysian waters.

. . . .

29. (1) No person shall, unless licensed, discharge wastes into the Malaysian waters.

. . . .

30. The Minister after consultation with the Council may by order published in the *Gazette*—

    (a) prohibit the use of any materials for any process, trade or industry;

    (b) prohibit whether by description or by brand name the use of any equipment or industrial plant,

within the areas specified in the order.

. . . .

Part V

Appeal and Appeal Board

35. (1) Any person who is aggrieved by—

    (a) a refusal to grant a licence or transfer of a licence;

    (b) the imposition of any condition, limitation or restriction on his licence;

    (c) the revocation, suspension or variation of his licence; or

    (d) the amount which he would be required to pay under section 47,

may within such time and in such manner as may be prescribed, appeal to the Appeal Board.

. . . .

36. (1) For the purpose of this Act there shall be appointed an Appeal Board consisting of three members, one of whom shall be the Chairman (hereafter in this section referred to as the Chairman).

. . . .

Part VI

Miscellaneous

37. (1) The Director General may by notice require the occupier of any premises to furnish to him within such period as may be specified in the notice such information relating to any equipment, control equipment or industrial plant found on such premises or as to any wastes discharged or likely to be discharged therefrom.

. . . .

48. (1) Where the Director General has reason to believe that any discharge or spillage of oil or mixture containing oil was from any ship, he may detain the ship and the ship may be so detained until the owner deposits with the Government such sum or furnishes such security as would in the opinion of the Director General be adequate to meet the costs and expenses which would be incurred to remove or eliminate the oil or mixture containing oil.

(2) If such detained ship proceeds to sea before it is released the owner, the master and any person who sends the ship to sea shall be guilty of an offence and shall be liable to a fine of not less than ten thousand dollars or to imprisonment not exceeding two years or to both.

. . . .

51. (1) In addition to and not in derogation of any of the powers contained in any other provisions of this Act, the Minister after consultation with the Council may make regulations for or with respect to—

> (a) prescribing fees for examining plans, specifications and information relating to installations or proposed installations the subject of applications for licences under this Act;

. . . .

> (f) prohibiting the use of any equipment, facility, vehicle or ship capable of causing pollution or regulating the construction, installation or operation thereof so as to prevent or minimize pollution;

. . . .

> (i) regulating the establishment of sites for the disposal of solid or liquid wastes on or in land;

. . . .

> (k) prohibiting or regulating bathing, swimming, boating or other aquatic activity in or around any waters that may be detrimental to health or welfare or for preventing pollution;

. . . .

> (m) requiring ships in Malaysian waters to be fitted with such equipment as may be prescribed for the purpose of preventing or reducing oil pollution;
>
> (n) requiring ships in Malaysian waters to carry such oil record books as may be prescribed, the master of such ships to record such particulars as may be prescribed and to transmit such books to such persons as may be specified,
>
> (o) restricting the transfer of oil to or from a ship in Malaysian

waters and prescribing the circumstances when such transfers may be carried out;

(p) requiring the master of any ship and the owner of any oil refinery to report discharges and spillages of oil or mixture containing oil into Malaysian waters;

(q) requiring the oil refineries carrying on business in Malaysia to store such substance or material and equipment necessary to deal with any oil pollution of the Malaysian waters that may arise in the course of their business;

(r) requiring the oil refineries carrying on business to install such equipment as may be prescribed for the purpose of reducing or preventing any trade effluent from containing oil;

(s) requiring ships using any port of Malaysia to discharge or deposit oil residues or wastes into oil reception facilities, the fees to be levied for the use of such facilities, and conditions upon which the vessels may use such facilities.

(2) Any such regulation may be general or may be restricted in operation as to time, place, persons or circumstances whether any such time, place, person or circumstance is determined or ascertainable before, at or after the making of the regulations.

(Date of Publication in Gazette, 14 March, 1974)

Appendix 2
Law Concerning Special Measures for Conservation of the Environmenf of the Seto Inland Sea (Japan)
(Law No. 110, Oct. 2, 1973)
(Amend. 1976, 1978)

Chapter I General Provisions

(Purpose)
Article 1
The purpose of this Law is to promote the conservation of the environment of the Seto Inland Sea by stipulating matters necessary for the
formulation, etc. of a plan for the conservation of the environment of
the Seto Inland Sea in order to promote the implementation of effective
measures in the conservation of the environment of the Seto Inland
Sea and by providing special measures in connection with restrictions
on the installment of specified facilities, the prevention of damage from
the eutrophication and with the conservation of the natural seashore,
etc.

(Definitions)
Article 2
1. The term "Seto Inland Sea" as used in this Law shall mean the sea
area enclosed by the straight lines described hereinbelow and the
shorelines, and other sea areas designated by Cabinet Order:
    (1) Straight lines drawn from Kii Hinomisaki Lighthouse in Wa-
kayama Prefecture to Ishima, Maejima of Tokushima Prefecture and
then to Gamoda Misaki of the same prefecture;
    (2) A straight line drawn from Sata Misaki of Ehime Prefecture to the
Sekizaki Lighthouse in Oita Prefecture; and
    (3) A straight line drawn from the Hinoyamashita Lighthouse in
Yamaguchi Prefecture to the Mojizaki Lighthouse in Fukuoka Prefecture.
2. The term "prefectures concerned" shall mean Osaka Prefecture,
Hyōgo Prefecture, Wakayama Prefecture, Okayama Prefecture,

Hiroshima Prefecture, Yamaguchi Prefecture, Tokushima Prefecture, Kagawa Prefecture, Ehime Prefecture, Fukuoka Prefecture, Oita Prefecture and other prefectures designated by Cabinet Order as being related to the environmental conservation of the Seto Inland Sea.

3. The term "governors of prefectures concerned" shall mean the governors of the prefectures concerned.

Chapter II Plan for Conservation of the Environment of the Seto Inland Sea

(Basic Plan for Conservation of the Environment of the Seto Inland Sea)
Article 3

1. In view of the benefits of the Seto Inland Sea, both as a place of scenic beauty unmatched by any in the country or elsewhere in the world and as a storehouse of rich fishery resources and of the fact that the Seto Inland Sea should rightly be enjoyed equally by all citizens of the nation and bequeathed to posterity, it behooves the national government to formulate a basic plan (to be referred to as the "Basic Plan" hereafter in this Chapter) for the conservation of the environment of the Seto Inland Sea in respect of preservation of water quality, conservation of scenic beauty, etc. of this Seto Inland Sea in order to promote the implementation of effective measures.

2. In determining or altering the Basic Plan, the Prime Minister shall in advance hear the opinions of the Seto Inland Sea Environmental Conservation Council and the governors of prefectures concerned.

3. When the Basic Plan has been determined or altered, the Prime Minister shall without delay send the Basic Plan or the change therein to the governors of prefectures concerned and, in addition, publicly announce the same.

(Prefectural Plan for Conservation of the Environment of the Seto Inland Sea)
Article 4

1. The governors of the prefectures concerned shall, on the basis of the Basic Plan, establish a prefectural plan for conservation of the Seto Inland Sea in respect of the measures to be implemented for the conservation of the environment of the Seto Inland Sea in the area of the prefectures concerned (to be referred to as the "Prefectural Plan" hereafter in this chapter).

2. The governors of the prefectures concerned shall, when they intend to establish the Prefectural Plan, report the content thereof to the

Prime Minister in accordance with what is prescribed by Ordinance of the Prime Minister's Office.

3. When the Prime Minister has received the report mentioned in the preceding paragraph, he may, upon consulting with the heads of the administrative organs concerned, issue necessary instructions regarding the drafting of the Prefectural Plan concerned.

4. When the governors of the prefectures concerned have established the Prefectural Plan, they shall, without delay, send it to the municipalities concerned and, in addition, publicly announce the same.

5. The provisions of the preceding three paragraphs shall apply *mutatis mutandis* to changes in the Prefectural Plan.

(Promotion of the Achievement of the Basic Plan and the Prefectural Plan)
Article 4–2
The State and local public bodies shall endeavor to take measures required for achievement of the Basic Plan and the Prefectural Plan.

Chapter III   Special Measures for Conservation of the Environment of the Seto Inland Sea

Section 1   Restrictions, etc. on the Installation of Specified Facilities

(Permit for the Installation of Specified Facilities)
Article 5
1. When a person who discharges effluents into a public water area [meaning a public water area stipulated in Article 2 paragraph 1 of the Water Pollution Control Law, Law No. 138 of 1970; the same hereinafter] from a factory or an establishment in the area of the prefectures concerned (excluding areas designated by Cabinet Order) plans to install a specified facility [meaning a specified facility stipulated in Article 2 paragraph 2 of the same Law but not including a specified facility installed in a factory or an establishment from which the maximum quantity of effluents (meaning the effluents stipulated in paragraph 3 of the same Article; the same hereinafter) discharged per day does not exceed fifty cubic meters or a specified facility prescribed by Cabinet Order; the same hereinafter], he shall obtain a permit from the governor of the prefecture in accordance with what is prescribed by Ordinance of the Prime Minister's Office.

2. A person seeking to obtain the permit mentioned in the preceding

paragraph shall file with the governor of the prefecture an application describing matters set forth in the following sub-paragraphs:

(1) Name or appellation and address, and, in the case of a juridical person, the name of its representative;

(2) Appellation of the factory or establishment and its address;

(3) Kind of the specified facility;

(4) Structure of the specified facility;

(5) Method of operation of the specified facility;

(6) Method of treatment of sewage or waste liquid (hereinafter referred to as "sewage, etc.") discharged from the specified facility;

(7) Quantity of effluents (including the quantity for each drainage system);

(8) State of pollution of the effluents (including state of pollution of effluents by each drainage system) and such other matters as are stipulated by Ordinance of the Prime Minister's Office.

3. The application referred to in the preceding paragraph shall be accompanied by a statement describing matters concerning prior assessment based on the findings of investigation on the impact which the proposed installation of the specified facility is likely to have on the environment.

4. Upon receipt of an application for permit referred to in paragraph 1, the governor of the prefecture shall, without delay, make an announcement of an outline thereof and shall make the statement referred to in the preceding paragraph open to the inspection by the public for three weeks from the date of such announcement.

5. When the governor of the prefecture has made the announcement referred to in the preceding paragraph, he shall, without delay, notify the governor(s) of those other prefectures concerned and the head(s) of those municipalities which are relevant on the ground of environmental preservation to the proposed installation of the specified facility and shall seek the opinions of the said governors of the prefectures concerned and the heads of the municipalities, fixing a period for their reply.

6. When the announcement referred to in paragraph 4 is made, any person who has interest in the proposed installation of the specified facility may file with the said governor of the prefecture a statement of opinion on matters regarding the prior assessment referred to in paragraph 3 any time up to the last day of the period for public inspection referred to in paragraph 4 hereof.

7. Matters to be dealt with in the statement of prior assessment referred to in paragraph 3 shall be prescribed by Ordinance of the Prime Minister's Office.

(Criteria for Permitting the Installation of Specified Facilities)
Article 6
1. The governor of the prefecture shall not issue the permit referred to in paragraph 1 of the preceding Article unless he finds that the proposed installation of the specified facility covered by an application filed under the provisions of said paragraph meets either of the following conditions:

(1) That the proposed facility is concerning a factory or establishment the purpose of which is to treat waste; or

(2) That the sewage, etc. discharged from the proposed facility present no serious hindrance to the conservation of the environment of the Seto Inland Sea.

2. Even when the specified facility covered by an application for permit filed under the provision of paragraph 1 of the preceding Article meets the condition set forth in sub-paragraph (1) of the preceding paragraph, the governor of the prefecture shall take into account the impact which the installation of such specified facility may have on the environment in relation to the permit referred to in paragraph 1 of the preceding Article.

(Transitory Measures Relating to Specified Facilities)
Article 7
. . . .

(Changes in the Structure, etc. of Specified Facilities)
Article 8
. . . .

(Changes in Name, etc.)
Article 9
. . . .

(Succession)
Article 10
. . . .

(Order of Measures against Contravention)
Article 11
In the event that any person has installed a specified facility in contravention of the provisions of Article 5 paragraph 1, or that any person has effected any change in matters prescribed in Article 8 paragraph 1, in contravention of the provisions thereof, the governor of the pre-

fecture may order the person to remove or discontinue the operation of the facility or take such other measures as may be necessary to remedy the situation caused by such contravention.

(Application of the Water Pollution Control Law, etc.)
Article 12

1. The provisions of Article 5 to Article 10 inclusive, Article 11 paragraph 1 to paragraph 3 inclusive and Article 23 paragraph 3 to paragraph 5 inclusive of the Water Pollution Control Law (only those parts of these provisions which are related to Articles 5, 7, 8, 8–2, 10 and 11 of the same Law), and those of Article 37 paragraph 1 of the Law relating to the Prevention of Marine Pollution and Maritime Disaster (Law No. 136 of 1970) shall not apply to the specified facilities installed in factories or establishments located in the area designated in Article 5 paragraph 1.

2. With respect to the application of the provisions of Article 22 paragraph 1 of the Water Pollution Control Law to the area designated in Article 5 paragraph 1, the term "this Law" appearing in the same paragraph shall read "this Law (Law concerning Special Measures for Conservation of the Environment of the Seto Inland Sea, Law No. 110 of 1973)."

(Reduction of Total Amount of Pollution Load)
Article 12–2

1. In order to prevent water pollution in terms of chemical oxygen demand in the Seto Inland Sea, the Prime Minister shall, in respect of the area stipulated in Article 5 paragraph 1, establish the fundamental policy for reduction of areawide total pollutant load mentioned in Article 4–2 paragraph 1 of the Water Pollution Control Law relative to the reduction of the total amount of pollution load expressed in terms of chemical oxygen demand.

2. As regards the application of the provisions of the Water Pollution Control Law relative to the fundamental policy for reduction of areawide total pollutant load mentioned in the preceding paragraph and the reduction of the total amount of pollution load on the basis of the same policy, the parts of the provisions of the same Law which read "Pollution Load," "Specified Water Areas," "Specified Items" and "Specified Regions" shall read "pollution load expressed in terms of chemical oxygen demand," "Seto Inland Sea as stipulated in Article 2 paragraph 1 of the Law concerning Special Measures for Conservation of the Environment of the Seto Inland Sea," "chemical oxygen demand" and "area stipulated in Article 5 paragraph 1 of the Law

concerning Special Measures for Conservation of the Environment of the Seto Inland Sea," respectively.

Section 2 Prevention of the Occurrence of Damage from Eutrophication

(Guideline for Reduction of Specified Substances)
Article 12–3

1. When the Director General of the Environment Agency deems it necessary for the prevention of the occurrence of damage to the living environment by eutrophication in the Seto Inland Sea, he may, in accordance with what is prescribed by Cabinet Order, instruct the governors of the prefectures concerned to establish a guideline for reduction of specified substances (referred to as the "guideline" hereafter in this Section) relative to the reduction of phosphorus and other substances specified by Cabinet Order (referred to as "specified substances" hereafter in this Section) discharged into the public water areas in the area stipulated in Article 5 paragraph 1, indicating the reduction target, the target fiscal year and other necessary matters.

2. In the guideline, there shall be stipulated the policy for guidance relative to reduction of the specified substances and other matters for the purpose of realizing the aim of attaining the reduction target in the target fiscal year.

3. When the governors of the prefectures concerned intend to establish a guideline or make a change in the same, they shall, in accordance with what is prescribed by Ordinance of the Prime Minister's Office, report to the Director General of the Environment Agency on the matters mentioned in the preceding paragraph.

4. When the governors of the prefectures concerned have established a guideline or made a change in the same, they shall publicly announce the guidelines or the change therein.

(Guidance, etc.)
Article 12–4

The governors of prefectures concerned may, in accordance with the guideline, give a person who discharges a specified substance into a public water area in the area stipulated in Article 5 paragraph 1, any guidance, advice or recommendation which may be required.

(Collection of Reports)
Article 12–5

The governors of prefectures concerned may, when they deem it necessary for giving guidance, advice or recommendation under the preceding Article, request a person who, in connection with his business activities, discharges a specified substance into a public water area in the area stipulated in Article 5 paragraph 1, and who is designated by Cabinet Order, to submit a report on his method of treating sewage or waste liquid and any other necessary matters.

Section 3 Conservation of the Natural Seashore, etc.

(Designation of National Seashore Conservation Areas)
Article 12–6
The prefectures concerned may, in accordance with what is prescribed by an ordinance, designate as a natural seashore conservation area those parts of the seashore and its adjacent sea areas of the Seto Inland Sea which fall under either of the following sub-paragraphs:

(1) Those parts where sand beaches, reefs or other similar natural conditions are maintained near the water-boundary line.

(2) Those parts which are used by the public for sea bathing, gathering sea shells and other similar purposes and which are recognized as being suitable for such use both at present and in the future.

(Notification of Acts, etc.)
Article 12–7
The prefectures concerned may, in accordance with what is prescribed by an ordinance, require a person who intends to build a new structure, change the form or nature of the land, mine minerals, quarry stones or conduct other acts in a natural seashore conservation area to submit a notification and may give a person who submitted such a notification any recommendation or advice necessary to assure the conservation and proper utilization of the natural seashore conservation area.

(Special Consideration Given to Reclamation, etc.)
Article 13
1. In considering the license referred to in Article 2 paragraph 1 of the Public Water Body Reclamation Law (Law No. 57 of 1921) or the approval referred to in Article 42 paragraph 1 of the same Law for projects undertaken in the Seto Inland Sea, the governor of the prefecture concerned shall take into account the peculiarites of the Seto Inland Sea referred to in Article 3 paragraph 1 hereof.
2. The basic policy of the application of the provision of the preceding paragraph shall be studied and considered by the Seto Inland Sea Environmental Conservation Council.

Section 4 Promotion of Projects for Conservation of Environment, etc.

(Construction of Sewerage Works and Waste Disposal Facilities, etc.)
Article 14
In view of the current state of water pollution of the Seto Inland Sea, the State and the local public bodies shall make endeavors to promote the construction of sewerage works and waste disposal facilities, the dredging of bottom deposit, the installation of facilities and equipment for monitoring and measuring the water quality and other projects necessary for the conservation of water quality in the Seto Inland Sea.

(Financial Assistance, etc.)
Article 15
The State shall make endeavors to extend financial assistance to, arrange loans of necessary funds for and make other forms of assistance available to, those who undertake the projects referred to in the preceding Article.

(Formulation of Plans for Projects Designed to Purify the Seto Inland Sea)
Article 16
The national government shall make endeavors for the formulation of plans for large-scale projects designed to purify the polluted water of the Seto Inland Sea and in this regard shall promote the development of the technology, etc. necessary for such projects and take necessary financial measures.

(Prevention, etc. of the Spillage of Oil through Marine Disaster)
Article 17
In order to prevent the pollution of the Seto Inland Sea by oil, the national government shall, in connection with the prevention of the spillage of large volumes of oil through marine disaster and the elimination of spilled oil, make efforts to strengthen its guidance and control, organize a system for the elimination of spilled oil and take any other necessary measures.

(Promotion for the Development of Technology, etc.)
Article 18
The national government shall promptly make efforts to clarify the mechanism by which red tides occur and to develop technology for the prevention and elimination thereof and also make efforts to develop

technology for treatment of oil in ships and other technology for the conservation of the environment of the Seto Inland Sea, and shall take necessary measures based on the result of such technological development.

(Relief for Persons Engaged in Fishery Suffering Damage Caused by Red Tides, etc.)
In view of the large number of instances of fishery damage caused by red tides and oil spillage in the Seto Inland Sea, the national government shall promptly take necessary measures for the relief for persons engaged in fishery who are suffering such fishery damage.

Chapter IV   Miscellaneous Provisions

(Recommendations or Advice)
Article 20
. . . .

(Transitory Measures)
Article 21
. . . .

(Delegation of Administrative Services, etc.)
Article 22
. . . .

(The Seto Inland Sea Environmental Conservation Council)
Article 23
1. The Seto Inland Sea Environmental Conservation Council shall be established within the Environment Agency (hereinafter referred to as "Council").
2. The Council shall study and examine important matters relating to the conservation of the environment of the Seto Inland Sea upon request from the Director General of the Environment Agency or other ministers concerned.
3. The Council may present its opinions to the Director General of the Environment Agency or other ministers concerned on important matters relating to the conservation of the environment of the Seto Inland Sea.
. . . .

Chapter V   Penal Provisions

Article 24
Any person who falls under the following sub-paragraphs shall be imprisoned not more than one year or fined not more than five hundred thousand yen (¥500,000):

(1) Any person who violates the provision of Article 5 paragraph 1 or Article 8 paragraph 1;

(2) Any person who contravenes an order issued under the provision of Article 11.

[Articles 25–26 and Supplementary Provisions omitted.]

Appendix 3
Coastal Zone Management Act
of 1972 (U.S.A.)
(Pub. L., 92–583; 16 U.S.C.A. §§1451–1464; 86 Stat. 1280,
Oct. 27, 1972)
(Amend. 1976, 1978, 1980)

Sec. 301. Short Title. This title may be cited as the "Coastal Zone
Management Act of 1972."

Sec. 302. Congressional Findings. The Congress finds that—
(a) There is a national interest in the effective management, beneficial
use, protection and development of the coastal zone;
(b) The coastal zone is rich in a variety of natural, commercial, recreational, industrial and esthetic resources of immediate and potential
value to the present and future well-being of the Nation;
(c) The increasing and competing demands upon the lands and waters
of our coastal zone occasioned by population growth and economic
development, including requirements for industry, commerce, residential development, recreation, extraction of mineral resources and
fossil fuels, transportation and navigation, waste disposal and harvesting of fish, shellfish and other living marine resources, have resulted
in the loss of living marine resources, wildlife, nutrient-rich areas,
permanent and adverse changes to ecological systems, decreasing open
space for public use and shoreline erosion;
(d) The coastal zone, and the fish, shellfish, other living marine resources and wildlife therein, are ecologically fragile and consequently
extremely vulnerable to destruction by man's alterations;
(e) Important ecological, cultural, historic and esthetic values in the
coastal zone which are essential to the well-being of all citizens are
being irretrievably damaged or lost;
(f) Special natural and scenic characteristics are being damaged by
ill-planned development that threatens these values;
(g) In light of competing demands and the urgent need to protect
and to give high priority to natural systems in the coastal zone, present

state and local institutional arrangements for planning and regulating land and water uses in such areas are inadequate; and

(h) The key to more effective protection and use of the land and water resources of the coastal zone is to encourage the states to exercise their full authority over the lands and waters in the coastal zone by assisting the states, in cooperation with Federal and local governments and other vitally affected interests, in developing land and water use programs for the coastal zone, including unified policies, criteria, standards, methods and processes for dealing with land and water use decisions of more than local significance.

Sec. 303. Declaration of Policy. The Congress finds and declares that it is the national policy (a) to preserve, protect, develop and, where possible, to restore or enhance, the resources of the Nation's coastal zone for this and succeeding generations, (b) to encourage and assist the states to exercise effectively their responsibilities in the coastal zone through the development and implementation of management programs to achieve wise use of the land and water resources of the coastal zone giving full consideration to ecological, cultural, historic and esthetic values as well as to needs for economic development, (c) for all Federal agencies engaged in programs affecting the coastal zone to cooperate and participate with state and local governments and regional agencies in effectuating the purposes of this title and (d) to encourage the participation of the public, of Federal, state and local governments and of regional agencies in the development of coastal zone management programs. With respect to implementation of such management programs, it is the national policy to encourage cooperation among the various state and regional agencies including establishment of interstate and regional agreements, cooperative procedures and joint action particularly regarding environmental problems.

Sec. 304. Definitions. For the purposes of this title—

(a) "Coastal zone" means the coastal waters (including the lands therein and thereunder) and the adjacent shorelands (including the waters therein and thereunder), strongly influenced by each other and in proximity to the shorelines of the several coastal states, and includes transitional and intertidal areas, salt marshes, wetlands and beaches. The zone extends, in Great Lakes waters, to the international boundary between the United States and Canada and, in other areas, seaward to the outer limit of the United States territorial sea. The zone extends inland from the shorelines only to the extent necessary to control shorelands, the uses of which have a direct and significant impact on the coastal waters. Excluded from the coastal zone are lands the use of which is by law subject solely to the discretion of or which is held in trust by the Federal Government, its officers or agents.

(b) "Coastal waters" means (1) in the Great Lakes area, the waters within the territorial jurisdiction of the United States consisting of the Great Lakes, their connecting waters, harbors, roadsteads and estuary-type areas such as bays, shallows and marshes and (2) in other areas, those waters, adjacent to the shorelines, which contain a measurable quantity or percentage of sea water, including, but not limited to, sounds, bays, lagoons, bayous, ponds and estuaries.

(c) "Coastal state" means a state of the United States in, or bordering on, the Atlantic, Pacific or Arctic Ocean, the Gulf of Mexico, Long Island Sound or one or more of the Great Lakes. For the purposes of this title, the term also includes Puerto Rico, the Virgin Islands, Guam and American Samoa.

(d) "Estuary" means that part of a river or stream or other body of water having unimpaired connection with the open sea, where the sea water is measurably diluted with fresh water derived from land drainage. The term includes estuary-type areas of the Great Lakes.

(e) "Estuarine sanctuary" means a research area which may include any part or all of an estuary, adjoining transitional areas and adjacent uplands, constituting to the extent feasible a natural unit, set aside to provide scientists and students the opportunity to examine over a period of time the ecological relationships within the area.

(f) "Secretary" means the Secretary of Commerce.

(g) "Management program" includes, but is not limited to, a comprehensive statement in words, maps, illustrations or other media of communication, prepared and adopted by the state in accordance with the provisions of this title, setting forth objectives, policies and standards to guide public and private uses of lands and waters in the coastal zone.

(h) "Water use" means activities which are conducted in or on the water; but does not mean or include the establishment of any water quality standard or criteria or the regulation of the discharge or runoff of water pollutants except the standards, criteria or regulations which are incorporated in any program as required by the provisions of section 307(f).

(i) "Land use" means activities which are conducted in or on the shorelands within the coastal zone, subject to the requirements outlined in section 307(g).

Sec. 305. Management Program Development Grants. (a) The Secretary is authorized to make annual grants to any coastal state for the purpose of assisting in the development of a management program for the land and water resources of its coastal zone.

(b) Such management program shall include:

(1) an identification of the boundaries of the coastal zone subject to the management program;

(2) a definition of what shall constitute permissible land and water uses within the coastal zone which have a direct and significant impact on the coastal waters;

(3) an inventory and designation of areas of particular concern within the coastal zone;

(4) an identification of the means by which the state proposes to exert control over the land and water uses referred to in paragraph (2) of this subsection, including a listing of relevant constitutional provisions, legislative enactments, regulations and judicial decisions.

Sec. 306. Administrative Grants. (a) The Secretary is authorized to make annual grants to any coastal state for not more than 66 2/3 per centum of the costs of administering the state's management program, if he approves such program in accordance with subsection (c) hereof. Federal funds received from other sources shall not be used to pay the state's share of costs.

Sec. 307. Interagency Coordination and Cooperation. (a) In carrying out his functions and responsibilities under this title, the Secretary shall consult with, cooperate with and, to the maximum extent practicable, coordinate his activities with other interested Federal agencies.

(b) The Secretary shall not approve the management program submitted by a state pursuant to section 306 unless the views of Federal agencies principally affected by such program have been adequately considered. In case of serious disagreement between any Federal agency and the state in the development of the program the Secretary, in cooperation with the Executive Office of the President, shall seek to mediate the differences.

Sec. 308. Public Hearings. All public hearings required under this title must be announced at least thirty days prior to the hearing date. At the time of the announcement, all agency materials pertinent to the hearings, including documents, studies and other data, must be made available to the public for review and study.

Sec. 309. Review of Performance. (a) The Secretary shall conduct a continuing review of the management programs of the coastal states and of the performance of each state.

Sec. 310. Records. (a) Each recipient of a grant under this title shall keep such records as the Secretary shall prescribe, including records which fully disclose the amount and disposition of the funds received under the grant, the total cost of the project or undertaking supplied by other sources and such other records as will facilitate an effective audit.

Sec. 311. Advisory Committee. (a) The Secretary is authorized and directed to establish a Coastal Zone Management Advisory Committee to advise, consult with and make recommendations to the Secretary on matters of policy concerning the coastal zone.

Sec. 312. Estuarine Sanctuaries. The Secretary, in accordance with rules and regulations promulgated by him, is authorized to make available to a coastal state grants of up to 50 per centum of the costs of acquisition, development and operation of estuarine sanctuaries for the purpose of creating national field laboratories to gather data and make studies of the natural and human processes occurring within the estuaries of the coastal zone.

Sec. 313. Annual Report. (a) The Secretary shall prepare and submit to the President for transmittal to the Congress not later than November 1 of each year a report on the administration of this title for the preceding fiscal year.

Sec. 314. Rules and Regulations. The Secretary shall develop and promulgate, pursuant to section 553 of title 5, United States Code, after notice and opportunity for full participation by relevant Federal agencies, state agencies, local governments, regional organizations, port authorities and other interested parties, both public and private, such rules and regulations as may be necessary to carry out the provisions of this title.

Sec. 315.
[Approved October 27, 1972.]

Information on Contributors

Cheong Chup Lim has been a member of the Drainage and Irrigation Department, Malaysia, since 1960, and now serves as Deputy Director General. He was born in 1932 and received a B.Sc. (Civil Engineering) from the University of Hong Kong in 1957. He is the author of "Irrigation Development and Present Status of Farm Water Management in Malaysia," *Tropical Agriculture Research Series* No. 9 (Ministry of Agriculture and Forestry, Japan, 1976).

M. W. Ranjith N. De Silva is Associate Professor, Faculty of Fisheries and Marine Science, Universiti Pertanian Malaysia. He was born in 1939 and received a B.Sc. (Special Botany, Hons.) from the University of Ceylon (Sri Lanka) in 1964, and Ph.D. (Marine Ecology-Algology) from the University of Liverpool in 1969. Dr. De Silva is the author of many scientific articles and coauthor of "An experimental assessment of the status of species *Enteromorpha intestinalis and Enteromorpha compressa* Grev," *Journal of the Marine Biological Association* U. K. 53, 895 (1973). He was president of the Malaysia Society of Marine Sciences in 1980 and is a consultant to the IUCIN Committee on National Parks and Protected Areas.

Ichirō Katō has been chancellor of Seijō Gakuen Institute in Tokyo since 1983. Dr. Katō was born in 1922, graduated from the University of Tokyo in 1943, and received an LL. D. from that University. He was Professor of Civil Law at the University of Tokyo from 1957 to 1983, and served as president of the University from 1969 to 1973. Dr. Katō was a visiting scholar at Harvard University (1962–1963) and the University of California, Berkeley (1967–1968), was Vice-rector of the United Nations University (1975–1976) and is president of the Japan Center for Human Environmental Problems. He is the author of many books and articles, among them *Fuhō koi* [Law of torts] (Yūhikaku 1959). He is also editor of *Kōgai hō no seisei to tenkai* [Formation and development of environmental law] (Yūhikaku 1965), and coeditor of *Environmental Law and Policy in the Pacific Basin Area* (University of Tokyo Press 1981) and *Water Management and Environmental Protection in Asia and the Pacific* (University of Tokyo Press 1983).

Akira Kimizuka is Senior Government Officer in the Road Bureau, Ministry of Construction (MOC), Japan. He was Deputy Director of the Water Use Coordination Section, Water Administration Division, River Bureau (MOC) from 1977 to 1982. He was dispatched to the Malaysian government as Colombo Plan Expert (legal/institutional expert on water law) from 1979 to 1982. He was born in 1942 and graduated from the University of Tokyo, Faculty of Law in 1967. He is the author of "Nōgyō yōsui no gōrika" [Optimization of water use for agricultural purposes] (Jichikenkyū 1978) and *General Conception of the National Water Resources Code—Recommendation on Water Law and Institution Malaysia* (Economic Planning Unit of the Malaysian Government and Japan International Cooperation Agency 1982).

Nobuo Kumamoto has been Professor of Administrative Law at Hokkaigakuen University since 1974. Born in 1935, he received an LL.B. (1961), LL.M. (1964) and LL.D. (1973) from Hokkaido University, and LL.M. (1974) from the University of California, Berkeley. Dr. Kumamoto was a Fulbright visiting scholar at the University of Michigan Law School (1968–1970), and visiting professor at the Hebrew University of Jerusalem (1981), Tulane Law School (1982) and the University of Georgia Law School (1984). In 1983–1984 he was legal consultant to the Economic and Social Commission for Asia and the Pacific in Bangkok. Professor Kumamoto is coeditor of *Environmental Law and Policy in the Pacific Basin Area* (University of Tokyo Press 1981) and *Water Management and Environmental Protection in Asia and the Pacific* (University of Tokyo Press 1983).

Lee Choong Loui is Corporate Environmental Coordinator for ESSO Production Malaysia Inc.

Appadurai Maheswaran has been Director-General of Environment, Malaysia, since 1984. He was formerly Director of Water Pollution Control in the Ministry of Science, Technology and Environment, Malaysia. He was born in 1932, and is a chartered chemist and Fellow of the Royal Society of Chemistry, London. Mr. Maheswaran is author of "Nightsoil treatment by anaerobic digestion," in *Waste Recovery by Microorganisms* (University of Malaya 1972).

William H. Matthews is director of the Environment and Policy Institute, East-West Center, Hawaii. He was born in 1942 and received his S.M. in electrical engineering (1968), Professional E.E. (1968), S.M. in political science (1970) and Ph.D. in socio-technology engineering (1970) from Massachusetts Institute of Technology. He is the coeditor of *Renewable Energy Prospects* (Pergamon Press 1979), *Environmental Law and Policy in the Pacific Basin Area* (University of Tokyo Press 1981) and *Water Management and Environmental Protection in Asia and the Pacific* (University of Tokyo Press 1983).

Mohd. Ibrahim bin Haji Mohamad is Associate Professor of Fishing Technology and Head of the Fisheries and Marine Science Center, Universiti Pertanian Malaysia. He was born in 1952 and has a Dip. Tech. Naut. Sc. from the College of Fisheries, Newfoundland, Canada (1973), Certificate of Competency as Fishing Master, D.O.T., Canada (1973) and MMA, Rhode Island (1981). Capt. Mohamad is the author of "Impact of the Exclusive Economic Zone on Malaysian Fishery" in *Proceedings of the Fifth Marine Science Seminar, Universiti Pertanian Malaysia*.

Masahisa Nakamura is an Environmental Systems Engineer with the World Health Organization, Western Pacific Regional Centre for the Promotion of Environmental Planning and Applied Studies. He was born in 1945 and received a B. Eng., Hokkaido University (1962), M. Eng., University of Washington (1969) and Ph.D., University of Illinois (1977). Dr. Nakamura was formerly Assistant Professor at the University of Louisville, Kentucky. He is the author of "A multi-objective branch-and-bound method for network-structured water resources planning problems," *Water Resources Research* 17 (5), 1981.

Ng Cheng Siong is Senior Lecturer in the Department of Chemical Engineering, National University of Singapore, and Managing Director of the Applied Research Corporation. Born in 1942, he received a B.Sc. (Hons.) from the University of Singapore (1965) and M.Sc. (1966) and Ph.D. (1968) from the University of Manchester. Dr. Ng is the author of "Survey of the electroplating and metal finishing industry in Singapore (Seminar on the Electroplating and Metal Finishing Industry in Singapore, 1980), and coauthor of "Curriculum planning and development in chemical engineering at the National

University of Singapore (Seminar on Chemical Engineering Training in Singapore, 1980) Dr. Ng was a contributor to the Second Asian-American Conference on Environmental Protection.

Yoshihiro Nomura has been Professor of Civil Law at Tokyo Metropolitan University since 1978. He was born in 1941 and graduated from the University of Tokyo in 1963. Professor Nomura is a member of the editorial board of the *Environmental Journal* and Secretary-General of the Japan Center for Human Environmental Problems. He is also a member of the Committee on Environmental Law and Policy of the International Union for Conservation of Nature and Natural Resources. Professor Nomura is the coauthor of *Kōgai Hanrei no Kenkyū* [Studies on environmental cases] (Gyōsei 1971) and *Kōgai no Hanrei* [Environmental cases] (Yūhikaku 1971). He was a contributor to both the First and Second Asian-American Conferences on Environmental Protection.

Henry Ong Wah Kim is Associate Professor of Chemistry in the Department of Chemistry, National University of Singapore. He was born in 1937 and received a B.Sc. (Hons.) from the University of Singapore in 1963 and a Ph.D. from Cambridge University in 1966.

Ong Jin Eong has been a lecturer at Universiti Sains Malaysia since 1970. He was born in 1943 and received a B.Sc. from the University of Melbourne in 1966 and a Ph.D. from the University of Tasmania in 1971. Dr. Ong is the author of "Mangroves and aquaculture in Malaysia," *Ambio* 11, 252.

Twesukdi Piyakarnchana is Professor of Marine Science, Chulalongkorn University. He was born in 1930 and received his B.S. (Chulalongkorn University, 1953), M.S. (University of California, Scripps Institution of Oceanography, 1960) and Ph.D. (University of Hawaii, 1965). Dr. Piyakarnchana was Director of the Institute of Environmental Research, Chulalongkorn University, from 1975 to 1979. He is the author of "Oil pollution from tankers in the Straits of Malacca: A policy and legal analysis," Open Grants No. 6, 1979. He was a contributor to the First and Second Asian-American Conferences on Environmental Protection.

Nik Abdul Rashid Majid was appointed Director of the Mara Institute of Technology, Selangor, Malaysia, in 1980. He was previously Deputy Dean and Professor of the Faculty of Law, University of Malaya.

Mr. Rashid was born in 1936 and received his LL.B. from the University of Singapore (1967) and M.P.A. from the University of Pittsburgh (1969).

Surin Setamanit has been Director of the Institute of Environmental Research, Chulalongkorn University, since 1979. He was born in 1935 and received his B.Sc. (Eng.) in 1958 and Ph.D. (Eng.) in 1962 from the Imperial College of Science and Technology, University of London. Dr. Setamanit became a Fellow of the Institution of Public Health Engineering, London, in 1968. He is the author of *Staff and Faculty Development in Southeast Asian Universities: A Case Study of Thailand*, Research Series, Regional Institute of Higher Education and Development (Maruzen Asia 1981).

Sieh Kok Chi is in the Drainage and Irrigation Department, Ministry of Agriculture, Malaysia.

P.B.L. Srivastava is Chief Research Officer in the Office of Forestry, Department of Primary Industry, Boroko, Papua New Guinea. He was lecturer in the Faculty of Forestry, Universiti Pertanian Malaysia from 1975 to 1982, and consultant to the Food and Agricultural Organization in Bhutan in 1982–1983. Dr. Srivastava was born in 1938 and received his Ph.D. in Forest Ecology in 1963. He is the author of "Effect of final fellings on natural regeneration of mangrove species in Matang Reserve," *Pertanika* 2 (34), 1979.

Ariffin Suhaimi is Vice-Rector of the International Islamic University, Selangor, Malaysia. He was formerly Professor and Deputy Vice-chancellor of the Universiti Pertanian Malaysia. Dr. Ariffin was born in 1937 and received his B.Sc. (Hons.) from the University of Malaya in Singapore (1960), Dip. E. (1962) and M.Sc. (1965) from the University of Singapore and Ph.D. (1973) from the University of Reading. He has been a member of the Environmental Quality Council of Malaysia.

R. Tjang Mushadji Sutamihardja is lecturer in Environmental Toxicology and Pollution in the Graduate School, and Water Quality Manager at the Center for Studies of Natural Resources and Environment, Bogor Agricultural University. He is also Deputy Assistant Minister, Office of the State Minister of Development Supervision and Environment. He was born in 1939, graduated from Bogor Agricultural University in 1963, received his Master of Agriculture degree from Gifu

State University, Japan, in 1968, and Doctor of Pharmacy from Gifu College of Pharmacy in 1972. Dr. Sutamihardja is coeditor of *Water Management and Environmental Protection in Asia and the Pacific* (University of Tokyo Press 1983), and was a contributor to the First and Second Asian-American Conferences on Environmental Protection.

Hipolito C. Talavera is Deputy Commissioner for Enforcement, National Pollution Control Commission, Ministry of Human Settlements, Philippines. He was born in 1928 and received his LL.B. (1954) from Manuel L. Quezon University. Mr. Talavera is the author of *More Responsibilities to the Marine Environment* (Philippine Seas 1982), and was a contributor to the Second Asian-American Conference on Environmental Protection.

Mark J. Valencia is a Research Associate in the Resource Systems Institute, East-West Center, Hawaii. He was born in 1944 and received a B.S. (Hons.) from the University of Massachusetts, Amherst (1966), M.A. (University of Texas, 1968) and Ph.D. (University of Hawaii, 1972). Dr. Valencia is author of *South China Sea: Oil Under Troubled Water* (Oxford University Press 1985), editor of *The South China Sea: Hydrocarbon Potential and Possibilities of Joint Development* (Oxford: Pergamon Press 1981) and coeditor of *Shipping, Energy, and Environment: Southeast Asian Perspectives* (Halifax 1983) and *Marine Policy in Southeast Asia* (University of California Press 1985).

Stephen Yong Kuet Tze is Minister of Science, Technology and Environment, Malaysia. Mr. Yong graduated from Nottingham University in 1953 (LL.B., Hons.) and became a Barrister-at-Law, Lincoln's Inn, London, in 1953.

Index